School Days

In our memories they remain days to treasure,
whether we learned in one-room rural
schoolhouses or sturdy brick buildings.
From the Pledge of Allegiance to the Palmer
Method to Dick and Jane, we'll never forget
the ways we learned…as the fond memories
and photographs in this book attest.

from
the readers of
Reminisce magazine

SMILING FACES. School was hard work, but it also was fun, as this picture shows. The photo of the first- and second-grade classes from 1939-40 in Rathdrum, Idaho was sent by Thora Marie (Hansen) Sheaman (back row, second from right), Torrance, California. Her sister Dorothy (middle row, third from right) also was in the picture.

1st & 2nd GRADE
RATHDRUM, IDA.
1939 — 1940
PHOTO BY LEO'S STUDIO

Editor: Mike Beno

Managing Editor: Lee Aschoff

Contributing Editor: Clancy Strock

Assistant Editors: John Schroeder, Deb Mulvey, Kristine Krueger, Mike Martin

Art Director: Linda Dzik

Art Associate: Jim Sibilski

Photo Coordinator: Trudi Bellin

Editorial Assistants: Blanche Comiskey, Joy Bartol-Snyder, Jean Steiner, Mary Ann Koebernik

Production Assistant: Ellen Lloyd

Publisher: Roy J. Reiman

©2000 Reiman Publications, LLC
5400 S. 60th St., Greendale WI 53129

Reminisce Books
International Standard Book Number:
0-89821-287-1

Library of Congress Control Number: 00-132050

On the Cover: After a day of learning, no sound was sweeter than the final bell of the school day, as reflected in the happy faces of these children in 1949 racing to school buses for the trip home. (Photo: Bettmann/CORBIS)

For additional copies of this book or information on other books, write: Reminisce Books, P.O. Box 990, Greendale WI 53129-0990; call toll-free 1-800/558-1013 to order with a credit card; or visit our Web site at **www.reimanpub.com**.

Contents

CONGRATULATIONS! That's the comment this little guy gave his big sister after her graduation from kindergarten. You'll find their story on page 87, along with hundreds of others in this heartwarming celebration of the years we fondly remember as "School Days".

Prologue

By Clancy Strock, Contributing Editor

RICH OR POOR, man or woman, Texan or British Columbian, something all of us share in common are memories of our school days. It's the one common bond that North American adults have no matter where they grew up.

To some, school was a creaky one-room structure standing alone on the prairie. For others, it was a sprawling brick edifice with thousands of students. To many of our grandchildren, school is now a prison-like place with armed playground guards and metal detectors on the doors.

Whatever and wherever, school was where we spent most of the days of our childhood. It was where we learned the Pledge of Allegiance as we faced the flag, flanked by portraits of Washington and Lincoln. It was where we learned about our patriots and heroes, and how to sing *Good Morning to You.*

Education Means Progress

Few places on Earth believe so deeply in the importance of educating their young as we do here in North America. And hooray for us! Without schools and teachers, we quite likely would have continued repeating the same dumb mistakes from one generation to the next, century after century.

Progress depended upon finding a way to build on what was so tediously learned year by year, instead of having to start fresh with every generation.

Socrates long ago had pronounced that, "There is only one good, knowledge; and only one evil, ignorance." Farsighted people decided they'd do something about the evil of ignorance. The solution was schooling.

Still, for a long time, a school education was mostly the privilege of the upper classes. After all, how much wisdom did it take to be a chimney sweep or a shepherd? Why did any woman need formal education to tend the home fires?

Public schools eventually opened their doors to one and all, and just in time! It was clear that the future would call not only for brawn but for brains.

MEMORIES OF SCHOOL DAYS still echo for Clancy Strock, who grew up in the 1930s and whose mother was a teacher. He often reads and edits such recollections in his role as Contributing Editor for *Reminisce*, North America's most popular nostalgia magazine.

So as the frontier moved west, we built schools and trained teachers to staff them.

By the end of the 1800s, the profession opened up for women, mostly young women, looking for something to do before finding a husband.

The turnover was so great that many school employment contracts specified that dating was forbidden, or that the teacher could only socialize one night a week. And even though a young woman married, pregnancy would mean automatic dismissal.

All it took to become a teacher was completion of a 2-year course at a state "normal school". My mother graduated from the one at De Kalb, Illinois in 1916. She treasured her graduation picture showing three dozen or so new teachers in pretty white dresses, eager to go to work.

Some of them were as young as 18, barely older and often smaller than many of the students they'd teach. Because salaries were a pittance—as little as $70 a month—they frequently "boarded around the district", meaning that families took turns providing a room and meals for the "schoolmarm".

More Than Just Teachers

We expected a lot of our teachers, especially those in the rural one-room schoolhouses that dotted the countryside.

For their meager salary, teachers were expected to arrive early each day, carry in firewood, start a fire in the cast-iron heating stove, check the outhouses and lug in a pail or two of water from the pump...oh, and teach all eight grades.

Mother remembered that while working with the kids in one grade, she had to keep an eye on rambunctious youngsters in all the other classes. From her stories of those days, I got the vivid impression that her job was much like a circus lion tamer's.

But even constant vigilance wasn't enough. Inflicting misery on the teacher was a full-time preoccupation—especially for the boys.

Mom never knew what might lurk inside her desk drawer when she opened it. Sometimes it was a frog, sometimes a green garter snake, sometimes a handful of wiggly earthworms. Every kid in the room knew what the surprise was and waited breathlessly for the teacher's reaction. The trick, of course, was to never scream or even show surprise. If you did, you became a permanent target for mischief.

There also was the matter of raccoons, skunks, squirrels, mice, bats and other pests that set up homes inside the schoolhouse. Mom would recruit two or three of the bigger boys for help, and pandemonium would reign until the interloper was captured or chased outside.

All in all, it was quite a challenge for a young woman. Some stuck it out for a year, then fled. Others, like Mom, prayed for the day when the board of education offered a promotion to the city school system.

Imagine! Just one grade to teach. No water to carry or fires to start. Wouldn't that be heaven!

Regardless of where you taught, your job was considerably more than teaching the three R's. You also were the school nurse, social worker and confidant. You arbitrated playground fights, supervised games at recess and coped with parents who saw no need for their kids to have education of any kind.

When Halloween, Thanksgiving and other holidays came along, you dug into your own pocket for the art supplies needed to decorate the schoolroom…and baked a treat for refreshments.

A few years ago, *Reminisce* carried the story of a lady who remembered a special kindness from her teacher. Her family was desperately poor and there was no money for a graduation dress. But a compassionate teacher bought yard goods and a pattern, then worked

"It was quite a challenge for a young woman. Some stuck it out for a year, then fled…"

nights to sew a dress so her student could attend graduation properly attired.

Not all teachers were saints; some weren't even competent. But considering the hours and the compensation, most of them did a remarkably good job…just as they do today.

Toward the end of my working days, I was privileged to spend 5 years teaching at a Midwestern university. It was the only job I ever had where I went home every night with a happy smile on my face.

I discovered why so many people stay in what is too often a poorly paid job with no hope for advancement and precious little recognition. Teaching is simply one of the most personally rewarding jobs anyone could hope for.

You have the opportunity to change lives—for the better, and often for years to come.

Dad's entire formal education was acquired in a one-room schoolhouse; just the basic three R's. But something more important happened. A fine teacher gave Dad a thirst for learning that enhanced his life for all of his 78 years. Thanks to the inspiration and curiosity instilled by that teacher, he made himself one of the best-read and most intelligent men I ever met.

Now turn the page and revisit your own childhood…your first day at school, the embarrassing moments, most memorable teachers, school clothes, holiday celebrations and all the other things that made up the fabric of school life.

And fear not if you don't finish it at one sitting…we promise not to make you stay late and clean the blackboard erasers. ❖

Bob Artley, the cartoonist who adds visual chuckles to chapter introductions in this book, has produced several collections of farm-related cartoons and memories. His latest collection, *Once Upon a Farm*, which covers his family's farm in the 1920s and '30s, will be in bookstores in the summer of 2000. Bob divides his time between retirement in Florida and the family's century farm near Hampton, Iowa. His brother, who operates the farm, claims that Bob's published works have "worked" the farm more thoroughly than he has.

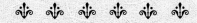

Chapter 1

First Day of School

First Day of School

Truth to tell, I have absolutely no memory of my first day in kindergarten at Lincoln School in Sterling, Illinois. That is a bit odd, because several traumatic childhood firsts are etched in my memory. My first haircut, for example, when I vaulted from the little merry-go-round horse the barber used for kiddies and fled howling into the busy downtown street.

But I draw a blank on that first day of all first days—my entry into the educational system. Little did I suspect what was ahead!

What I do recall was my delight at discovering a nice-looking young woman whose only apparent concern in life was to make me happy. She never lost her temper, never told me to go away until she finished stuffing the turkey, never chastised me for jumping up and down and making the angel food cake fall.

She told us stories. She led us in songs. She taught us the rules of fox-and-geese in the playground snow. She didn't scold us for spilling the sugary white sand out of the sandbox in the corner of the classroom. She helped us put on our four-buckle galoshes and made sure we had mittens—*someone's mittens*—for the trip home.

There were days when I would have swapped her for my own mother, except I wasn't sure she could cook.

Most likely the real reason going to school was a non-event in my life is because my mother, a former school-teacher, made school sound like the ultimate adventure, somewhere between Christmas morning and a circus parade. I couldn't wait to get there!

Some of my classmates had not been as well sold on the experience. They clung to their mothers' skirts, red-faced and baying to the heavens. Others simply bolted for freedom, as I had done in the barbershop.

Every time a Western movie shows bronc-busting in the dusty old corral, I think of opening day at school.

The "first days" I do remember came later. There was a new teacher every year, each with his or her own teaching style—a mystery requiring study and adjustment.

There was the second-grade teacher who drew bad reviews from kids a grade or two ahead of me. And no wonder! She had a hair-trigger temper that was awesome to behold. To this day I am convinced that her teeth turned bright green when she was at her angry worst. They did! I can see them still.

And then there was my fourth-grade teacher, who ruled a class the way Clyde Beatty dominated a cage of angry jungle cats. She consumed wooden rulers by the gross, breaking them on any backside within reach.

Although I draw a blank over my very first day in school, many others recall theirs perfectly, even as far back as 1910. Just follow along and share their memories.

—*Clancy Strock*

Rowdy Twins Struck Terror in the Hearts of Teachers

By Joe Juntunen, Carlton, Minnesota

AT HOME, my twin and I were always called Jum and Joe. But when we started school in the late 1930s, Mother told us to use our middle names. My name would be Melvin, and my brother's would be Merton.

Had the teachers known our true identities, they probably wouldn't have allowed us in public school. To this day, our older sisters say we were the most obnoxious kids they've ever seen.

Mother bought us matching playsuits with blue short pants and white tops from the Montgomery Ward catalog. "Now you have to be big boys," she told us as she combed our hair and tied our suspenders.

We boarded a bus for the half-mile trip to Esko, Minnesota, where we'd transfer to another bus for the 2-mile ride to Washington School. Our brother Art had told us if we got on the wrong bus in Esko, we'd wind up in China. In

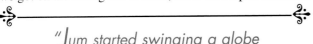

"Jum started swinging a globe that hung from the ceiling..."

Esko, Jum and I asked the bus driver, "Does this bus go to China?" He said no, so we hopped on board, ready to begin our school careers.

Before class began, the teacher took Jum and me aside. "Aren't you Jum and Joe, the Juntunen twins?" she asked. She spoke as if she was trying to weed out crabgrass before starting a new garden.

Jum rested his elbow on his bare knees and put his chin in his cupped hands. "Our names are Merton and Melvin Juntunen, and our pa's name is Hjalmer."

The teacher continued to view us suspiciously.

"Our mom bought us new clothes and shoes," I volunteered. From the expression on the teacher's face, this was not the information she was looking for.

"Follow me," she said and led us to our seats. Then she ran to the superintendent's office to see if she could get a year's leave of absence.

One day several weeks later, I felt sick. The teacher sent me to the sickroom, which was next to the principal's office. I'd been there only a short time when I noticed the telephone on the principal's desk, so I decided to call home.

OBNOXIOUS TWINS. Author (above left and far left) and twin brother Jum struck fear on first day of school when their first-grade teacher realized she had the infamous "Juntunen twins". She left school after Christmas break.

"I've been throwing up all afternoon," I shouted to my mother. "I think I've got pneumonia."

This should've struck a responsive chord. These were the pre-penicillin days, and pneumonia could be fatal. My brother Earl almost died of it several years earlier.

"Who is this?" Mother demanded. She had 13 children and didn't always know who was calling.

"This is Joe," I said.

"Where are you?"

"I'm in the sickroom at school," I said. "Will you make me cocoa when I get home?"

"Yes, after you drink your cod liver oil."

One day when the teacher stepped out of the room, Jum started swinging a globe that hung from the ceiling. Suddenly it broke loose and landed on the teacher's desk, breaking her eyeglasses. When the teacher got back, she gave Jum a public flogging with her blackboard pointer. She put him over her knees and pummeled away.

I was secretly pleased when something like this happened to Jum, because I could go home and tell Mother about it. But this time my smugness was short-lived. A few weeks later, I was flogged myself.

I'd been unable to spell a word, and the teacher accused me of "leaving my thinking cap in the ditch". I called her a nincompoop. She left school after the Christmas break.

At the end of the year, we had our all-school picnic at Hay Creek, east of the school. I remember the second-grade teacher eyeing Jum and me with disdain. That night, as always, we boarded the bus holding hands. We'd heard of two brothers who didn't hold hands. One missed the bus, and the janitor had to take him home. Luckily, he didn't end up in China. ✂

Sight of Teacher Sent Him Running for Home

WHEN I WAS 5, we lived in the small mining town of Clymer, Pennsylvania. On the first day of school, my mother took me to school, enrolled me and went back home.

When I walked into my classroom, I was terrified—the first-grade teacher was wearing red rouge on her cheeks and the brightest red lipstick I'd ever seen. My mother and her friends never wore makeup. I was so scared that I fled the building and ran the eight blocks home, crying all the way.

Mom had to have me placed in another class. I refused to return to school otherwise!
—*Dale Zimmerman*
Miami, Florida

HE RECOVERED. Dale Zimmerman obviously made it through first grade. He was a fourth grader when this picture of him and his pet rooster was taken in 1940.

"Landmark" Vanished Along with Her Route Home

IN 1930, we left our farm and moved to Medford, Oregon. When I started fourth grade, I was to attend a new school—and I'd have to walk there by myself.

My mother, a single parent who taught at another school, patiently drove me over the route several times. She suggested I pick out special landmarks on each street so I didn't lose my way.

The plan worked beautifully. I got to the school just fine and enjoyed my first day there. But when I started home, I had a problem. I'd picked a big yellow steamroller as one of my landmarks, and it was gone!

In tears, I found my way back to school. The teacher made arrangements for me to walk home with a boy from my class, whose parents would then take me home. This

THREE GENERATIONS. Author was all smiles on this day in 1930, when she posed with her grandmother, Irene Conger Wells, and mother, Edna May Beeson. After her walk to her first day of school, Charlotte's much-needed landmark wasn't in sight.

proved to be doubly frustrating—when we got to the boy's house, he was having a birthday party, and I wasn't invited to stay.

I always picked non-mobile landmarks after that.
—*Charlotte Toon*
Fairfield, California

Will the Real Joseph John Kelly Please Stand Up?

IN 1933, I enrolled as a freshman at Campion Prep in Prairie du Chien, Wisconsin. It was an ROTC boarding school for boys, operated by the Jesuits.

On our first day, we sat at our desks facing the teacher, Father F.X. Nebrich, who held an attendance roster in one hand. After an opening prayer, Father Nebrich said, "So that we all get acquainted, I will read your names alphabetically. When I call your name, please stand up. Does everyone understand?" All 20-plus of us nodded.

It wasn't long before Father Nebrich called out the name "Kelly". Three of us stood up. "All right, sit down," Father said.

Then he called, "John Joseph Kelly." Again all three of

THREE OF A KIND. When Joseph J. Kelly stood up after his name was called on the first day of ROTC boarding school, two other boys with the same name also stood up. The teacher soon settled the matter ...and settled it for good!

us stood up. Father pointed to the lad on my right and announced, "From now on, you are John Joseph Kelly."

Pointing at me, he said, "From now on, you are Joseph J. Kelly." To the Kelly on my left, he said, "And you are J.J.K. Now, all three of you Kellys please resume your seats." I've been "Joseph J." ever since.
—*Joseph Kelly*
Albuquerque, New Mexico

Pussy Willow Taffeta Was No Match for Frog-Hunting

By Eleanore Lofgren, Olympia, Washington

I THINK my mother was more excited about my first day of school in 1922 than I was. She went into a frenzy with the sewing machine, measuring tape, scissors, pins, needles and some reddish-pink material she called "pussy willow taffeta".

"It whispers when you walk," she said.

On the first day of school, Mother got me up early, washed and scrubbed me and finally slipped the taffeta dress over my head. She tied the sash, fastened a big floppy ribbon of the same material to a braid atop my head, then stepped back to admire her handiwork.

She looked up and said, "Here comes Jimmy. Be careful. Here's your lunch box. Use the napkin. Don't spoil your dress."

Jimmy was my next-door playmate. A year older, he knew all about going to school and was going to show me the way.

We walked along, holding hands, as we approached the end of the block. This was one of our favorite places to play in our Idaho Falls, Idaho neighborhood.

There was a large irrigation ditch with head-gates, frogs and pretty rocks. We could hear the water running out of the corrugated pipe that brought the water into the deepest part of the ditch.

Jimmy wanted to stop and check for frogs. I turned back to see if Mother was watching from the porch. I didn't see her, so I followed Jimmy onto the ditch bank, where we peered along the water's edge. When I took one more step for a closer look, my new shoes slipped on the grass, throwing me into the deepest part of the ditch. I started to scream—not because I was hurt, but because of the trouble I'd be in when I had to face Mother.

Jimmy pulled me out. I was soaking wet from the tip of my new shoes to the top of my pussy willow bow. Jimmy went on to school while I ran for home, screaming and dripping streams of pinkish water.

Mother heard my screams and met me just inside the screen door. When she saw me, she screamed, too. She scooped me up in her arms and ran into the bathroom, where my older brother was combing his hair in front of the mirror. I can still see the surprised look on his face when he asked, "Gee, what happened?"

Mother didn't answer. She kicked him out of the bathroom, slammed the door and started stripping the sopping mess off me. My screams subsided to great shaking sobs as Mother washed, scrubbed and combed me for the second time. She wrapped me in an old towel and plunked me down on the toilet seat lid.

As the pinkish bathwater ran down the drain, Mother leaned on the wash basin and looked in the mirror. Her blue dress was soaked with pinkish-purple stains.

"Why me?" she sighed. Suddenly Mother turned, opened the door and yelled, "Edward, you will have to take your sister to school."

"But Mom," he argued, "I'll be late!"

"I know, but it can't be helped. You'll just have to do it anyway. Take her on your bicycle."

By now Mother had me ready to go. I was still kind of pink in spots, and sore from all the scrubbing, but at least I was in a comfortable old dress and shoes.

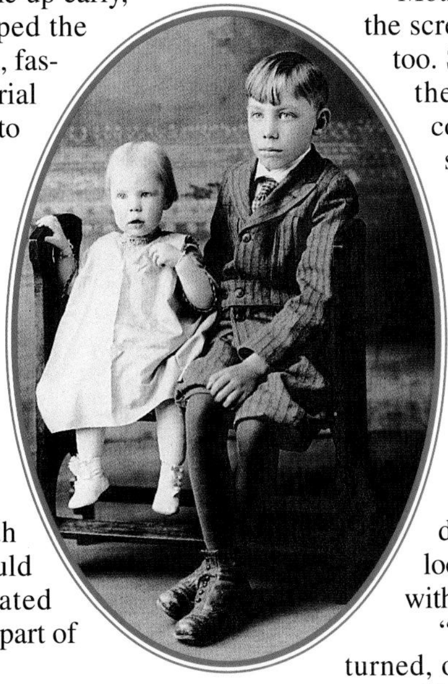

GENTLER TIMES. **Four years after this picture of Eleanore Lofgren and her brother Edward was taken in 1918, Eleanore went off to her first day of school, but fate and a ditch full of frogs intervened.**

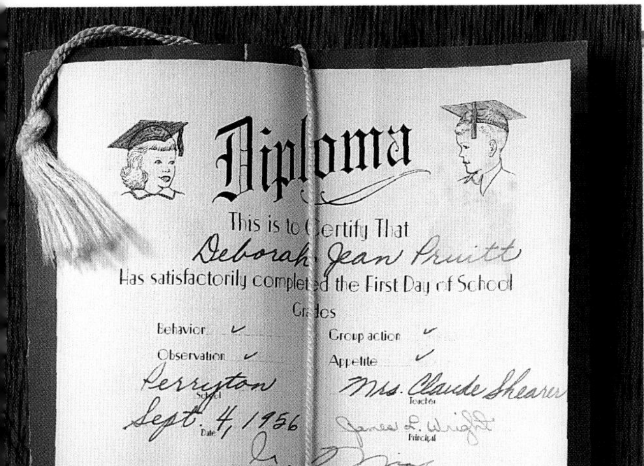

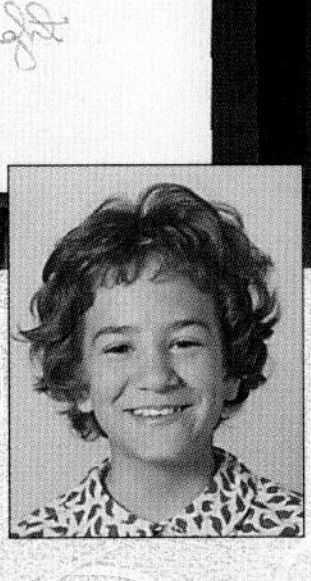

QUICK LEARNER. **Debbie Pruitt happily thought her first-day school diploma meant she was done with school after only 1 day.**

"Diploma" Convinced Child She Was a One-Day Wonder

I REMEMBER experiencing so many emotions on my first day of school in 1956—fear, happiness, pride, dread. But the best feeling of all was relief.

At the end of the day, I was given a diploma. It read: "This is to certify that Deborah Jean Pruitt has satisfactorily completed the first day of school." I was so proud. And I was glad, too. Now I was finished with school and didn't have to go back!

I wanted to tease my big brother and sister as we walked home that day, but I didn't. I felt sorry for them. Look at how old they were, and they still had to go to school. Maybe they were a little slow. But not me.

When we got home, I ran into the house and proudly told Mom and Dad, "I finished school. Here's my diploma!" Dad looked at it and said, "No, honey. This is just for the first day. You have to go back for many years."

Years! I was heartbroken. *—Debbie Pruitt, Dallas, Texas*

Teacher's Fairy-Tale Charms Turned First Grader's Head

I STARTED first grade in the fall of 1953 in Hamilton Township, New Jersey. Having attended the previous term as a half-day kindergartner, I was proud to join the ranks of the full-time students.

Our new teacher, Mrs. Woodward, welcomed us warmly. Once we were seated and counted, she said that too many pupils had been assigned to her class and asked if anyone would be willing to transfer to Mrs. Alpert's room.

I raised my hand. When Mrs. Woodward asked me why I wanted to be in Mrs. Alpert's class, I blurted, "Because she looks like Snow White."

Obviously amused, Mrs. Woodward left the room and returned with Mrs. Alpert. They whispered to each other, smiling in my direction. Then Mrs. Woodward asked me again why I wanted to switch classrooms.

I was more self-conscious now that the young, pretty Mrs. Alpert was beaming down at me, but I managed to repeat my earlier response. The teachers giggled and exchanged a

FIRST GRADE - MRS. ALPERT

PRINCE CHARMING. When Phil Feinberg (inset photo) started first grade, there were too many children in his classroom. He was offered a chance to transfer to Mrs. Alpert's class and he readily agreed. Read his story to learn why.

few words, then Mrs. Alpert beckoned me to come with her.

It was the beginning of a memorable year. Mrs. Alpert's instructional skills and attentiveness ultimately carried far more significance for me than the initial attraction that so impressed me on the first day of school. —*Phil Feinberg*
Penndel, Pennsylvania

Scent Brings Back Memories Of Kindergarten "Rest Time"

IN SEPTEMBER 1935, I started kindergarten at Lindbergh School in Dearborn, Michigan. I was not quite 4-1/2.

The room seemed very large to me, and I was surprised to see a sandbox and a slide indoors.

For "rest time", each student brought a small rug to nap on. To this day, whenever I'm in the rug department of a large store, the scent of the rugs brings back my kindergarten days.

—*Nora Cripps, Howell, Michigan*

SLEEPY STUDENTS. A certain scent reminds Nora Cripps of "rest times" like this.

First-Timer Found Himself In Right Church, Wrong Pew

MOVING UP. Jim Henderson just took a seat on his first day of school. Unfortunately, it was in the wrong classroom.

OUR FAMILY was living on a tenant cotton farm in Elmore County, Alabama when I started school in fall of 1930. I walked the 1-1/2 miles to Holtville School with my two older brothers.

When we got there, I had no idea where to go, so I walked into the fourth-grade room and sat down. I can still see those big kids snickering at me. I didn't see anything funny, so I just sat there.

After a while, the first-grade teacher came to the room and asked me to come with her. She took me to the first-grade classroom where I belonged.

When I returned for our 50th class reunion, I had dinner with that teacher. I told her that if she'd left me alone, I would've gotten out of high school 4 years sooner.

—*Jim Henderson Sr.*
Siloam Springs, Arkansas

"Odd Girl Out" Found Herself in a Hairy Situation

THE NIGHT before I started classes at Lincoln School in Reno County, Kansas, Mother put a home permanent in my very straight hair. In 1940, these perms contained a slimy green waving lotion, so that was an experience in itself.

The next day, I went to school all curly-haired, wearing a crisp new wine-colored dress that my mother had sewn for my big day. I also carried my lunch, which included some purple grapes.

Lincoln was a one-room school that had grades one through eight. I was one of four first graders.

The other three were already friends, but I didn't know any of them, so I stood back at morning recess while they enjoyed the three playground

RABBIT STAYED HOME. Sylvia Richmond left her pet rabbit behind when she went to her first day of school. She didn't know the other three first graders, but they introduced themselves in a most memorable way.

swings. At noon, "the other three" decided I needed wine-colored hair to match my dress, so they rubbed the grapes from my lunch into my hair.

The teacher had to wash my hair—in cold water from the well—so there went my curls.

At afternoon recess, "the other three" were detained. I ran from swing to swing while they watched from their desks.

Although I looked bedraggled when I came home that afternoon, those first few weeks were good ones.

I'll always remember the sound of doves cooing outside the school, and the yellow goldenrod that was the same color as the delicious egg salad sandwiches Mother put in my lunch. She never packed purple grapes again
—*Sylvia Richmond, Grandin, Missouri*

Kindergartner Unfazed By Rigors of Education

WHEN OUR son Timm was 5 years old, in 1949, he started kindergarten in Los Angeles, California. I don't think he was very impressed. When he came home the first day, I asked him what he did.

He replied, "Today we learned to read. Tomorrow we're going to write. Then I won't have to go anymore and I can stay home and play."

I'm pleased to report that he turned out okay and is now an excellent car repairman with four busy teenagers of his own. —*Babs Foley, Lake Havasu City, Arizona*

❧ ❧ ❧ ❧ ❧

HE REALLY RECESSED. When his teacher dismissed the class for recess the first day of school in 1910, Verne Phelps misunderstood. This was his class picture, but Verne didn't identify himself.

At Recess, He Was First Out the Door

I BEGAN SCHOOL in August 1910. Our teacher, Miss Cantey, called the roll, then had us stand and pledge allegiance to the flag.

She told us where the boys' and girls' toilets were located, and to raise our hands to get her attention.

Before much longer, she announced it was time for recess. I was seated near the door, so I was the first one to leave. I headed straight for home, which was only a block away.

When I told my mother why I'd come home, she laughed and explained that "recess" was time to go outside and play. She gave me a loving pat on my bottom and sent me back to school.

I was the last one to return to the classroom. I raised my hand to tell Miss Cantey what I'd done at recess, and she had a hearty laugh. —*Verne Phelps, Edina, Minnesota*

Beanbag Mishap Transformed His Teacher into 'Angel of Death'

By Wally Windscheffel, Grand Junction, Colorado

WHEN MY FIRST DAY of kindergarten arrived in Smith Center, Kansas, I was a little bit scared, but happy. I would be 5 in just 2 weeks.

My 12-year-old brother, Frank, left for school before I did. "I'll see ya after school, Wally," he hollered with a grin.

Frank had been telling me about school for days. According to him, all teachers were treacherous, the work was hard and if you weren't careful, a girl might kiss you at recess in front of your friends.

Mom walked the short distance to school with me. The two-story redbrick building, surrounded by a bare-dirt playground with a few swings and slides, was familiar to me. But it seemed different now that I was an official student. I hadn't come just to use the playground.

The kindergarten room was in the basement, with its own side entrance. Mom and I went down the steps and into the large room filled with noisy kids and their mothers.

"Oh, Mrs. Windscheffel! So this is little Waldemar. I'm sure we'll get along fine," my new teacher said. She was bending over with her hand on my shoulder, smiling brightly at me. She was very pretty, and she smelled nice, too. Could this teacher be treacherous? I thought not.

After the mothers left, the teacher talked for a long time about all the rules of going to school. Some rules were clear to me, but others were a little hazy.

Why did we have to hold up one or two fingers? What was a fire drill? (Grandpa had a wheat drill; surely that wasn't the same thing.) And what about "marching in an orderly file"? (Grandpa had a file, too, for sharpening his tools.)

When the teacher finished, we were given our first play period. My old friend Bobby Don Burr asked if I wanted to play in the classroom sandbox. But our attention soon shifted to the beanbags. Bobby thought it would be more sporting to throw his beanbag at a moving target—me—than at a cardboard clown's mouth.

Maybe it was more sporting, but when this moving target ducked, the beanbag crashed into the clock on the teacher's desk, knocking it to the floor. The glass front was shattered.

The teacher grabbed us by our shirt collars and marched us to the front of the room. Her transformation from smiling teacher to Angel of Death kept me from even trying to plead self-defense. We were scolded in front of the class and ordered to stand in the cloakroom until it was time to go home. Frank had been right. ✁

Brown Brothers

FULL OF BEANS. Playtime in kindergarten classes like this one could be great fun. But when Wally Windscheffel and his pal started tossing beanbags, they got in a hill full of trouble.

Child Knew Her Name— She Wasn't Just Whistling Dixie

By Dixie Caughel, Fort Myers, Florida

THE WHOLE SUMMER OF 1925, I looked forward to starting school. When the day finally arrived, I was excited. I was 5 years old and couldn't wait to go to school and make new friends.

The principal met each of us at the door and directed us to our rooms. Our kindergarten teacher, Miss Brown, assigned us chairs at a large round table. She gave each of us a coloring book and crayons and told us to select a picture to color. As we worked, she would call each of us to her desk to answer some questions.

When my turn came, I sat in a chair next to her desk. Miss Brown asked me what my name was.

"Dixie Glanton," I said.

Miss Brown replied, "No, I want your real name, not your nickname."

"That is my real name," I said.

"No," Miss Brown said, "that is your nickname."

I didn't know what a nickname was, but I knew my name was Dixie, and I said so. Finally she gave up and moved along to other questions. How old was I? When was my birthday? What was my address?

Miss Brown was satisfied with my answers—until she asked what my father's name was. "Shorty," I said. Again she said this wasn't a real name, but a nickname. I stuck to my guns. It was his name. That's what everyone called him.

Miss Brown said she would send a note to my mother

TRICK QUESTIONS? Like Dixie Caughel, this schoolgirl looks ready to answer any queries her new teacher might ask.

when I went home for lunch, and she wanted an answer when I returned.

I arrived home upset and very mixed up. When I gave Mother the note, she began to laugh. "Sit down," she said. "We'll have lunch and I'll help you understand what a nickname is."

It turned out that many of the people in our family—including my father, Horace—had nicknames, but I wasn't one of them. It might have been unusual in those days, but Dixie was my real name, and I made sure Miss Brown knew it when I took that note back after lunch! ⚜

Kindergartner Preferred Moniker to "Monica"

WHEN I started kindergarten at public school in Buffalo, New York in 1952, the teacher sent a note home to my parents, asking them to have my hearing checked. She said that when she called on me in class, I didn't respond.

The teacher called me "Monica", which was the name on my birth certificate and school papers—but everyone had called me "Mitzie" since I was a baby.

When the teacher called on "Monica",

I had no idea she was speaking to me.

At that time, the Catholic schools did not offer kindergarten. For first grade, my parents sent me to a Catholic school —St. Monica's. Believe it or not, all the sisters called me "Mitzie" so I wouldn't get upset.

—*Mitzie Lewandowski
Rochester, New York*

⚜   ⚜   ⚜

WRONG NAME. Mitzie Lewandowski (right) didn't answer to her given name, Monica, when she started kindergarten.

Rural Alabama School Gave Her Many Happy Memories

MY FAMILY MOVED from Texas to Alabama in January 1926, when I was 6. I hadn't gone to school yet—children in Texas didn't begin until age 7 then—but Mother taught me the alphabet and how to count to 100 by ones, fives and tens.

My formal education began that September at the three-room country school in Allgood. I was very eager to begin. Daddy hitchhiked to town and bought me a primer, a tablet, one pencil and a blue lunch box.

The school was 2-1/2 miles away, and we didn't have a car. Mother arranged for the teacher, Lula Belle Lacey, to pick me up in her Model T. Miss Lacey was a pretty 18-year-old, and I adored her.

I quickly learned to read and loved it so much that my family soon began calling me "the bookworm".

The school had no running water or electricity, and there were two outhouses out back. At recess and lunchtime, the girls played in the pine trees near the school, outlining rooms of "play houses" with low walls of pine needles.

We had chapel once or twice a week, with Bible reading and prayer.

The school had a bell tower with a long rope, and we took turns ringing the bell to call the children to classes. It was considered a great privilege to be the one to ring the bell.

The summer after first grade, Miss Lacey got married and became Mrs. Wilson. That fall, my sister Lillie Ruth started school, and we both had Mrs. Wilson as our teacher.

We moved back to Texas in 1928, but I never forgot that little country school, or my beloved teacher. About 10 years ago, my sister and I went back to Alabama and visited Mrs. Wilson. She still looked young and pretty.

—*Martha Dudley, Nacogdoches, Texas*

GOOD-BYE, SIS. Martha Dudley was eager to start school in 1926. That's her brother O.R. and sister Lillie Ruth waving in the background. Inset is a 1989 photo of her teacher, Mrs. Wilson.

First-Day Footrace?

IT WAS 1935, and I was 5 and ready to start school. We lived just around the block from the school, so my mother walked me over and got me situated in the classroom.

But when she started to leave, I cried. She finally settled me down and left.

As soon as she left, I ran out of the room, out of the school, across the school grounds, through backyards, jumped fences and was sitting on the front steps of our house when Mother arrived.

You can imagine the surprised look on her face. She took me right back to school. This time I stayed.

—*Paul Ohlemacher, Sandusky, Ohio*

At Age 5, This Prospective Student Was Wise Beyond His Years

IN FALL 1945, my mother decided it was time for me to start school. I could've enrolled the previous fall, but she wanted to let me mature a little more before leaving her side. On a bright sunny day, we went to Frances Willard Grade School in Rock Island, Illinois to register.

Because I'd turn 6 that November, I could either attend kindergarten, or skip it and start with first grade. The registrar asked my mother where she wanted me to begin. She hesitated for a moment, then turned to me and asked, "Which would you prefer?"

The registration desk was in the hall, between the two classrooms. I looked into the first-grade room and saw desks, maps, textbooks, and big numbers and letters on the walls. I began to picture myself there all day.

Then I looked into the kindergarten room. It was filled with blocks, games and activity tables with paints and crayons. I would be there for only half the day, leaving me all afternoon to play at home.

I was no dummy. "I would prefer to start there," I said, pointing to the kindergarten room. And so I did.

—*Paul Castle*
Rock Island, Illinois

STUDENT'S CHOICE. Paul Castle was 5 when this picture of him and his mother was taken in 1944. He went to school the next year at age 6 and was given an interesting—and unusual—choice to make.

First-Day Jitters Took Their Toll on Mom, Too

By Dick Hanson, Mentor, Ohio

I HAD a great summer in 1938. I knew I would start school that fall at the Sixth Ward School in Bradford, Pennsylvania, but I wasn't thinking about that. I was having too much fun.

Our family spent several weeks in Sunset Bay, New York. What fun we had—swimming, cooking hot dogs over a campfire and enjoying the rides at a little amusement park. I knew it was August, but for a 6-year-old, September seemed a long way off.

We'd barely returned from vacation when my two older sisters began talking about going back to school. Suddenly I realized that school began the day after Labor Day—and Labor Day was only 2 days away. My heart sank. I didn't want to leave Mom and spend the day in that scary brick building!

We had a family picnic on Labor Day, but nothing looked good to me. Even Mom's applesauce cake stuck in my throat. I couldn't understand why.

It seemed very, very early when Mom woke me the next morning. I put on a new pair of brown oxfords with kneesocks, a white shirt with a collar and a fairly new pair of short pants. At least it wasn't cold enough to wear my scratchy old knickers.

After Mom combed my hair, I thought I looked pretty good. But I didn't feel good. My throat was so tight I could hardly speak. I didn't want to go to school, but I said nothing.

Mom had promised to walk to school with me and meet my first-grade teacher. My sisters had already left,

DRESSED TO LEARN. Like this young boy, Dick Hanson was all set for his first day of school in his short pants, white shirt, kneesocks and oxfords.

so Mom took me by the hand, held onto my little brother, Bill, with the other hand and off we went.

Mom tried to talk to me, but I remained silent. Bill was talking up a storm, saying he wished he was going to school like me.

Our 1-mile walk ended much sooner than I'd hoped. I stood at the bottom of the steps leading to the entrance. The steps looked so steep, as if they led to the top of the world.

When we found my room, I clasped Mom's hand tighter and tighter. The teacher pointed out my desk, and Mom took me to it. Then it happened—I started to cry. Oh, did I cry. There was no way I was going to stay with these strange kids and this strange teacher!

Mom put her arm around me and assured me everything would be fine. Before long it would be lunchtime, and she'd be back to walk me home. She promised to fix me almost anything I wanted, if only I'd stop crying.

Finally, the teacher told Mom to leave. Mom was so nervous and upset by that time that she was relieved to go. As she hurried toward home, she kept thinking about me, hoping I'd be all right when she returned at noon.

Then Mom realized she'd forgotten something—my brother. Bill was still at school with me! By the time she returned to retrieve him, I was fine and happily waved good-bye to both of them.

I went on to graduate from high school and Penn State University, but every year I dreaded the first day of school. Maybe it just brought back memories of that day in 1938, when Mom left two boys at school instead of one. ❧

School Like a Foreign Land For Czech-Speaking Child

MY FIRST DAY of school was like going to a foreign country. Up until that September in 1932, all I'd ever known was Czech. I spoke, wrote and read only Czech.

My mother took me to Central School in South St. Paul, Minnesota and left me with the first-grade teacher.

Miss Smith directed me to a desk piled with several black metal boxes. Curious, I opened one and found eight thick pencil-shaped objects in different colors. Thinking they were can-

dy, I picked up the blue one—my favorite color—and bit off the pointed end. It tasted awful!

Miss Smith took the rest of this strange blue object away from me, put it back in the box and slapped my hand. Later, I found out that I'd tasted a crayon!

I heard Miss Smith say something—I didn't know what—then saw pencils and pieces of paper being passed back from the front of each row. Miss Smith said something else I didn't understand. I saw the other

students write something on their sheets of paper and pass them forward.

I had no idea what to do, so I scribbled on my paper and passed it forward. I really felt like a foreigner that day.

But I did learn English that year. I brought my first reading book, *Dick and Jane*, home with me every day. With it, I was able to teach my mother and sister to read and speak English as well.

—*Mary Stich*
Mendota Heights, Minnesota

When All Else Failed, Mom Tried Reverse Psychology

By Alice Marks, Colorado Springs, Colorado

I'D RARELY been away from my parents, so starting school in 1928 was traumatic. I'd never even had a baby-sitter. My folks seldom went anywhere, and if they did, my grandmother was always there to watch me, because she lived with us at our home in Cedar Rapids, Iowa.

I cried and carried on every single day of school. After 2 weeks of this, my mother was worn out. She tried everything—pleading, begging, scolding, bribing, even spanking. Still, I wailed every morning. To make things more miserable, it rained almost every day.

One morning I got up and found my school clothes weren't laid out as usual. As I ate breakfast, the older neighbor girl who usually walked to school with me walked right past our house. This was a new twist, and I was worried. It was getting late.

"Where are my school clothes?" I finally asked Mom.

"Oh, I decided you couldn't go to school today," she replied.

"Why not? Teacher says we're supposed to come every day unless we're sick!"

"Do you want to go?"

"YES!"

"Well, we'll have to hurry," Mom said. "The 8:30 bell

HAPPIER DAYS. Alice Marks looks a little more relaxed in this October 1928 photo than she did during the first 2 weeks of school that year.

has already rung." (School started at 9 o'clock.)

My 3-year-old brother, Bob, piped up, "I want to go, too, and see sister's school."

"You'd better stay with Grandma," Mom told him. "It's raining."

"No, I want to go," Bob protested. Now he was crying.

So Mom bundled us into raincoats and rubbers, and we hurried the five or six muddy blocks to Edgewood School. Bob lost his rubbers in the mud, but we made it to my room just as the last bell rang. My teacher greeted me at the door.

"I'm so glad to see you, Alice," she said. "We're going to make pigs today."

"I don't want to make any old pig," I retorted.

She thanked my mother for bringing me, took me by the shoulders and guided me none too gently into the cloakroom. Later, Mom said she could hear me shouting, "Good-bye, Mama! Good-bye, Mama!" through the cloakroom window until she and Bob got back to the muddy road.

It was a miserable beginning, but I grew to like school and became an educator myself. I spent 4 years teaching and another 15 as a speech therapist. ✦

Early Enrollee Was Overwhelmed Without Cousin at Her Side

EARLY START. Martha Marsh (left) attended the one-room schoolhouse in Macon County, Missouri (below).

FOR CHRISTMAS in 1920, my parents gave me a primer. They promised that, as soon as I read it, I could go to school with my cousin Iris, who was in eighth grade.

I quickly discovered the joy of reading and started school about 2 months after Christmas. I shared a double seat with Iris in the back of our one-room country school. To me, Iris was the epitome of intelligence and goodness, and I was completely happy with her beside me.

However, when Iris left her seat to go to the blackboard or the recitation bench at the front of the room, my feelings of security vanished and I started to cry. This went on for days.

One evening when I got home, I told Mother, "I'll be glad when this old school business is over."

Mother asked, "Why, did you cry again today?"

"I most certainly did," I said.

That ended my school career until the next fall. By then I was 6 years old and Iris was in high school, so I was on my own. I went on to graduate from high school and college, then taught school until I married at age 25. In 1963, I resumed teaching and continued until my retirement in 1981.

It took a long time for "this old school business" to be over.

—*Martha Marsh, Gladstone, Missouri*

Brave Entry into New World Crumbled Before Class Began

By RubyLee Schneider, Portland, Oregon

WE MOVED to Portland in time for my sixth birthday, in January 1933. At that time, the school district had a two-track system. Depending on your age, you could start first grade in either September or January.

Since I'd already been to kindergarten, mostly in dark church basements, I'd start first grade right away.

In "real school", I'd learn to read exciting books, like my parents and brothers did. Even at age 6, I didn't find Dick, Jane and Spot particularly exciting. From my brothers' concentration, I suspected their adventure books contained pure magic.

My parents had pre-registered me, so my favorite big brother walked me to school the first day.

I wore a brand-new Pendleton jacket and hat of creamy wool with rainbow stripes. In my hand was my own First Reader.

My brother says I waved at the policeman at the corner of 42nd and Fremont, marched across the street and walked right into Beaumont School, set to conquer the world.

A "big person" monitor, probably a fifth grader, took me to a huge, bright classroom, where I was assigned a seat and told to leave my precious Reader in the desk. Then the monitor took me down a hallway lined with what ap-

> *"I did what any intelligent 6-year-old would do—I howled..."*

peared to have 10,000 identical lockers. She told me to leave my beautiful new jacket and hat in one of those steel coffins.

We started back to the classroom—and then the monitor disappeared.

There I was, not tall enough to peek into a classroom to spot the desk that held my very own Reader, and unable to remember which locker had swallowed my gorgeous new coat. What was I to do?

I did what any intelligent 6-year-old would do. I sat down right in the middle of the hallway and howled.

Obviously, someone rescued me, since I'm not still sitting there with tears running down my face. But that's all I remember of my first day of "real school".

Kid Sister Tantalized by Siblings' School Adventures

MY OLDER brother and sister were already in school, and I envied them. I wondered what great adventures they were having, and I wanted to go, too. "When can I go, Mom?" I asked over and over.

The day finally came in September 1945. Mom pulled our 1936 Packard out of the garage, and I proudly got in beside her. We lived close to town and usually walked everywhere, but this day was special.

When we arrived at school, I was holding my mother's hand. She looked so beautiful with her long black hair, brown hat and long coat. She always reminded me of Ingrid Bergman.

As we entered the first-grade classroom, I became aware of the unusual scents—floor polish, crayons—and of all the other children. My sense of adventure left quickly. I was scared.

"Let's go home, Mom," I said. "We can come back tomorrow."

Mom sat me down at a table with a picture book, and I became engrossed in it. "Look, Mom," I said after a while.

TOOTHLESS GRIN. Doris Christensen was excited about going to school... until she got there. In this first-grade picture in Safford, Arizona, she's in the back row, third from the right—the smiling one without front teeth.

"Here's a picture of a little calf." There was no response. Mom had left!

I must have been wide-eyed as the teacher came toward me and said, "It's all right. You'll be going home shortly, and your brother will be waiting outside for you. You can walk home with him."

Sure enough, when the school day was over and I went outside, my third-grade brother was there. But he wanted to walk with his friends, not a kid sister. "You can follow me home," he said. "But you have to walk on *that* side of the street, and we'll walk on this side."

I often wonder if children have the same feelings today when they start school. To me, that first day will always be a precious memory.

—*Doris Christensen*
Buckley, Washington

Mama Was Just Down the Road

I REMEMBER my first day of school in Lake Arthur, Louisiana in 1946. Mama took me and stayed with me as long as she could, then left with all the other mothers.

I didn't cry. But I was very sad, except when we went out to play at recess and lunch.

There were four large oak trees on the edge of the school property. I'd sit on one of the large roots of the first tree, and from there I could look down the street and see the very last stop sign.

I knew my mama was right down that street, and when I looked that way, which I did through recess and lunch, I'd feel all warm inside and wasn't sad anymore.

—*Joetta Bussy La Point*
Lake Arthur, Louisiana

DOWN THE STREET. Joetta La Point (right and above) discovered she could sit on the root of a large oak tree and focus on the far stop sign, showing the street where her family lived. Her mother, Lena Mae Bussy (top left), was only that far away.

Anticipation Gave Way to Anxiety on Long Walk to School

By Irene Rader, San Jose, California

I'M OKAY NOW. Author (on the right) posed with her older sister and brother, Renata and LeRoy, and younger sister Delores in 1937, about 2 years after Irene's unfinished first walk to school.

ONE OF MY first memories is from the spring of 1935, when I was 4 years old. Day after day, I watched my older brother and sister start off to school, books and lunch pails in hand, to spend the day in what I imagined was a special and exciting place.

Each afternoon, I eagerly awaited their return so I could listen to their accounts of the day's happenings. The things they learned, their tales of playtime and their mischievous escapades were so intriguing.

Looking over the papers and books they brought home made me happy. I even learned to read the *Dick and Jane* books with my sister's help.

I began badgering my mother to let me go to school someday. I whined, complained, begged and cried until she finally decided to let me walk to school by myself one afternoon.

The small country schoolhouse was nestled in a valley just below a gently sloping hill, about a half mile south of our farm

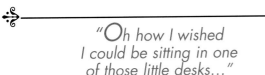

"Oh how I wished I could be sitting in one of those little desks..."

in Walworth County, South Dakota. I'd seen it many times from our car on our occasional trips to town, and I'd peered in its windows on summer walks with my siblings.

Oh, how I wished I could be sitting in one of those little desks near the front of the room!

Eagerly Started Down the Road

On this day, however, I'd go to school all by myself to join the children who were already there. Scrubbed and wearing my best dress, I started down the road in eager anticipation. I walked all the way past the garden gate before turning to wave good-bye to my mother.

At the far end of the garden, I saw the clump of plum trees where we played in summer and stopped to admire the pink blossoms. Finally I trudged past the pasture gate, where the milk cows were lazily munching the first blades of new grass.

Our big red barn now seemed far in the distance—but I could not yet see the little white schoolhouse ahead. The school never seemed this far away. A feeling of uneasiness came over me.

Where Was the School?

Before long, I was near the top of the hill, next to the gate that led to Uncle John's farm. Surely the school should be in sight by now! My legs began to tire, and suddenly I wondered why I ever wanted to go to school in the first place.

The next thing I knew, I was running as fast as my little legs could carry me, but in the opposite direction. With tears streaming down my cheeks, I headed for the safety of home and the security of my mother's arms.

That September, I started first grade, just a few weeks short of my fifth birthday. I walked to school holding on tightly to my older sister's hand. That was my first real day of school—but I don't remember anything else about it! ✧

HELPING HAND. Older brothers and sisters such as these can make the transition to school easier for a first-timer.

First Day of High School Was a Study in Misery

By Anna Gray, Boca Raton, Florida

AFTER 6 HOURS as a high school student, I made a vow to myself: I was never going back there again.

My parents had moved to the outskirts of Mars, Pennsylvania in 1931, after I graduated from a two-room country school. I didn't know anyone who'd attend my new school. As a shy 13-year-old, I looked on this new venture with some trepidation, but my parents painted a picture of the joys and opportunities that awaited.

On the first day of school, I got up with what would've been diagnosed as flu if we'd had a doctor. My mother was my doctor. After a week of chicken broth and Jell-O, I was ready to start high school.

In my best homemade jumper and blouse, brown-bag lunch in hand, I started down our rutted country road on a sunny September morning. It was a 1-mile walk to school, and there were no buses in those days.

Building Was *Big*

The building looked even bigger than I'd imagined. I saw kids standing around the entrance, and they all appeared to be eyeing me as I approached. I found a doorway with "OFFICE" lettered above it and timidly entered.

BAD START. This high school was daunting for Anna Gray because she moved from a small school and started a week late.

The principal was seated behind his desk and looked up at me. When I shyly explained that I was a freshman who'd missed last week because of illness, he handed me a sheet of paper without saying a word.

I saw a lot of kids entering Room D—the freshman room, according to my paper. I followed them in and sat down in the back. Another girl promptly told me that I was in her seat. I apologized and took another, with the same results.

After trying three or four seats, I got brave enough to approach the teacher and explain my plight. It seemed all the seats were assigned, and overflow kids were using the library as their homeroom. By now I was dying of embarrassment. The thought that everyone considered me a country bumpkin was almost unbearable.

After blundering around, looking into strange rooms where hundreds of strange faces seemed to turn in my direction, I finally found the library.

There was only one empty seat—at a table of five boys, three of them big upperclassmen. As a senior, I might have loved this situation, but for a bashful child, it was crushing. The boys teased me for being a "little girl". I wanted to die!

I found myself in the wrong room more than once that day, too dazed to attempt to figure out my schedule. What confusion, after the security of attending a school that had four grades in one room.

How I longed to be back in eighth grade in my little country school!

She Couldn't Quit

When this misery of a day ended, I made it through town without any show of emotion, but as soon as I hit our country road, I started bawling and couldn't stop. My poor mother was torn between sympathy and firmness, but when I said my school days were over, she made it clear that wasn't an option.

The embarrassment of that first day remained with me through my entire freshman year. I rarely recited in class, though I got good grades on written exams. My teachers weren't the ogres I'd imagined them to be—I think they understood.

But all bad things, if endured, can get better. I even managed to love high school by the time I graduated. ❧

First Grader Couldn't Stop Crying for Weeks

KINDERGARTEN was no problem for me—after all, we lived right across the street from my first school.

First grade at "real" school, however, was a whole different story. Our family had moved to a new neighborhood, and the school was six long blocks away.

When the big day arrived, my older brother, Freddie, was no more eager to go to second grade than I was to go to first.

Mother drove us to school in her new 1931 Chevrolet and escorted us to our respective rooms. As soon as she was out of sight, I began to cry. Another little girl, Betty Marie, was crying, too. Our teacher, Miss Olive Davis, tried to comfort us. She was sweet, but she wasn't Mama.

This scene was repeated every day for the first couple of weeks. Then, one wonderful day, I didn't cry.

Betty Marie's tears continued for several more days. I was so proud of myself for being the first one of us to stop crying.

Freddie's story was different. His second-grade teacher was stern—and stern-looking—and handled his display of tears with a terse announcement.

"There will be *no* crybabies in *this* room!" she pronounced.

Then she wisely assigned another pupil, Richard, to be a friend to Freddie. Richard looked after Freddie like a mother hen caring for her little chick.

The two boys became best of friends and continued their friendship through the years.

—*Betty Mintz*
Memphis, Tennessee

EAGER AND SMILING. Beverly Ferris was more than ready for her first day of school, even though she was only 5 years old and entering as a first grader.

In Nebraska, First Day Wasn't Always in Fall

BACK in the "good old days", the first day of school didn't always occur in fall. In some parts of Nebraska, children were allowed to start school any time after they turned 5.

My fifth birthday was in December. In March 1937, I was dressed in warm clothes and equipped with a lunch box, tablet and crayons, and off I went.

Mom said she sent me to school that spring so I'd "learn to sit still and be still". In later years, I realized she needed the peace and quiet so she could rest in preparation for the birth of my brother, who arrived that June.

There was no kindergarten in the rural school I attended, so I was considered a first grader. Mom had prepared me well by teaching me the numbers and alphabet.

When the new first graders arrived that fall, I was pushed ahead to second grade, resulting in my graduation from high school at age 16. —*Beverly Ferris Hastings, Nebraska*

28 Years Later, Son's Day Mirrored His Own

I STARTED attending Ogden Grade School in Ogden, Kansas in September 1930, when I was 5 years old. I wasn't ready for school, didn't like it, didn't know the other kids, was afraid and cried the first day.

At lunchtime, Dad showed up with some of his homegrown watermelons and sliced them for my sister, brothers and me to share with our classmates.

That made the day easier for me—the other kids wanted to befriend anyone who had watermelons to share.

Twenty-eight years later, my wife and I tried to  prepare our eldest son, Mitch, for his first day at Seven Dolors Elementary School in Manhattan, Kansas. He, too, was 5 years old.

We expressed confidence in him and assured him all would go well. I promised I'd be waiting for him when school was out.

I considered showing up at lunchtime with some doughnuts for Mitch to share, but I didn't. The nuns preferred to handle the first couple of weeks their way, without interference, and I wasn't going to argue.

When Mitch's school day ended, I met him eagerly and asked how it went.

"Okay," he replied rather nonchalantly.

"Did anything unusual happen?" I asked.

"No," he said. "Well, one little boy did cry a bit."

"Oh!" I said. "Was he anyone you knew?"

"Yes," Mitch said, hooking a thumb at his chest. "Me."

I hugged Mitch with tears of empathy in my eyes as memories of my own first day of school came racing back. —*Carl Crumpton Topeka, Kansas*

"Initiation" Made First Day Rough at All-Girls' School

FRESHMAN INITIATION certainly made for a traumatic first day at Bishop Muldoon, a girls' high school in Rockford, Illinois. Each senior was assigned a freshman as her "slave" for the day.

My senior had me braid my long hair in about 20 different directions. I had to wear a high-heeled shoe on one foot and a four-buckle rubber boot on the other, with a nylon and garter over the top.

At lunchtime, I had to eat a bunch of grapes one at a time, with a fork. Before each bite, I had to say, "Supercilious seniors do supercilious things."

My sister was a junior at the same school. As I walked down the hall, I saw her and called out to her. She turned around and stared at me. "Janice?" she said. I was such a mess my own sister didn't recognize me.
—*Janice Julius, Oceanside, California*

INITIATION SURVIVORS. **Janice Julius (on the left) and friends wore traditional attire for their 1953 high school graduation. Initiation on the first day was a different story.**

Sister Had "Lucky" Attendance Streak

MY YOUNGER SISTER, Carolyn, began kindergarten in 1934 at P.S. 87 in Windsor Hills, a suburb of Baltimore, Maryland. Our German shepherd, "Lucky", accompanied her the four blocks to school.

The big kindergarten room had a door directly to the yard with a little stoop, so Lucky settled there to wait for her. When the children came out to the playground, he sat on a little hill and watched over all the class. And when school was over, he walked Carolyn home.

From then on, he came to school with Carolyn every day. Although Lucky was a big dog, he was very gentle and had a good reputation in the neighborhood. Everyone, especially children, loved him.

One day while Carolyn was inside the school, it started to rain. The children stared out the windows at their pal getting soaked on the roofless porch. Soon, 25 children were crying so loudly that the principal, Miss Emily Eversfield, came out of her office to see what was the matter.

When their teacher, Miss House, told her the situation, Miss Eversfield said, "Well, bring Lucky in, but he must stay in the cloakroom."

Soon Lucky was lying in the cloakroom on top of some coats the children claimed had "fallen" on the floor. From that day on, he was a regular member of the class.

In fact, Miss House put his name on the attendance chart that hung on the wall. Just under my sister's name, she printed "Lucky Whitaker". Just like the other kids, Lucky earned stars for every day he was in school—and he and Carolyn had perfect attendance that year.
—*Jeanne Price, Naples, Florida*

ON GUARD. **"Lucky" (below) kept a close watch on the kids in Carolyn Whitaker's kindergarten class. That's Carolyn and her big sister, Jeanne, at right on a day off of school in 1934.**

Chapter 2

Getting To and From School

Getting To and From School

Perhaps the most important lesson we learned at school was that, no matter what, *you had to get there!* Somehow. Anyhow. Through snow, sleet, rain, howling wind or a sky filled with falling frogs… whatever. *You had to get there!*

Not all those tales Grandpa tells about slogging 4 miles through hip-deep snow in a pitiless blizzard, uphill both coming and going, are total fiction.

Back in the early part of the last century, most people lived on farms and ranches and plantations. School buses hadn't been invented yet and automobiles were scarce. So most kids walked to school, and not just down the block, either.

Or they had a docile, semi-retired horse that would tolerate as many as three school-bound tots on its back and patiently stand under a shade tree all day waiting to make the return trip.

When winter took over, many families had a horse-drawn sleigh or sled, usually with a layer of insulating straw covering the floor and heavy lap robes for the passengers. In really wretched weather, Dad would heat up flat slabs of stone and wrap them in burlap sacks for foot warmers.

Whatever your mode of transportation, getting to school during winter months in northern states years ago was a daily adventure. Snowplows had not been invented yet, although a few counties pressed their horse-drawn road graders into service with mixed results.

Would it astonish you to learn that as recently as 1990, there were kids in western Nebraska who rode 50 miles each way to get to school—and probably still do? (You should hear them giggle when the city schools close because of a 2-inch snowfall!)

I'm not sure when school buses were invented, but a *Reminisce* reader who grew up in North Dakota has vivid memories of the first one he rode. The ingenious driver installed a wood-burning stove that worked quite well, except on occasions when hot embers spilled out onto the wooden floor and set it afire.

My primary good-weather transportation to school was my bicycle. I was so fond of it that one winter I decided to design chains for the tires so I could plow along through snow, mud or icy streets. Chains worked on Dad's car, so why not my bike? It was a total flop.

Getting to school was a heavy responsibility that you honored, come what might. Floods or axle-deep mud on thawing country roads or blinding blizzard whiteouts were only inconveniences to be met and overcome.

Woody Allen once said that half the secret of success was "just showing up". No argument here. And most of us learned that great truth during our school days. Ha! And they thought they were teaching us the three R's!

—*Clancy Strock*

Seasons of the Year Were Part of Education

By Sheryl Jansma, Spring Valley, California

HERE'S what I heard a mother say recently when she dropped off her child at school: "Honey, I'll meet you here by the fire hydrant after school. If I'm late, go to the office and wait for me there. Don't ever walk home—it's far too dangerous!"

As I watched her drive away, I thought with sadness about what her little girl was missing by not walking to and from school every morning and afternoon.

For those of us who attended McKinley Public School in St. Thomas, Ontario in the '50s, that walk was as much a part of our education as hours spent in the classroom.

Followed Same Route

The walk was a kind of ritual. Every day my friends and I went down the sidewalk, past the corner store and onto the wooden slats of the boardwalk across the bridge.

Then we'd cut through the gully to school. That gully shared the pulse of the earth in her seasons. When school began in September, the path came alive with goldenrod...and with children making friends, choosing sides and setting the social order for the coming year.

On warm Indian summer days, my friends and I would pause awhile at the rotten stump, recalling the memories of our last school year.

As the brown leaves underfoot slickened with morning frost, our pace through the gully quickened. We felt a restless excitement in anticipation of the first snow and the snow-

WALK WAS A RITUAL. Sheryl Jansma and her brother Brent were ready to start their walk to school—always an adventure—on a sunny day in 1953.

ball fights soon to follow. To an outsider, those battles might have appeared to be hit-and-miss, disorganized frays, but those of us involved managed to keep accurate accounts and draw a fine line between love and war.

The afternoon Simon Smith threw snowballs exclusively at me, it was an obvious declaration of love. I walked home with new-found stature that day.

Skipped in Spring

When winter slushed into spring, our walks to and from school became a literal dance as we skipped along the paths in our newly bared legs. We'd bend to catch pollywogs in the stream, stretch to pick apple blossoms or kneel to find sweet wild strawberries bordering the path.

Boys and girls even explored the gully together, as petty jealousies and irritations melted with the snow. It seemed as if the gully and the seasons, my friends and our walks would go on forever.

For me, they have. Sometimes I'll consciously transport myself back to that gully. Other times, a flash of recognition—after the taste of the season's first strawberry or maybe the scent of damp earth—will take me there.

Either way, I'll step out of my present world of deadlines and tensions and let my heart beat once again with the slow, even meter of the earth's cycles as I walk with my friends from a school that's always there...to a home that never changes. 🎵

Brother Bud Had a Stowaway

THE YEAR was 1924, and my brother Bud was in his first year of high school in Gnadenhutten, Ohio. He had a rather complex way of getting to school each morning.

First, he hitched one of our horses to a buggy and drove 2 miles to the church. There he unhitched the horse, put it in the "preacher's barn" and rode the rest of way in a car driven by an older student. The horse and buggy were retrieved on the way home.

One weekend my family was surprised to see a Rhode Island Red hen eating with the rest of our chickens—

especially since we didn't have any Rhode Island Reds!

After eating her fill, the red hen wandered toward the barn. Curious, my parents followed her as she flew up on the buggy and went under the seat (where they soon discovered a nest of eggs she'd been sitting on).

Evidently my brother had been hauling the "preacher's hen" back and forth for quite some time. She could get out and eat at home after the school day was over, but on the weekends, she got hungry enough to dine out... with strangers!
—*Donna Rinehart, Dover, Ohio*

Getting There Was Half The Fun

By Margaret Adams
Dennis, Massachusetts

NOW, don't get me wrong. I have nothing against kids being driven to school, either by a school bus or a parent.

But after reflecting on my 1920s elementary school days in East Milton, Massachusetts, I think there's a lot to be said for the neighborhood school.

We walked there, arriving no later than 8:30. We'd walk back home for lunch at 11:45, then return for the afternoon session at 1 o'clock.

Every season offered something unusual to enjoy along the way. After school began in September, one of the first things we did on our back-and-forth treks was to look for chestnuts that had fallen from an ancient tree.

We'd eagerly scoop up all we could find and take them home. With a knife, we fashioned chestnut necklaces by gouging out holes and inserting string.

Late in autumn, after the leaves came tumbling down, more fun was in store. Back then, everyone raked their leaves into the street before burning them later.

We enjoyed scuffing through these piles on our way to school. I still miss the aroma of burning oak and maple leaves that would permeate the neighborhood for weeks.

Each Season Was Special

Winter brought its own pleasures… and not just snowballing or knocking down icicles to suck on. Hitching a ride on a "pung" was a joy!

The pung was an open-sled vehicle on runners, which was pulled by a horse and used by milkmen and grocers to make deliveries in snowy weather.

Spring? That was the time to search vacant lots for wildflowers—butter and eggs, bluegrass, five fingers, daisies and buttercups (we'd hold these under a friend's chin to see if she liked butter).

We even picked a weed that tasted like pineapple and chewed on sour grass with no ill effects. Other times we'd gather a bouquet for a mother or teacher…and get a botany lesson in return.

On rainy days, going to school meant trudging in our oilskin slickers, with an umbrella and those hated black rubbers!

There was no school lunch program then, and lunch was always ready when we got home. That gave us a chance to unwind and relate our "highs" ("I got 100% in spelling!") and our "lows" ("Ginny kicked me at recess!").

Obviously, a return to those days is impossible. Economically, it makes sense to build a regional or consolidated school, bus the kids in and let them off in late afternoon almost at their doors.

I'm afraid most of the "wonders" we encountered on our way to and from school are largely gone, but that's progress…or is it? ♣

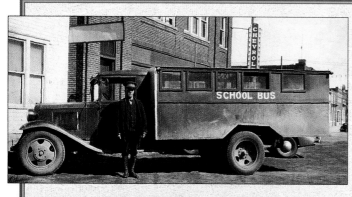

A Blast from the Bus

FROM 1937 to 1939, Casey Phelps' school bus would start at Badger, South Dakota and pick up us farm kids on the way to Arlington High School. Casey, a World War I veteran, was the owner and driver.

The homemade bus was mounted on a Chevy truck chassis, and the heater was a long pipe along the floor from the motor to the rear, with a protective grille so nobody would get burned.

While we were in school, Casey passed the time of day at the Chevrolet garage.

One time during our ride home, he spotted some pheasants from the driver's seat. Slowing down, he reached for the shotgun he carried beside his seat. Then he stopped the bus, got out and, as we kids watched in excitement, bagged two roosters!
—*Clint Nielsen, Sioux Falls, South Dakota*

BUS GANGSTERS. Clint Nielsen (sixth from right) and the other students who rode Casey Phelps' bus in the late '30s called themselves "The Bus Gangsters". That's Casey and his homemade bus in the top photo.

He Walked to School Alone...He Thought!

By Bob Vaisey, Rogersville, Tennessee

IN September of 1941, I was 4-1/2 years old and about to begin an exciting time. I was starting first grade!

We lived outside Camden, New York, and I was going to be allowed to begin school a year early because the district needed one more student to keep the school open.

My presence would give our school a total of three students, a brother and sister named Royce and Delores Babcock and me. There was no kindergarten in rural districts back then, so I'd start in first grade. Boy, did I feel important!

As you might expect, our school district had no bus. Dad worked about 20 miles away and left early, so the only way I could get to school was to walk the mile and a half by myself. I felt excited about doing such a "big person" thing and could hardly wait for that first day so I could get started.

Felt 7 Feet Tall

Finally, it was time to go. Off I marched down the road, feeling about 7 feet tall—especially since my "little brother" couldn't tag along!

For once, I was all by myself...or so I thought. As I passed the first house, I noticed Mrs. Peck looking out her window. I waved as I trudged by. At the next house, Mrs. Regan was out on the front porch, so, of course, she said hi and waved before going back inside.

So it went as I passed each home on the way to school. It

BIG BOY. Bob Vaisey (left) sat with his father and brother in 1940, the year before he started his "unaccompanied" walks to school.

seemed like somebody from each family was out early to wish me luck or just say hello.

Neighbors Were Wonderful

Little did I know that, to ensure my safety, Mom and Dad had worked out a deal with the neighbors. As I neared each house, someone was watching. And after I'd passed, they'd call Mom and let her know I'd gotten that far with no problems.

Although I was nowhere near as alone on my journey as I thought, it wasn't until years later that I learned about these arrangements. I was allowed to keep my "big boy" feeling, yet I was completely safe. This went on every day school was in session. Neighbors sure were wonderful back then!

Besides the pleasures of my "solo" walks to our little three-student school, I also had a great time learning to read and do math while sitting on Miss Marsh's lap. ✧

Granddad Only *Seemed* Confused

IN THE EARLY 1930s, my granddad, W.A. Settle, was a minister in Columbus, Indiana and didn't have time to visit with us during the school week. Since we hated to miss the wonderful stories he told, we'd linger with him at breakfast.

With more than a mile to walk to school, we were always delighted when Granddad said, "You'll be late for school, so I guess I'll have to drive you."

With that proclamation, my sister, my two cousins and I rushed to the car. As soon as we were on our way, Granddad would start another story (after reminding us all to watch for our turn onto North Street).

Of course, he'd drive right past North Street and we'd all squeal, "You missed the turn! You missed the turn!"

After he apologized, Granddad would say, "Well, we'll just go on to the next turn then, but since you don't normally come on these streets, maybe we better stop at Mr. Hooper's grocery store just to be sure we know the way."

Before we entered the store, Granddad would caution us, "Now you shouldn't go into a man's store without buying something, so here's a nickel for each of you."

In my mind's eye, I can still see the array of candies placed behind the glass at nose level. It took some time to pick out a nickel's worth of candy when some of it was five for a penny or six for a penny.

Mr. Hooper would point out that we could get a Baby Ruth or a Butterfinger for a nickel. Phooey on that! As budding young economists, we knew we had to have as many different kinds of candy as that nickel would allow (we each left with a sackful).

Granddad's sense of direction would soon seem to return as we heard him say, "Oh, we forgot to ask the way, but I'm sure if we turn here on Vineyard, it'll take us directly to Indiana Avenue."

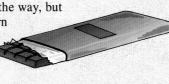

It's funny, but Granddad's confusion with directions reappeared almost every time he drove us to school. —*Jo Carey, Homer, Alaska*

Horse Really Knew the Way

WE LIVED about six blocks from school when I was in sixth grade. The school was near the railroad yard, and the switch engine passed near our house. On the way to school, I'd wave at the engineer and fireman.

One day they gave me a ride to school in the engine. What a treat!

My father also got rides to school, but it was in a horse-drawn wagon. That was in the early 1900s, when they lived on a farm.

Grandfather would hitch "Cap" to a wagon, and my dad and his brothers would drive to school, picking up other kids on the way. At school, they'd turn Cap around and he'd head for home on his own.

When it was time for school to let out, Grandpa would hitch Cap back to the wagon, and Cap would walk back to school to pick up the kids.

This might not seem all that unusual, except for the fact that Cap was blind.

—Jean Luehr
Racine, Wisconsin

Riding the "Jingle Bell" Bus Was No Chore

IN THE EARLY '30s, my father, Frank Barnes, took over the job of transporting children to the Edgewood School District in the outskirts of Bristol, Connecticut. After morning milking, Dad would hitch up our two horses, "Nip" and "Queen", to the school wagon.

Then he'd drive around to designated points and pick up students. The trip took about an hour, and the horses usually walked, but if Dad was running a little late, he'd let them trot a little. The other children and I loved that!

The wagon was about 12 feet long with wooden benches attached on either side. There was a seat in front for the driver, a step in back for climbing aboard and curtains along the sides.

There were a lot of blankets, and when the weather was below freezing, we often stamped our feet as we rode along. Dad had to calm us down sometimes because he thought our feet would go through the floorboards!

When the weather was nice, the curtains were rolled up and it was a fun ride. My father really loved that job, even if he occasionally would have trouble with the older boys. Sometimes

TWO TYPES OF RIDES. "Nip" and "Queen" (left) were decked out for the holidays to pull the school wagon Belle Brown's father drove in the early 1930s. In the winter, a bobsled (below) replaced the wagon.

they'd sit hanging out the back or try to ride on the step. If this happened, Dad would stop the wagon and straighten them out.

For the holidays, Dad would decorate Nip's and Queen's halters. At Christmas they got red bows and bells, while on St. Patrick's Day they'd be wearing green ribbons. Of course, the children enjoyed this.

The best fun of all was in winter. Dad hitched the team to the bobsled and added lots of hay and blankets. When he approached the school at 3:30 in the afternoon with bells ringing, classes would be dismissed right away.

We were in no hurry to go home—we'd laugh and sing *Jingle Bells* all the way. I rode that wagon to school with Dad many times, and those are such special shared memories.

—Belle Brown, Bristol, Connecticut

Early Bus Rides Were Both Ordeals and Adventures

By Mary Ann Kunselman, Longmont, Colorado

SOON AFTER we moved to Colorado in the late '20s, I rode a school bus for the first time. It was just a wooden box fastened onto the back of a truck that rattled and swayed over the sagebrush hills. Since my twin sister, Martha, brother Shelton and I were the last kids let off, we were often dizzy from the ride.

Then we moved to a farm near Iliff, Colorado. We still rode a school bus, but it was through farmland instead of prairie, which was easier on our stomachs.

It was a quarter mile walk from the house to the bus, and on frigid winter days, both the walk and bus ride were *cold*. Despite good leather shoes, cotton stockings and four-buckle overshoes, our feet would be so numb that we couldn't feel our toes.

Once we arrived at school, it took several minutes before we stopped shivering and warmed up enough to concentrate on our lessons.

We later moved to another farm, but we still had the same bus driver, Mr. Herman—and one time we had some real excitement with him. It was during the "Dirty '30s", when we were having all those terrible dust storms. We were coming home in a storm when suddenly we heard a loud ripping sound. Then there was a loud bang, and off flew the rubberized bus top!

It really scared us kids. Meanwhile, Mr. Herman held tight to the steering wheel and stopped the bus safely. Then he walked back, picked up the top and stowed it in the back of the bus.

Without that top over our heads, we were awfully dirty and dusty by the time we made it home that day.

Another time, our bus got a flat tire on the way to school. We got out of the bus and stood at the side of the road while Mr. Herman jacked up the wheel and pumped up the tire with a hand pump.

Several of the bigger boys took turns with that pump. For them, it was fun to see who could pump the longest and put the most air in.

One winter day, a blizzard blew in while we were at school, and the school board wouldn't let the buses take the children home. Of course, our parents were worried, since there were no telephones to call the school.

One father and his grown son, who lived about 5 miles away, started out with a wagon and team of horses, looking

RICKETY RIDE. Mary Ann Kunselman (center), twin sister Martha and brother Shelton had the longest ride on this bus in the 1920s because they got off at the last stop.

> *"Without that top over our heads, we were dirty and dusty by the time we made it home..."*

for a stranded busload of kids. They'd piled the wagon bed full of quilts and blankets to use when they found us. When they stopped at our house to see if Daddy wanted to join the search, he added more blankets to the stack.

As you can imagine, they were greatly relieved when they reached the schoolhouse and found everyone safe and warm inside.

There were six or eight of us kids from three different families. We all got in the wagon and bundled up cozy, wrapped in so many quilts that not even our heads peeked out.

It was a slow trip with those old workhorses plodding along through the wind and cold. My brother, sister and I were the luckiest ones. We only lived 2-1/2 miles from school and we could all keep each other warm. The last two or three kids must have been really cold when they finally pulled into their yard.

Still, we all survived those school bus rides—and learned our lessons, too!

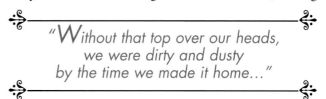

ALWAYS MEMORABLE. School bus rides—good and bad, hot and cold, fun or fearsome—have remained etched in our minds for decades.

Her Model T "Muddled" Its Way to School

AFTER 61 years, the most vivid memory of my high school days is how I got to school. From 1934 to 1938, I drove a Model T Ford coupe the 4 miles to Western High School in Saline County, Nebraska.

There were steep hills to climb and low places where the car dragged through the deep rutted tracks in the dirt road. Sometimes I held my breath, thinking the car would slide into the ditch or drop off the end of a culvert. The way it bounced around on those slippery roads, I never knew where it would go.

Only once did I have to walk away from my Model T, when mud balled up under the wheels and the engine wasn't up to pulling it any farther.

During rainstorms, the roof leaked, and when we hit a puddle, the water splashed up through the cracks of the floor onto my legs.

Model T's were hard to start in cold weather, and on occasion I'd miss school because of it. To get my car going, we'd sometimes use a horse to pull it around the yard. Or, if the ground was dry, my parents would push it down the sloping lane with me behind the wheel.

When my car did start, I often took the family's cream to town. After school was dismissed for the day, I'd pick up the check and the can, then stop at Brown's Store for a 1¢ candy bar.

After my graduation in 1938, it took another 4 years of driving in the mud to get my sister through high school. Those 8 years left me with many fond memories of negotiating muddy roads in my 1927 Model T.

—*Ruby Zabel, Daykin, Nebraska*

ALL-TERRAIN VEHICLE. **Ruby Zabel (above) drove her 1927 Ford Model T (left) to high school in Nebraska in the 1930s and '40s. She encountered dirt roads, rainstorms, mud and cold snowy weather (below).**

Bootless in a Blizzard

IN 1950, as a student in junior high school in Duluth, Minnesota, I usually walked the eight blocks downhill to school, so I didn't carry bus fare with me.

In northern Minnesota, it wasn't unusual to get snowstorms during spring. As a teenager, I was tired of wearing boots all winter. So when my mother warned there was a snowstorm coming and that I should wear my boots, I naturally thought I could outsmart the weather.

Of course, Mother was right. The snow came, and school closed early. If I walked home, I'd get wet without boots, so I borrowed money to take the city bus.

I'd have been better off walking, getting my feet wet and listening to Mother's anger. The snow forced the bus to take an alternate route that got farther and farther from home.

I tried to get off, but the driver wouldn't stop. He was afraid he wouldn't regain traction and was determined to get to the top of the hill and to the end of the route.

I rode all the way to the end of the line, and all the other passengers had gotten off. When the driver turned the bus around, he came back to me and demanded another fare for the return trip.

I started to cry and explained I had no more money. Reluctantly, he let me stay on. But then his mood improved and he even advised me where to get off for the shortest walk.

I was so relieved to get home that it didn't bother me to listen to Mother's tongue-lashing.

—*Gloria Albrecht*
Duluth, Minnesota

BETTER IN BOOTS. **Gloria Albrecht didn't listen to her mother. When a snowstorm closed school, she was bootless.**

Walking Off That School Day Lunch

By Charlotte Spiegel, White Oak, Pennsylvania

WHEN MY SISTER, Binky, and I attended McKeesport (Pennsylvania) High School in the '40s, we had to walk home for lunch.

There was no cafeteria at school, and only some students were allowed to bring a lunch and eat in specially assigned classrooms. Those of us who lived within walking distance went home.

We had to walk down a steep hill about a mile long. Then we crossed busy Walnut Street and the B&O Railroad tracks. There was usually a train, and it was often stopped. At times it took as long as 20 minutes for that train to get moving.

We also crossed Market Street, which was busy at lunchtime, then we still had another half block to our house. All this, and eating lunch had to be accomplished

THEY MADE IT. Charlotte Spiegel (left) and her sister, Binky, graduated in 1945 after 4 years of walking to school in the morning, home for lunch and back again.

in an hour. Mother always had a nice lunch on the table. But we often had to eat quickly to get back to school before the bell at 1 p.m.

If it got close to 1, or if the weather was bad. Mother would call our father at his gas station at Ninth and Walnut and have him give us a ride back up the hill.

When it was icy, walking that hill was tricky. We fell on our backsides more than once.

We walked 5 days a week for 4 years. But we made it to graduation in May 1945. ⚜

FORMER DESTINATION. Nan Rowan and her brother walked or used bikes, horses or sleighs to get to this now-closed school in Peterborough, Ontario.

School Rides Took Many Forms

MY BROTHER Mervin and I first attended Fairmount Public School, a rural one-room school in Peterborough, Ontario, in 1938. Although we usually walked the 1-3/4 miles, we used other modes of travel, too.

The two of us shared a bicycle. Once in a while, neighbors driving along the road would give us a lift, letting us stand on the running boards as we hung on to the open windows.

In winter, we'd get rides with horses and sleighs or cutters. For a while, we even rode our workhorse, "Nellie", and tied her up in the school yard.
—*Nan Rowan, Brighton, Ontario*

Beautiful Ride While It Lasted

MY PONY, "Beauty", and I rode to a one-room school in Jacobson, Minnesota in the '40s (pictured below). There was a small barn at school, where she could stay during the day with hay to eat.

I rode only a couple of months out of the year in the fall and spring of 1948 and 1949. From home to school was 5-1/2 miles of country roads, and Beauty was always in a hurry to get home in the afternoons.

One day she took the turn out of the school driveway too sharply and we both fell into the ditch!

Long grass and the soft shoulders of the ditch broke our fall, but we were both shaken up a bit. After that, we were careful not to cut corners again.
—*Anna Maupin, Northome, Minnesota*

HAPPY TRAILS. Louise Basse and her horse, "Jane", navigated seven fields and gates to get to school in Goldendale, Washington in the early 1900s.

Little Horsewoman "Fenced In" by Time Constraints

IN 1904, when I was 4 years old, my father filed for a homestead 30 miles east of Goldendale, Washington. We moved there by horse-drawn wagon, which was all we could afford.

My mother taught me at home until I was 8, as there was no other school to attend. Finally, when I was a third grader, a school was built—7 miles away!

My daily trek to school (on horseback) was across seven fields, and each of them had wire gates to open. My father built little steps on either side of each gate so I could climb off my horse on one side of the gate, then back on after closing it.

Tardiness was a special problem for me. Try as I might, if the weather was rough, I would be late for class. In addition, I'd sometimes pick up another student and give her a ride.

On the days when we came in late, the teacher determined that my rider had a good excuse, but I was always punished for tardiness. Later, though, I graduated first in my class (I was the only one in my class).

—*Louise Basse, Portland, Oregon*

Dad's Durant Got Them Through the Depression

IN THE winter of 1927-28, our family drove a Durant from Iowa to California and settled in San Diego County at a place called Winterless Gardens. There we opened a store and service station.

My father drove us four children to the nearest school at San Marcos. There were a dozen or so children along the way, and it wasn't long before the school board convinced my father that he was ideally situated to bring all those children in also.

Since the Durant was only a five-passenger car, he had to make several trips to get the job done. My father replaced seats with narrow wooden benches to increase the numbers of children he could carry—no cushions or seat belts in those days!

But the population of San Marcos was growing fast, and the school board realized it was time to purchase a bus. Would my father drive it for them? Would he! The Depression was on, and we needed that money badly.

The Ford agency drove my dad to Bakersfield, California, where he picked up a brand-new 1930 Model A Ford school bus.

He drove it for the next 13 years before taking a job with Consolidated Aircraft in San Diego, helping build B-24 Liberator bombers. By that time, the income from his school bus driving had saved our family's little store and service station from foreclosure.

—*Chet Mersman*
Lincolnshire, England

Memories of Live-in Teacher

WHEN I was a little girl, I went to a one-room country school near Pearl, Illinois with eight or 10 students. The teacher lived with my family, which I thought was pretty special!

In nice weather, we walked to school, but when winter came, my father would put bales of hay on the bobsled and hitch up two big horses wearing sleigh bells.

Teacher and I would climb on the hay and wrap ourselves up in a woolen lap robe. Then we'd drive around the neighborhood and pick up all the other schoolchildren.

Often we'd sing songs as we rode to class. When we got to school, we'd have to build a fire in the potbellied stove to warm up. I shall never forget those wonderful school days!

And those sleigh bells still hang in my dining room today.

—*Virginia Wyatt, Troy, Illinois*

BUS EXPANSION. Chet Mersman (above, standing highest) was among the children his father took to school in San Diego County, California in the family's Durant. Later, the school board reacted to a population boom and asked Chet's father to drive the new 1930 Model A Ford bus (below).

DESPITE my present age of 91, I vividly remember being a 7-year-old attending the country school about a mile from our farm home in the tiny rural town of Passport in southern Illinois.

Each day, my classmates and I would walk down the paths alongside the fences on our way to school. Then we'd cross the road in front of school. That was fine in dry weather, but after a rainstorm, the road turned muddy.

As we crossed the road, our feet would be sucked into the deep mud, and we'd sometimes walk right out of our boots. Then the bigger boys would have to come and carry us smaller kids across to the schoolhouse.

When the weather grew frigid, my daddy took me to school in a buggy that had a storm front so we'd be out of the cold. If there was enough snow on the ground, he'd come for me in a bright red sleigh with fluffy straw in the bottom and lots of heavy robes to keep us warm.

The ride home was wonderful. It was so merry hearing those sleigh bells jingle as our team of horses, "Maude" and "Babe", headed for home. —*Evelyn Cochran, Noble, Illinois*

GUMBLE SCHOOL. Evelyn Cochran attended this school (left) in Passport, Illinois from 1915 to 1923. In her third-grade picture in 1918 (top), Evelyn is in the back row, third from right, wearing a bow in her hair.

❖ ❖ ❖ ❖ ❖ ❖

Sisters' Sense of Direction Slightly Askew

BACK IN 1919, our family lived on a farm in Michigan's "thumb". I was 7, my sister Eleanor was 5 and we had a long walk to the one-room school.

One fall morning as we walked to school, our teenage uncle was husking corn in a field. He called us over to see a nest of baby mice that he'd found.

Because we were already in the field, I decided Eleanor and I should take a shortcut to school that someone had shown me the year before.

We came to a creek and had to go a long way before we could cross. Of course, we went in the wrong direction and got lost. We heard the first school bell ring and then the final one as we randomly wandered the fields.

Eventually we found the road, but we had walked well beyond the school.

When we finally arrived at the schoolhouse, the door was closed, so we knocked. Although I'm now in my 80s, I can still remember the astonished look on the teacher's face when she recognized the two little bedraggled girls standing there.

After Eleanor innocently explained, "We took a shortcut," teacher immediately called recess. The older girls took us in hand, washed our faces, combed our hair and pulled the cockleburs and "pitchforks" out of our clothing.

Although exhausted from our harrowing experience, we were made to feel like the heroines of the day.

—*Lucille Vance Krause, Davisburg, Michigan*

SHORTCUT WASN'T. Lucille Krause (left) and her sister Eleanor (right) were all cleaned up for a photo with their baby sister, Vi—not like they looked when they got to school one memorable day.

MINISTER HAD TWO FLOCKS. Vern Wardlow of Tulsa, Oklahoma has fond memories of this school bus and the man standing next to it. Vern's father, Lester, who was a minister, also was a bus driver for the Mannford, Oklahoma schools in 1930-31. A first grader at the time, Vern loved it when his dad let him ride along.

Stay Away from That Stove!

A NUMBER of us kids rode our horses to the little one-room schools I attended in Oklahoma during the Depression. My horse was a little half Shetland-half quarter horse named "Joker".

He got his name from all the tricks he played on me. On my first day of school, after I'd tied him up by the bridle reins, he rubbed the bridle off and I had to walk home.

When I was in the third and fourth grades, I trapped skunks. The hides sold for 25¢ or 50¢ and gave me a little spending money besides the 25¢-a-week allowance I got for doing chores at home.

I'd check my traps on the way to school, putting any skunks I'd caught in a gunnysack I threw over Joker's neck. By the time we got to school, both Joker and I smelled pretty bad.

My desk was next to the big stove, and many times the teacher would move me somewhere else—that heat really brought out the full richness of the skunk aroma!

After school, I went home to do my chores, then skinned the skunks and put the hides on stretcher boards to cure. Sometimes I saved the fat from the skunks and put it in an old coffee can, which would be placed over a fire and rendered to make skunk grease that we used on leather harnesses and to waterproof our shoes.

One of my teachers is still living at 90. I asked her if she remembered moving me away from the stove. She said, "Oh, yes—a number of times!"

As I was not the only one trapping skunks, you can imagine what that school must have smelled like!

—*Homer Crouch, Grand Junction, Colorado*

SKUNK HUNTER. Homer Crouch (front row, second from left) made some spending money by trapping skunks on the way to school in the '30s.

School Wagon a Comfy Ride No Matter What the Season

By Rita Haban, Reynoldsburg, Ohio

WHEN my good neighbor, Lucinda Kaiser, told me about her elementary school years, I could hardly believe her stories of going to school.

I'd grown up in Columbus, Ohio and walked to school, while she rode to school on a farm wagon with nine other children in the early '30s. All of those children, including Lucinda, lived on small farms 30 miles north of Columbus.

As the weather grew colder, the wagon was filled with straw, and each child carried a "comfy". She described a comfy as a quilted bag that held a heated rock.

The children would snuggle in the straw, holding the comfy close to their body for warmth. Once they arrived at school, they'd take the rock from the quilted sack and place it atop the potbellied stove to ensure a warm trip home.

As spring came and the weather improved, the straw and comfy were no longer needed. Lucinda's most pleasant memory was of the driver whistling as he drove.

If the kids grew rowdy, he'd throw a potato over his shoulder into the wagon bed, and the children would toss it back and forth until he stopped whistling.

Whoever was left holding the "hot potato" when the driver stopped was out of the game (kind of like "musical chairs"). He always managed to dig some kind of sweet out of his pocket for the last one out.

Lucinda has passed on, but as I watch loaded school buses pass our house these days and see the solemn faces of the children inside, I remember her and think of all the fun she had riding in her school wagon. ❧

WELCOME RIDE. Carol Smith, back row, second from left in 1933 photo above, got to school in Coos Bay, Oregon by boat (left). Sometimes students jumped ship and raced to the next landing for fun. If they lost, it was a long walk home.

Their School 'Bus' Floated!

By Carol Smith, Allegany, Oregon

OUR SCHOOL was on a bluff overlooking the two main forks of Oregon's Coos River. Until the early 1930s, people in the area had no way of getting to the closest town (Coos Bay, Oregon) except by boat.

Along the river were dairy farms that shipped 10-gallon cans of milk to the creamery daily. In addition to milk, the boats carried passengers, mail, supplies for the general store...and schoolchildren like me.

There was a separate boat to serve each fork (and a smaller one to bring children upriver from below the forks). The boat I rode was the *Welcome*. She served the North Fork and was captained by my brother, Harold Ott.

Those living near the school didn't have a very long ride, but those of us living farther upriver had a trip of about an hour and a half. We didn't mind, as we were free to wander the cabin.

Studied En Route

There were benches running the length of either side and shelves in one corner for our schoolbooks and lunchpails. Many used the time to read; others set up the card table to do their homework. Procrastinators usually had time to do it during the morning trip.

The boats always dropped us off in good time for morning classes, but the schedule didn't mesh as well in the afternoons.

Usually the boats arrived before dismissal time, tied up at the dock and waited for school to let out. But in winter, when the weather was stormy and the river was running dangerously high and carrying floating debris, the boats had a hard time fighting their way upstream.

At those times it wasn't wise to risk being overtaken by darkness before reaching home. A lookout would be posted on the upper floor of the school building, where there was a good view

> *"The boats never failed to deliver their passengers safely..."*

downriver. He or she would call out the name of whatever boat came into view. All students who rode that particular vessel would be dismissed so the boat wouldn't have to delay.

In all those years of river travel, never did a boat fail to deliver its passengers safely (and more or less on time). That safety record may have been due in part to the fact that children in those days had respect for authority.

The older ones also could be trusted not to do anything foolhardy. Of course, there was inevitably a high school boy or two who liked to show his expertise in rolling aboard those heavy milk cans.

Every farm had a floating dock that allowed the can to be tilted slightly and rolled aboard (rather than lifted). It was a tricky maneuver, and I suspect some of the boys were more hindrance than help, but the good-natured deckhands did not rebuff their efforts.

Raced the Boat

On nice evenings, we sometimes played "Let's Run Awhile!" A small group of us would get off at a dock and race the boat upriver to the next landing. If we failed, it was a long walk home!

The river curved away from the road in many places, giving the runners the advantage of a more direct route. Naturally the skipper would accept the challenge, and the puffs of diesel engine smoke would show he was "pouring on the coal" in an effort to leave the smart alecks behind.

Sometimes the girls would join in the run, but that was something I only did a couple of times. I wasn't a very good sprinter and wasn't that anxious to try my hand at long-distance running.

Brother or not, I had the feeling that Harold would gleefully leave me behind just as he would anyone else. Maybe not, but I wasn't about to put my suspicions to the test! ❧

Grandpa's Team Took Her to School

I WAS 5 years old, in 1923, when I started school in a one-room schoolhouse near Pavilion, New York. The teacher had all eight grades, and I was the only first grader.

However, that first year, my mother became very upset because she thought I should have been taught more. Since she was a trustee, she called a meeting of the other trustees. They decided to close the school and contract with the village of Pavilion to educate students there.

The trustees found a horse-drawn bus and hired my grandfather to transport all of the pupils to the village school. I remember how safe I felt with my grandfather sitting up front driving his team.

Although I didn't know what to expect at the big school, the teacher made me welcome and said I'd be in the second grade. Our classroom was one large room, which held the first three grades. I soon made friends with my classmates and truly enjoyed school.

—*Elizabeth Norton, Pavilion, New York*

FUN TIME. "The bus was painted yellow with a door in the back. Grandpa parked it next to the barn, where kids would play in it," recalls Elizabeth Norton. "That's my sister Alta and brother Charles in the wagon."

Bus Stop Became a Bush Stop

SURPRISE! Vera Tarantino and her brother, shown in 1949 photo, thought they'd skip school one day in 1952. Their bus driver intervened.

ONE DAY in 1952 my brother and I wanted to skip school. So when the bus arrived at the stop in the area of the Bronx where we lived in New York City, we hid in the bushes.

The plan was to tell Mom that we'd gotten to the bus stop late and had missed the bus.

What we didn't realize was how much higher the bus was than ground level. While we peeked out from behind the bushes, there stood the hated bus with all the children laughing at us from the windows.

Meanwhile, the driver (whose nickname was "Tiger") hollered, "C'mon, get in the bus. What are you doing in the bushes?" How humiliating!

—*Vera Tarantino, New Brunswick, New Jersey*

Tumbling Tumbleweeds Are Part of His School Memories

WE DIDN'T HAVE busing in the rural school district I attended in West Texas during the '30s, so the only way we could get to school was on foot or horseback.

In fifth grade, I had a Spanish pony I rode to school—but I never rode it back home because it always threw me off before I got there! Since my brother and I lived only 1-

1/2 miles from school, it wasn't too bad unless there was a blizzard blowing in from the north. When that happened, we'd walk awhile, then crawl into the ditch and warm ourselves by starting a little fire with tumbleweeds.

—*Gene McGehee, Colorado City, Texas*

"Kerosene Kids" Sledded to School

I LIVED the first 42 years of my life in northwestern Wyoming, where the elevation was over 7,000 feet and the winters long and cold. My dad drove the school "bus" for years. He'd harness up the team, hitch it to a covered sled and drive us about 5 miles to school every day. Then he'd return home, harness another team and feed 300 head of cattle.

By the time he finished, it was time to return to town to pick up the schoolchildren on our route. There were usually seven or eight of us on the bus. Mother would heat rocks in the woodstove to put in the sled, and we'd hold our feet to them.

Later, we had a kerosene heater. Although the heat was appreciated, it seemed that the "town kids" would roll their noses up at us because we smelled like fuel oil.

It was a few years before I learned that slights like that don't matter in the long run.

—*Ellen Lozier Quesnel, British Columbia*

WARMTH MATTERED. Ellen Lozier (right) rode to school in a heated sled.

Chapter 3

The Three R's...and Other Subjects

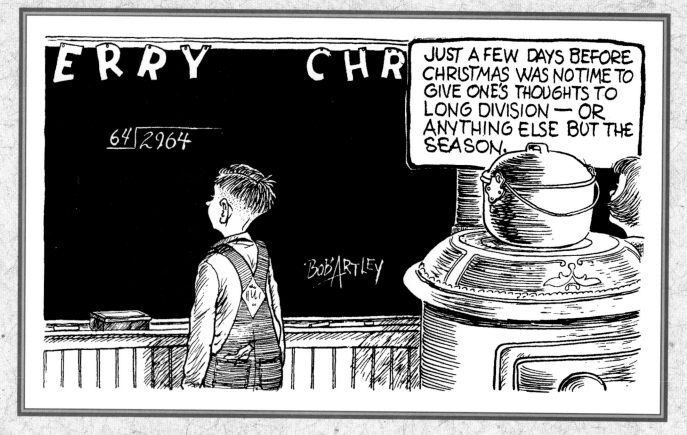

The Three R's...and Other Subjects

Perhaps you, too, went to school when teaching consisted of the "three R's"—readin', 'ritin' and 'rithmetic. And let's not forget the fourth "R"...the ruler.

Educators figured if you could get kids interested in reading, give them the rudiments of understandable writing and teach them to do their sums, you'd equipped them with the basics necessary for a decent life. After all, the world wasn't all that complicated back then.

Learning about American history and the nation's heroes was deemed important. Patriotism was stressed. Spelling and grammar were given a lot of attention, as was world geography. Education was fairly straightforward, although not essential for most jobs of the day.

There were more important things for a farmer's son to master than book-learnin'. Planting crops, building fences and getting in the harvest had higher priorities than learning some Englishman's sonnets. My dad started high school three consecutive autumns, always to be pulled out to help pick corn. He never did get a diploma.

Rural areas were dotted with one-room schoolhouses where young women taught all eight grades. A friend remembers his one-room school in Nebraska during the '20s. "In a way, we taught each other," he told me. "If you were in the second grade, you couldn't help but hear the third graders' reciting their lessons."

Sometimes busy teachers even turned older kids into assistants. A bright fourth grader, for example, might drill first graders in reading. Those were the days when reading was taught with flash cards. Words were printed large on cards that the instructor held up.

D-O-G. "Dog," chanted the class. It may have been slow and tedious, but it worked.

What a different world it is today! What a different curriculum! The three R's are long gone, along with the ruler. The debates in educational circles are sometimes startling, to say the least. Some point out that a perfectly good little calculator can be purchased for a few dollars, so why waste time teaching arithmetic?

Computers will, at the push of a button, check not only spelling but even spot poor grammar. So what's the point of spelling bees and learning to diagram sentences?

And absolutely no one writes anymore, so let's not waste valuable class time teaching penmanship.

Meanwhile, my grandchildren can't point out India on a world map and could care less. George Washington was some rich old geezer who possibly was a president or governor or something. And the Great Depression is a rock group that has a really neat Top 10 record.

Or so it sometimes seems. I'm not advocating that we return to the one-room schoolhouse, but I do often wonder if we had it right 80 years ago. Can there be such a thing as too much progress?

—Clancy Strock

Fun with Dick and Jane?
You Bet We Did!

By J.H. Johnson, Greenwood, Indiana

MAYBE I led a sheltered life in 1950, but I don't recall knowing much about the world until I met Dick and Jane.

I made their acquaintance in the first grade in Beech Grove, Indiana inside a book called *Fun with Dick and Jane*. I guess you never forget the first book you ever learned to read. On the cover were Dick, Jane and Spot chasing a toy airplane.

For me, that little book brings back a flood of memories...an old wooden desk with the large drawer at the bottom and the inkwell on top, the aroma of chalk dust mixed with that of the cloakroom on a rainy day, the excitement of learning to read.

"See It Go" was the name of the first story I ever read. "Look," said Dick. "See it go. See it go up." After it went up, Jane saw it, Sally saw it and Spot chased it.

The excitement reached a climax when the plane knocked Father's hat off—exciting stuff for a first grader who'd never seen television.

Saw a Whole New World

Dick and Jane introduced me to a world outside my own. There were Mother and Father and sister Sally. Spot was their dog, of course, and Puff was their yellow kitten.

Remember "A Funny Ride" when the kids accompanied Father to the service station? The car went up on the lift, and Spot and Puff stayed on board. They, along with Tim (Sally's teddy bear), eventually had to be rescued.

FUN READING. The *Dick and Jane* series of storybooks opened a wonderful world for first graders like J.H. Johnson (at left in 1950). The simple stories and illustrations eased children into a lifetime of reading.

Dick and Jane had grandparents who lived on a farm, and they visited them often. One time they came home with a baby duck named Little Quack who didn't want to play or eat. He just sat and sat and sat—until the day a storm came up.

That's when Jane said, "Oh, Dick! Look up! Look up! We must run to the house. We must run fast!" Everybody but Little Quack ran to the house. When the storm was over, Dick and Jane found Little Quack floating happily in a puddle.

At the end of the book, Dick and Jane are waving goodbye to Mother and Sally and Spot. Sally said, "Oh, Spot. Dick and Jane went to school. They have fun with friends. They work and play at school."

"Bowwow," said Spot, ending the book on a high note.

Despite its simplicity, I owe a lot to this little book. It revealed to me the magic of the printed word, and I've loved reading ever since. Yes, I had fun with Dick and Jane. ❧

SCHOOL ON PARADE. In 1945, parents of the pupils at Oakdale School in Paso Robles, California built an exact replica of the school out of lumber and Sheetrock, says David Barlogio of Paso Robles. The miniature school was a prize-winning float in the city's annual Pioneer Day Parade. Afterward, it went to the Barlogios' yard, where David's sister used it as a playhouse!

CHECKERBOARD EDUCATION. This red-and-white checkered schoolhouse was erected in 1841 near Franklinville, New York. According to Marie Caldwell, who lives in Newark Valley, the story goes that residents' disagreement over whether the school should be red or white led to this unusual compromise.

Weekly Reader Scam Had Unforeseen Ending

I DIDN'T REALIZE I'd been a good student at my grade school in Wichita, Kansas back in the '40s until I saw some of my old report cards recently. I was surprised to learn I'd gotten all A's and B's.

School seemed difficult for me, and I disliked the standardized tests that the state used to gauge our intelligence. I knew I could do well on material I'd mastered, but those tests had so many questions and definitions I didn't know the answers to.

I remember one vocabulary test administered to us in eighth grade. The answers had been published in our *Weekly Reader* the week before.

A number of my classmates said they planned to memorize the answers. After listening to my classmates, I felt that if I were to compete, I, too, would have to cheat.

So I memorized all the numbers and letters. It was harder than if I'd just learned the words and definitions.

On the big day of the test, we cleared our desks and sat quietly with two pencils at the ready. When I read the words and their possible definitions, not one of them was familiar to me—it was demoralizing.

So then I used the code I'd memorized, deliberately making a few "mistakes" so my cheating wouldn't be obvious. Well, would you believe that, despite all the talk, I was the only student who'd actually gone

SNOW JOB. Pauline Crowley (on right), had fun with friends 4 years after learning a valuable lesson in school.

to the trouble of learning all of the answers!

Several weeks later, the teacher called me to her desk and confided in me, "Pauline, you made the highest grade on the vocabulary test." Then I felt so guilty. She never knew the answers had been made available to us before the test.

Now I wish someone would give me another vocabulary test. I've been working on my definitions for the past 50 years, and this time I wouldn't have to cheat. —*Pauline Crowley*
Virginia Beach, Virginia

Bulls and Bumblebees At the Bookmobile

ATTENDING a one-room school in Grand Rapids, Michigan from 1955 to 1958 was one of the most rewarding experiences of my life. One poignant memory involves the Bookmobile.

In my mind's eye, I can still see that big red vehicle. It looked like a bread truck and it came to our school once a month. We were allowed to pick out three books each visit. What a wonderful experience!

As I climbed the steps of the Bookmobile, I was in awe at the number of books—every nook and cranny was filled.

Along the stairwell up into the bookmobile were shelves of books, and when I stopped to look I'd get yelled at for holding up the line. Only five of us were allowed inside at a time, so the 16 of us in school took turns.

My favorite book from the Bookmobile was *Ferdinand the Bull*, the story of a very shy bull that sat on a bumblebee and had a violent reaction in front of the people picking ferocious bulls for the upcoming bullfight.

To this day, I love reading and believe it dates back to my trips up the Bookmobile steps. Being allowed only three books was a hardship, but it only made me want to read all the more. —*Joan Meyer, Grand Rapids, Michigan*

Dad's Dimes Helped Build Mt. Rushmore

THERE WERE two teachers for the first grade when I started school in North Dakota in 1926. One taught the English-speaking children while the other taught kids, like me, who could only speak German.

At the time I lived with my grandparents. Before the year was over, I'd not only learned English but taught my grandmother to speak it, too.

One vivid memory I have of that time is of sculptor Gutzon Borglum working on Mt. Rushmore.

Every now and then, our teacher would ask us students to bring pennies, nickels and even dimes to help with that monument being constructed in the Black Hills in our neighboring state. In those days, a dime would buy two dozen eggs or a large loaf of bread with a penny left over.

So it was no wonder that when I asked my father for a dime, he said, "Doggone it, kid! Are you building that thing all by yourself?" —*Viola Beeninga, Klamath, California*

Janitorial Duties Have Changed Over the Years

I CAN REMEMBER being 6 years old and walking a mile through deep snow to school in Sudbury, Massachusetts in 1913. There'd been a blizzard the night before.

When we reached the school, the janitor, Mr. Hadley, was waiting. If our shoes were wet, he took them down to the boiler room to dry. But first he put hot boards under our cold, wet feet. Oh, that felt good!

Mr. Hadley also came quietly into our room several times a day to read the thermometer. Keeping the correct temperature in every room in the building was no easy task.

Another important job involved our pencils. On our teacher's desk were two boxes—one for broken pencils and one for newly sharpened ones. Every afternoon, Mr. Hadley would come into our room to sharpen the pencils.

He'd sit beside the teacher's desk with the wastepaper basket between his knees and whittle each pencil to a sharp point with his jackknife.

In the years since, Sudbury had grown from 2,000 residents to over 15,000. I doubt that school janitors still provide students with hot boards and freshly whittled pencils!

—*Leona Johnson, Sudbury, Massachusetts*

His "Affliction" Had Its Advantages

LEFT OUT? Orval Schnarr's teacher didn't want him to write with his left hand, which for him was the right one.

DURING the 1930s, I attended the Bearinger School in Waterloo County, Ontario, a one-room, redbrick building with a teacher who taught all eight grades.

The teacher had a special problem with me. I was left-handed, and that was a big "no-no" in those days. That's why I write with my right hand today, although I do everything else with my left.

There was a bright side to my "problem". In high school, I was the only southpaw pitcher on the baseball team. I also learned to become a switch hitter.

A possible candidate for the big leagues? Unfortunately, I never found out, because we were farmers and Dad had other plans for me. At 14, I became a high school dropout…although my education has never ceased.

—*Orval Schnarr, Elmira, Ontario*

War Came Alive In Her Hands

IN 1934, I was in eighth grade in Colorado Springs, Colorado. Each student in my class was assigned to write a detailed report on the Civil War as our year-end project in history.

Mine consisted of 18 handwritten pages, interspersed with sketches of President Lincoln, famous generals from both sides and some of the notable sites of the war.

I had purchased an old American history textbook from which I'd clipped my illustrations, and I'd studied six other books from the library. Another illustration was of a real Confederate $100 bill my mother had found hidden in an antique book cabinet.

My teacher graded my paper as follows: "This book shows deep interest in your work. Cover, material and pictures couldn't be improved upon. 100%."

PERFECT GRADE. Eudora Thomas Sabo remembers working hard on her eighth-grade history project.

This report and its perfect grade were the highlights of my school career and, although faded now, they remain two of my most treasured mementos.

—*Eudora Thomas Sabo Boca Raton, Florida*

"Old-Time" Education Worked Out Fine

MY THOUGHTS often return to my wonderful boyhood in Cedar Falls, Iowa and the days between 1912 and 1919 when I attended the old St. Patrick's School.

Total enrollment was 60 pupils in two classrooms. We were taught by two Sisters of Charity nuns. Heat was supplied in the winter by a Holland furnace placed in a small excavation called the "cellar". Of course, the toilet facilities were "out back".

The effectiveness of our schooling was evident when we moved to Chicago in 1919. Although I was in seventh grade at the time, the principal gave me a series of tests, then advanced me to the eighth grade, and I graduated the following semester. —*Edward Brady, Delray Beach, Florida*

HIGHER LEARNING. Edward Brady attended this two-story school, which had one large classroom on each floor, in Cedar Falls, Iowa.

OLD, NOT FORGOTTEN. Belle Brown was Belle Barnes when she attended Edgewood School. That's her in the lower right corner in 1924 in the old school. Her mother was the teacher—she's above with her students outside the old school before they moved to a new building.

From One Room to Two Was a Big "To-Do"

A ONE-ROOM SCHOOL in Bristol, Connecticut was where my education began in the early '20s.

All eight grades were packed into that little building, so in 1924, we went into double sessions while the community built a bigger schoolhouse down the road. My mother was the teacher.

That little country school brings back so many precious memories. I remember entering the front door every day, hanging up my coat on the row of hooks and placing my boots on the old dirty floor.

The class troublemaker often had to sit behind the potbellied stove—now that was *really* a hot seat!

Next door was where the school janitor lived—his one big chore was keeping the stove stocked with wood.

If it was really cold, he'd keep the fire going all night. All day long we'd hear him chopping and stacking wood. Sometimes at recess we'd tease him and call him "Joe Potatoes", and he'd chase us around the school yard.

One recess we ran down to the hollow to play and were late getting back when the bell rang. Our teacher was waiting for us with ruler in hand. We had to line up by the classroom and hold out both of our hands. She hit us on the knuckles two or three times. It really didn't hurt much—but our pride was injured.

In spring of 1925, a new two-room school was finished. We were all excited about the move. On the day it was scheduled, we all lined up by twos outside the building after afternoon attendance was taken.

Holding our spelling blanks and pencil boxes, we said our good-byes to the old Edgewood School, then marched up the street to the new Edgewood School.

As we approached, we saw my mother standing on the front steps, ringing the old familiar school bell with a welcoming smile.   —*Belle Brown*
Bristol, Connecticut

Young Writers Endured Spotty Beginnings

By June Stromberg, Seaside, Oregon

WITH OUR FINGERS carefully placed around the holder, eyes on the teacher as if waiting for a music conductor to start a symphony, we fourth graders in 1934 were preparing to learn the fine art of penmanship.

There was excitement and anticipation in the air at the Franklin School in Jamestown, North Dakota—after all, this was grown-up stuff!

The holder was a wooden, pencil-length instrument, pointed at the top with the blunt end grooved to accommodate the pen point (the nib). The steel split point had curved sides to fit into the holder and a small hole in the middle that helped regulate the flow of ink.

After inserting the nib into the holder, we were ready. Carefully, I checked my ink bottle, snug in the well located at the upper right corner of my oak desk.

Supplies at the Ready

The fact that it was real ink—and it was entrusted to me—was impressive. Next I made note of my supplies. A new blotter lay neatly on the desk, ready to absorb the wet fluid from the paper.

Usually, blotters were rectangular and made of postcard-like paper with a picture on the front side and felt glued to the underside. I felt the pen cleaner my mother had made for me. It was made of pink flannel circles, multi-layered and sewn together in the center in a way that let the loose fabric free to wipe the nib "shiny clean" after each use.

Special paper had been passed out to each student—a piece was properly positioned on my desk. Smooth and white, almost glossy, it wasn't rough and gray like pencil paper.

Now the teacher was giving instructions. "Like this," she

INK-QUISITION. The transition from pencil to pen and ink was difficult and messy, as June Stromberg's story points out.

demonstrated, holding her pen in the air, "much as you hold a pencil, but not as tight. Practice it."

Then she walked up and down the aisles, making sure we were following directions. "When you dip into the ink, go just to the hole in the point," she emphasized. "Remember, too much ink will just drip on your paper. Write smoothly, not with too much pressure or you'll bend the delicate point."

It was time to begin. Trying to hold the pen correctly while reaching for the inkwell, I dipped, ever so slowly, into the blue fluid and then hesitantly wrote my name across the snow-colored paper. It worked!

Name in Blue and White

There it was: Wet and navy blue against the white was "Mary June Joyce". Admiring it briefly, I reached for my new blotter and placed it over my name, giving it ample time to drink up the excess ink.

When it was removed, my name appeared backward in the blotter. Then I wiped the pen with my new flannel cleaner, sighed happily and dipped again.

Thus began our pen and ink lessons. We worked on the process and practice of writing weekly. Many papers were ruined when big blobs of ink too heavy for the blotter to absorb suddenly dropped from the point. They left ugly blotches on the paper that could not be removed. Every pupil in the class was afraid of this happening on the last word on the page, ruining the exercise and causing us to start all over again.

Although no fountain pens were allowed at school, practicing with them at home was fun.

Under the precise directions of our teacher, we fourth graders struggled with pen and ink all year long, slowly learning to dip and write as we carefully placed our wet and shiny words on paper. ❧

GAVE HIM A LIFT. Back in September of 1959, Jim Bahm, then 8 years old, got to ring the bell at this school near Wisner, Nebraska. Jim, now of Norfolk, recalls being lifted completely off the ground "nearly half as high as the tower" as he clung tightly to the bell's rope.

Geography Class Was Salt-Enhanced

MY KNOWLEDGE of our world today is enhanced by the "salt maps" we were assigned to make at home during the early '30s for our fourth-grade geography class in Geneva, Ohio.

Our introduction to faraway places began by spreading the paste (made from salt, water and baking soda) within the outlines of various countries. Food coloring allowed us to make each country a different color—the countries on my map of Africa were pink, yellow and green.

When the paste was applied too generously (as in the case of mountain ranges), the paper tended to pucker—and, of course, carrying our maps to school was always a trip filled with peril.

—*Orla-Jean Williams*
Mayfield Heights, Ohio

Knitting Knot for Him

AS THE United States pulled together during World War II, everyone did what they could to support the troops. Both third and fourth graders in the rural one-room school I attended near Paso Robles, California strove to do their part.

Everyone in my grade and above at the Oakdale School, both boys and girls, were given large white knitting needles and yarn to knit squares for afghans for hospitalized soldiers. The completed squares were given to ladies who then sewed them together.

I knitted my squares so tightly that I couldn't pull the needles out!

I made a much better farmer.

—*David Barlogio*
Paso Robles, California

PREFERRED FARMING. David Barlogio was among students who knitted afghan squares to support the troops.

Rats and Ponies Gave Memory a Boost

ONE of my favorite memories is how the nuns at our school helped us remember how to spell difficult words.

One phrase I was taught to memorize helped me spell "arithmetic". "A rat in Tom's house might eat Tom's ice cream". To this day, that's the only way I can spell arithmetic.

And does anyone remember, "George Eagle's old grandmother rode a pony home yesterday."? That's how the nuns taught me to spell "geography".

—*Mary O'Toole*
Monroeville, Pennsylvania

They Couldn't Shake His Cake Conviction

THERE was just one other boy with me in the third grade in our one-room school near Zeeland, North Dakota in the early '40s. This was shortly after the Depression, and many of us were still quite poor.

One day in health class, we were assigned a work sheet with a list of various foods. On the line after each food item we were supposed to indicate whether the food should be eaten before a meal, during a meal or afterward.

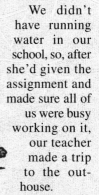

We didn't have running water in our school, so, after she'd given the assignment and made sure all of us were busy working on it, our teacher made a trip to the outhouse.

Of course, one of the older students kept a lookout for her at the window and would let us know when she was returning.

While she was gone, Johnny and I looked at each others' papers to compare answers. I noticed that after the word "cake", he had written "Sundays" instead of one of the three choices we'd been given.

I explained that the right answer would be "after a meal", but Johnny insisted that his family only ate cake on Sundays. Desperate, I went to Johnny's older sister's desk and asked her to explain to him why his answer was wrong.

Johnny was not to be swayed—he knew that Sunday was the only time his family ever had cake. Multiple choice or not, he wasn't about to change his answer. —*Leo Schatz*
Aberdeen, South Dakota

Success Was Spelled "P-O-P-S-I-C-L-E-"

MY SIXTH-GRADE TEACHER at Washington Heights School in Roanoke County, Virginia was Miss Lula Brown.

In the early 1940s, she encouraged our spelling studies by awarding a Popsicle to the last one standing during our weekly spelling bee.

Money was still so scarce then that a 5-cent Popsicle was a real enticement to study. But Mary Elizabeth Andrews and I won so often that the others in the class complained and the weekly bees were eventually discontinued.

—*Mae Sigmon, Vinton, Virginia*

Mom Knew How to Look On the Bright Side

DURING the late '50s, I attended a Catholic elementary school in southern Florida. My father passed away and left my mother to raise five children.

Due to financial constraints, my mother was about to enroll my sister and me in a public school. But the nuns said we could stay, and my tuition would be covered by my working in the cafeteria during recess.

They also told my mother that I'd have to repeat seventh grade. I'd missed a lot of school because of my father's death, and I also wasn't the brightest star in the sky!

WAR STORY. Sam Sinatra, with his godfather, Angelo Mancinelli, at Confirmation, learned years later that Mom told a fib.

One day soon after, my mother took me aside and said, "Son, I have some good news for you."

She then told me that I'd have to repeat the seventh grade because I'd missed so many days (skipping, of course, the part about me not being too bright). She explained that this was a good thing because it would keep me out of the Army and out of the war for at least another year.

It wasn't until later—when I finally started paying attention in history class—that I realized that there wasn't any war and that they don't draft 12-year-olds!

—*Sam Sinatra*
Davie, Florida

He Remembers Silver Badges And Shiny Faces

WHEN I attended the First Ward School in Seneca Falls, New York between 1938 and 1946, everyone had to be at their desks by the time the last bell rang. The only ones given permission to be late were the school crossing guards.

Being selected as a crossing guard was the ultimate honor in elementary school. If you were recommended by your teacher to be a crossing guard and approved by the principal, you were assigned a street outside the school and given an official white belt with a silver badge.

The best part of being a crossing guard was that you got to boss around the other students and stop cars. Those who were selected felt very special and important.

Those of us not chosen sneered at the guards and called them "teacher's pets", but secretly we envied them. I know, because I was finally selected as a crossing guard in sixth grade.

Our school day always began with reciting the Pledge of Allegiance. Afterward, especially in the early years of grammar school, we'd remain standing and sing:

> *Good morning to you,*
> *Good morning to you,*
> *We're all in our places*
> *With bright shiny faces,*
> *Good morning to you.*

—*William Congdon*
Levittown, Pennsylvania

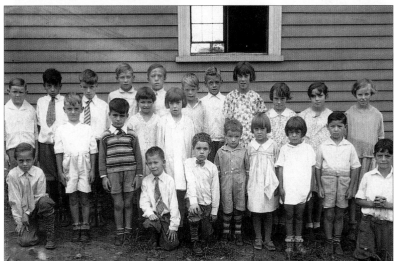

HER LITTLE RED SCHOOLHOUSE STILL STANDS. Shirley Torrey Campbell (third from right in the back row) attended this school back in 1931. It was in a section of Groveland, Massachusetts called Saveryville, says Shirley, now a resident of Haverhill. She recalls looking forward to Fridays because that's when their teacher would reward them by reading a chapter of an Uncle Wiggly book.

A CORNER FOR EVERY STUDENT. Back in the '40s, when Rudy Gavurnik and seven other students attended this unusual octagon-shaped school in Skaneateles, New York, the joke was when they all misbehaved at once, the teacher had a corner for each student to stand in. Rudy, who still lives in Skaneateles, is on the right in the back row. Later, the school became the home of another teacher.

WHEN I was in grade school at Public School 18, just outside the Bronx in Yonkers, New York, we had penmanship classes. We drew ovals, circles and lines with fat pens we dipped in inkwells.

We wrote on paper that had little pieces of straw-like material that would catch caught the nib of your pen and make holes in the paper. Mine was usually the messiest paper in the class.

To this day, I cannot write with ink. My fingers were always covered with that blue ink that never came off, and my papers had blue blobs on them. Weren't those great days?

That form of torture was called the Palmer Method. I don't know who Palmer was, but I'll bet he caused more trouble than he ever dreamed of. Inkwells never stayed full, and ink was always spurting onto people's fingers, desks and papers.

On Penmanship Day, I don't think there was a clean hankie in the room!
—*Rose Raimondi*
Wilmington, Delaware

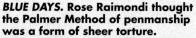

BLUE DAYS. Rose Raimondi thought the Palmer Method of penmanship was a form of sheer torture.

Perfection Did Not Begin with a Capital "P"

DURING THE '40s, I attended Fifth Avenue Elementary School in Beaver Falls, Pennsylvania. At that time, penmanship was taught in schools, and we used the Palmer Method with its looping characters.

One memorable day, my teacher, Miss Ague, decided I wasn't making my capital "P's" fat enough. So she made me stay after school and practice writing them over and over until they met her expectations of perfection.

When I did not arrive home at the usual hour after school, my mother came looking for me. When she found

me, she was properly irate that her 8-year-old daughter had been detained on a dark winter afternoon for such a trivial matter.

Fortunately for me, the next year the program was changed to the Peterson Method, which had "P's" that were more like stick figures.
—*Patricia Long, Ketchikan, Alaska*

Atmosphere in Village School Was Simple But Warm

By Wallace Shugg, Baltimore, Maryland

FOND MEMORIES. Wallace Shugg recalls the good times and helpful teachers at this three-room village school in Stamford Valley, Vermont, where he was a student in the '30s.

FROM 1935 to 1941, I attended a three-room schoolhouse in Stamford Valley, Vermont in which only three teachers taught eight grades.

Our day began with the bronze bell being tolled by the best-behaved boy of the week (never yours truly!).

We then lined up facing the entrance in three rows and filed into our respective classrooms to sit at initial-scarred wooden desks fixed onto iron frames and bolted to the floor.

In the ground-floor classrooms to the left, the ever-cheerful Tessie Clemens (grades one through three) held up flash cards with numbers for us first graders to add or multiply.

We'd shout the answers in unison (almost). Then she'd give us drawing to do and move over to hear the second-grade rows recite, assign them some work and move on to the third-grade row before coming back to us.

While in first grade, after finishing my assigned work, I'd listen to the second grade recite and join in.

Miss Clemens noticed my "volunteer efforts" and, after several weeks, told me to move over to the next row—I was now a second grader.

As I recall, it wasn't until third grade that our desktop inkwells were filled—the ones into which we dipped steel-nibbed pens and labored over Palmer Method penmanship.

We were taught that neat handwriting—like cleanliness—was close to godliness. The other subjects in our no-frills education included reading, spelling, music and "jargruffy" (geography).

In the other ground-floor classroom, grades four through six were taught by the elegant red-haired Miss Tolman, whom I still can picture blowing softly on a silver pitch pipe before leading us through a rousing version of *Alexander's Ragtime Band*.

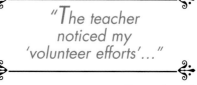

"The teacher noticed my 'volunteer efforts'..."

During those lean Depression years, the kids who walked down the logging trails from the surrounding hills brought in sandwiches made of coarse bread and a very dark meat that made me curious.

I swapped my peanut butter and jelly sandwich for one of theirs and got my first taste of venison (probably shot out of season because money to buy meat was so scarce).

In the middle of our schoolhouse cellar stood the long-unused town jail, now a rusty cage, really. It was littered with trash, its two bunks were broken-down and the door hung open at a crazy angle.

Passing it on our way to visit the boys' bathroom, we'd joke about which one of us would end up behind bars if he continued to get a D or F in behavior.

Seventh and eighth graders had to climb the creaky wooden stairs past the bell rope to the town meeting hall on the second floor. They sat at folding wooden tables and were taught by the calm and ladylike Iris McBride.

A simple stage stood at one end for meetings, theatricals and graduation ceremonies. Across the hall and over the schoolhouse entrance was the "liberry", an open space with shelves containing such solid fare as Horatio Alger's *Ragged Dick* and Victor Appleton's *Tom Swift and His Airship*.

I never did make it to that stage for graduation, because my family moved to Philadelphia in 1941. There I attended a city school, where the buildings and books were newer, the classes much larger and the teachers more numerous.

As good as it was, I missed that little village school. ❖

"Home Schooling" Put Her on the Fast Track

AFTER KINDERGARTEN had been in session for 2 weeks in 1927, the administration of our school in Geneva, Ohio decided that those, like me, whose birthday fell after the first of the year would not be allowed to start until the next school term.

With two older sisters already in grade school, I was brokenhearted when I was sent home. My mother must have been disappointed, too, since it meant I'd be "underfoot". But then she taught me how to crochet a simple chain stitch, using any length of heavy twine or yarn I could find. At first, I used just my fingers. Later, I graduated to a wooden hook.

She also taught me the game of solitaire, using only the aces and the 2,3 and 4 cards for starters. Then more numbers were added. When I got to know even the face cards, I could play with a full deck.

As it turned out, the school later eliminated the system of A and B semesters, and a bunch of us were allowed to "skip" half of the fifth grade. So we ended up graduating with those "older" kids after all.
—*Orla-Jean Williams*
Mayfield Heights, Ohio

Gopher Stew Wouldn't Do For Young Scientist's Mother

MY CHILDHOOD during the '20s was spent on a California plum, peach and orange ranch near Pomona. For our fifth-grade science class, each student had to do a project.

I chose the construction of the inner body and the bones in animals. My dad had caught a big fat gopher and told me I could use the carcass for my project.

After I'd skinned the gopher and cleaned him, all I had left were the bones. But I was at a loss as to how to remove the clinging pieces of meat left on the bones.

Then I hit on a neat idea—at least it seemed like a neat idea.

Mother was spending the day with relatives, so I had the kitchen to myself. I rummaged through the pots and pans and pulled out Mother's brand-new shiny stockpot. Into it went what was left of that gopher.

I covered him with water like I'd seen Mother do with stew meat and cooked him slowly for 2 hours. The house smelled awful, and when Mother walked in, she blew up!

I spent the next hour scrubbing and disinfecting that stockpot until it was as shiny as new. The story had a happy ending: I received a blue ribbon and an "A" on my project.
—*Ruth Ward, Victorville, California*

SWEET SOUNDS OF A SAVAGE SCHOOL. Back in 1954, all the students in Mrs. Brown's third-grade class in Savage, Maryland learned to play the flute, recalls Louise Mardones Horner, who now lives in New Windsor. That's Louise in the center of the picture, wearing a plaid jumper and white blouse.

HE TOOK THE SCHOOL HOME! Cleo Moore of Jefferson, New York attended District School 4 (built in 1837) near his home back in the '30s. After it closed in 1935, it sat for 50 years before the owner gave it to Cleo and he moved it a mile to his yard. Today, it's been restored, and Cleo proudly reports that when alumni of the school get together there each July, they often remark, "It's just like I remember it."

Katzenjammer Twins Were Terrific Reading Instructors

I'VE NEVER FORGOTTEN the first grader I taught around 1920 in a one-room schoolhouse. Her name was Dorothy and she lived near the school, so I boarded at her home during the week and then went to my own home in the St. Louis, Missouri area on weekends.

When I returned to Dorothy's house on Sundays, I always brought along the comics section of the *St. Louis Post Dispatch*. Dorothy and I read and studied it every day during the week.

From its pages, we entered the wonderful make-believe world of tall Mutt and short Jeff and the quarrelsome Maggie and Jiggs. But most thrilling of all were the fun-loving Katzenjammer Kids, Hans and Fritz—along with Mama, the Captain and the Old Inspector.

We laughed at the twins' outlandish antics and tricks, and we took marvelous journeys with them to foreign lands like Africa, Asia and Australia.

We became acquainted with native peoples and animals, hippos, rhinos and—best of all—the kangaroo with her marvelous pocket. What lessons in geography and science we experienced!

When we'd get come home from school, Dorothy and I would spread the funnies out on the kitchen table and have an hour or so of fun before supper.

At first, I did all the reading, but after 2 or 3 days, Dorothy had memorized all the dialogue and would not permit me to alter or omit a word. Soon, she was doing all the reading herself.

Years later, whenever I received a card from her, she'd remind me, "I'm the little girl who learned to read from the funnies."

—*Helen Hall, Carlyle, Illinois*

PROUD SON. Dean Thornton and his mother, Joe, posed in 1939, 2 years after her delayed high school graduation.

Her Diploma Made Everyone Proud

GROWING UP in the '20s, my mother had to leave school to help care for her younger brothers and sisters.

Still, Mom always wished she had her high school diploma. But in the 1930s, it was unusual for a woman with a 10-year-old son (me) to go back to school.

Mom had to meet with the principal and the Board of Education in Salt Lake City to get permission to attend. She did receive permission, so back to high school she went. There was a common fence between her school and the grade school I attended, and, as it turned out, our lunch hours coincided. I'd climb the fence and meet Mom in the cafeteria.

We'd go through the line together and have a nice hot lunch. It made me feel like a big shot to be around all those high school kids.

Mom introduced me to the principal and some of her teachers. I'd later have the same teachers myself when I enrolled in high school. I even got to use her activity card to attend football and basketball games.

Mom was like a big sister to her high school friends. She would have them over to our house after school so they could help each other study. I'm sure that 2 of the happiest years of my mother's life were those she spent at that high school.

On graduation day, my dad and I were two of the proudest people in the audience when Mom received high praise for being a straight-A student and was given her diploma.

—*Dean Thornton, Salt Lake City, Utah*

It Was Hard Not to Learn in Those Old 🍎 Country Schools 🍎

By Mildred Mitchell, Marion, Michigan

THE HARVEST was in full swing that fall of 1927, as I trudged along a dusty road in central Michigan on the way to my first day of school.

I was carrying a syrup pail containing my lunch in one hand, and a penny pencil and a thick red tablet filled with coarse blue-lined paper in the other.

My mother had made me a new outfit—a black-and-white-checked dress and black sateen bloomers with elastic in the legs that made them blouse around the knees. They billowed out beneath the hem of my dress and were a handicap when I wanted to run or jump. A tomboy at heart, I was excited about going to school, but I hated those bloomers!

Then an older girl showed me how to hide an apple in my bloomer leg. From then on, I used the bloomer legs to carry handkerchiefs or apples—even cookies and sandwiches.

At the Beebe School near Marion, Michigan, the day began with the raising of the flag. Then our names were called out one by one and we answered "present". After that, we placed our hands over our hearts and recited the Pledge of Allegiance together and sang a verse of *America*.

Reading and Recitation

Next, our teacher would read a chapter from a storybook. We enjoyed that since we had so few books to read. We sat in desks that held two people, and there was a long recitation desk in front of the room.

"Stand, pass, be seated" were the commands our teacher used when it was time to recite. Sometimes two classes recited at the same time. The younger classes were always eager to show up the older kids.

With all eight grades reciting lessons out loud, you couldn't help but absorb information that came in handy later on. We read aloud and, if we stumbled over a word, an older child helped us. If an arithmetic problem stumped someone, teacher worked it out on the blackboard and we all watched.

Poetry was learned, one verse at a time. Some of the best poetry ever written was contained in those old third- and fourth-grade readers. I'll bet I'm not the only former 7-year-old who can still recite *Darius Green and His Flying Machine* or *The Village Blacksmith*.

Recess came at 10:30 and lasted 15 minutes—time enough to choose sides for a game of "work up" baseball that would be played at noon. At lunchtime, we'd line up along the west wall of the school.

Everybody's lunch was about the same—peanut butter sandwich, a molasses cookie and an apple. How good it tasted as I sat among those laughing children in the shade of the school!

Occasionally we'd hear the drone of an airplane, and our teacher would rush us outside to try and see it. (That tiny speck high above was a true miracle back then.)

I suppose we weren't much different from students today. We spent part of our time developing our minds and the rest doing things like shooting paper wads or dropping pencils to distract the teacher when she was at the blackboard.

No Laughing Matter

I remember the time a small boy had to sit under the teacher's desk as punishment for something. Every time the teacher turned her back, an older boy motioned for him to open the teacher's dinner pail.

When he finally did, we tried not to laugh as he ate the teacher's lunch. We thought it was funny—until she reached down, grabbed him by the shoulder and marched him out to the woodshed for the rest of the day!

The rest of us had to stay in at recess and practice penmanship, which we didn't think was funny either. Despite incidents like this, we were expected to have good manners and usually did.

In those old country schools, the teacher cared about her students and the students cared about her. She visited our homes and knew who worked hard and could only attend classes part time. She'd spend extra time with these students so they wouldn't fall behind.

Yes, at that old country school, a good education was there for the taking—if we didn't absorb it, it was our own fault. 🍎

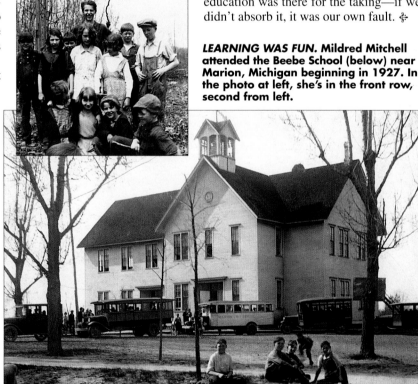

LEARNING WAS FUN. Mildred Mitchell attended the Beebe School (below) near Marion, Michigan beginning in 1927. In the photo at left, she's in the front row, second from left.

Chapter 4

Memories From Our Teachers

Memories From Our Teachers

Teaching is a profession that requires unshakable patience, a steady temper, a sense of humor…and the basic skills of a mule driver.

You start every year with new faces, and minds that are sure nothing very good is likely to happen in the months ahead. Most of the class would rather be anywhere on earth than fidgeting in an uncomfortable classroom desk. All they're looking forward to is Thanksgiving, the first school holiday on the calendar.

Despite all this, you'll seldom find a former teacher who doesn't treasure the good memories of the job.

Yes, youngsters were full of mischief, their feelings were easily bruised and they generally were positive that no one understood them. But to a teacher, a class of 25 kids wasn't merely a sea of faces. Rather, it was 25 individuals, each with special needs and unique abilities.

I'm in awe of teachers who can sort those kids out and provide some measure of attention for each one's needs. For that matter, I flat-out worship anyone who voluntarily chooses a job that requires 8-hour days in a room filled with small people who seem to have a permanent case of the "terrible twos".

But when you ask teachers about their memories, they'll invariably talk about the joys of the job. Recently, I chanced to sit beside a 40-something lady in a doctor's waiting room. She was (and is) a teacher.

"It used to be that our job was to teach," she began. "But these days, parents have babies, then turn them over to the school system to raise. I didn't take up teaching to become a full-time mama and daddy."

Yet, after we visited for half an hour, I knew she loved her work. She enjoyed the challenge of putting knowledge into young minds. She saw slower learners not as an annoyance, but a special test of her own ability. She saw the brighter ones as a different, no less challenging, demand on her talent.

"The key to teaching is to understand that it's 50% performance art," she said. "You have to stand up there and put on a performance that holds the attention of every kid in the room. You need to excite them, amuse them and occasionally mystify them. You can't teach kids a thing by boring them to death."

The other ingredient she didn't mention was courage. Teaching certainly requires a fair amount of that. Your students never doubt you know everything. But teachers—especially newer ones—know deep inside that isn't really the case.

Teachers were as prone to first-day jitters as their charges. Marilyn Byerley vividly recalls those feelings in the memory she shared for this book. I think you'll enjoy her story and the others in the pages ahead.

—*Clancy Strock*

Supervisor Gave High Marks to Hardworking Teacher

By Marion Weekly, Fresno, California

MADE THE GRADE. New teacher Marion Weekly (cameo) got an excellent grade from her supervising teacher, but her first class in 1942 (above) was the best reflection of her teaching skills.

AFTER GRADUATING from a 2-year teachers' college, I taught in a one-room school near Unity, Wisconsin.

Looking back, it's mind-boggling to think of the preparation we did to teach all subjects to all eight grades.

Besides the three R's, we taught agriculture, grammar, history, geography, art, music and many other things. Teachers also served as the school janitor and nurse as well as social director for the community.

The big Christmas program was probably the most important event on the social calendar. The other event generating excitement was the closing-day picnic with its contests and other activities.

In those days, there were supervising teachers who walked into the classroom unannounced to give you (and your school board) a report on your teaching and the needs of your school. This is the text of supervisor Eugene W. Laurent's review of my classroom on November 9, 1942. Note the recommendation of an asbestos covering for the furnace. How times change!

A Glowing Report

"The building is in very good condition. The board has made excellent improvements—walls redecorated, new well on the grounds. The schoolroom now has a very fine appearance.

"A covering of asbestos on the furnace would prevent the loss of much heat. Will it be possible to get a radio very soon? The programs sponsored by the Wisconsin School of the Air are excellent for schools. Considering the fine spirit of these pupils, I think they are entitled to this treat.

"Your room is very neat, well arranged and artistically decorated. I am pleased to see freehand work posted. There is evidence of a careful choice of decorations.

"I am always impressed by the wholesome atmosphere in this school. Pupils are very courteous, considerate of others and cheerful. They have commendable study habits. I like the fine spirit of cooperation here.

"You do very effective teaching, which is

the result of careful preparation. The poem for Language 7 and 8 was beautifully taught. The discussion for agriculture was interesting.

"Reading classes were very well conducted. Your little people are making fine progress. I am pleased to note how effectively *My Weekly Reader* is being used for reading. I liked the points listed on the blackboard for Reading 3 and 4. Upper-grade pupils are remarkable readers. There is value in giving attention to vocabulary and expression."

Teaching school then was a lot of work, but a lot of good teaching was done in those old country schools. I'm sure most of us loved what we were doing. I know I did.

EXCITEMENT IN THE AIR. Each fall, a new class offered challenges and opportunities for old and new teachers alike.

Never Too Old to Learn—or Churn

I'D ALWAYS LIVED in small towns and thought "city people" knew all the answers because of greater educational opportunities. But my first year of teaching in the big city of Dallas, Texas changed my mind.

Many of my first-grade pupils at Urban Park Elementary School were unfamiliar with farm life. When we talked about where our food came from, I realized some of the children thought butter came "from the store".

I'd seen my mother-in-law make butter many times, using fresh cream from the family cows, so I enlisted her help. What better way for my students to learn where butter *really* came from than to make it themselves?

The principal notified one of the newspapers, and he and a lady reporter watched as the children took turns cranking the handle on the churn. When the butter was ready, we salted it lightly, then spread it on crackers so all the children could sample it. They also got to try buttermilk, the liquid left over from the churning process.

The question I remember the most came not from the children, but from the reporter, who was older than me. "Does it taste like butter?" she asked.

I realize now that she probably meant to ask if it tasted like butter bought at the store, but I just told her, "It *is* butter."

As I recall, she asked the question more than once. The memory still makes me chuckle and reminds me that none of us is ever too old to learn.
—*Wilma Wade*
Emory, Texas

DOES IT TASTE LIKE BUTTER? Wilma Wade brought her small-town background to the big city and showed her students how to churn butter.

Students Helped Stoke Fires, Shovel Snow, Carry Water

I TAUGHT in a one-room country school during the 1930s and early '40s in Somerset County, Pennsylvania. The winters were severe. We built big fires in the furnace to fight off the cold and stoked the fire so it'd last overnight.

We used soft coal, which was stored in the unfinished basement and carried up a ladder. I paid one of the older boys to start the fire early in the mornings.

Our drinking water came from a spring nearby. The children loved fetching water—that took longer than a recess period. The toilets were outside, of course. The older students shoveled paths to them in winter.

The students brought their own lunches, which usually consisted of homemade bread with tomatoes in fall, home-cured ham in winter or plain apple butter. They often brought a peach or apple in season, and some had a piece of pie or cookies around Christmas. Children from farms had the better lunches, because food was canned and gathered in abundance.

I used a hectograph to make copies of work or artwork. I made my own gelatin base, put it in a cookie pan and used it over and over until it became too discolored from the ink to make any more master copies.

The township school board provided pencils, pens and pen points, textbooks (though many were outdated), and four writing tablets a year for children in grades three to eight.

I made ink from a powder, then had to hope it didn't freeze in winter. It often did. The only other materials we received were chalk, maps and a box of crayons. Anything I wanted to decorate the room I provided myself.

I realize how fortunate those children were. They shared in the joys and sorrows of others, and they had respect for life, their elders and their friends.
—*Clarice Winters*
Hershey, Pennsylvania

LIKE MOTHER, LIKE DAUGHTER. In 1908, Clarice Winters' mother, Marjorie Zimmerman (back row, center), was in her last year at Bellview School in Somerset County, Pennsylvania. The next year, she went to normal school and become a teacher. Some 30 years later, Clarice started teaching.

Student Teachers Learned How to Think on Their Feet

By Shirley Benson, Elk River, Minnesota

IN THE dead of winter 1945, four young women were sent to a rural Minnesota school for 6 weeks of student teaching. None of us had even set foot in a country school before, much less taught in one.

When we arrived at the farmhouse where we'd stay, we discovered our supervising teacher had been called away by a death in the family. We'd have to teach the classes on our own—and none of us had the slightest idea what to do.

Our college supervisor took us on to Hill School, where we found 30 children in grades one through eight sitting in the single classroom, staring at the "new teachers". Our supervisor apparently wanted no part of this situation, because he didn't stick around.

On the teacher's desk, we found four folders labeled "Block 1", "Block 2", "Block 3" and "Block 4". We had no idea what this meant. To us, blocks were something you walked around. Finally, with the help of a seventh-grade girl, we discovered "blocks" were sections of time and began working our way through the lesson plans.

Burned the Soup

We also discovered it was our job to prepare hot cocoa or soup at lunchtime. One day another student teacher and I burned a kettle full of canned bean soup and ended up throwing the whole mess into a snowbank. We covered it up with more snow so no one would notice, but we often wondered what that spot looked like when spring came.

A man came every morning before school to stoke the furnace, but it was our job to keep it going. We knew nothing about furnaces

HELPING HANDS. Student-teaching assignments gave teachers much-needed help in the days of larger classes. Three or four student teachers might be assigned to a class like this one. The author describes her student-teaching trials when the regular teacher was called away.

and went to the furnace room only when necessary. Whichever girl had furnace duty would run into the dark room, scoop up a shovelful of coal, throw it into the furnace as quickly as possible and run out just as fast.

One day the furnace began coughing black smoke. Convinced it was going to blow, we sent the children home, then raced toward the farmhouse, constantly looking back to see if the building was still there. It was, and still is.

But there were jobs we loved, like ringing the school bell. Several times the rope got away from us and flipped up into the bell area, and we had to climb a ladder to pull it back down. One day as I stood on the ladder, I looked down into the face of a woman—the teacher whose school we'd been running. She was back. What a way to meet her!

Loved Recess, Too

At recess and noon hours, we slid down the hill with the children. We loved it as much as they did. On Friday nights, the parents held card parties at the school, and we went to several. They were so much fun that we came back to attend them even after returning to college.

Hill School holds such fond, fun memories for me. The teacher I met while standing on the ladder became one of my best friends. The building is now someone's home, but whenever I drive past it, I visualize that darling little white schoolhouse, and all of us sliding down the hill. ❧

Chew on This: No Gum Allowed

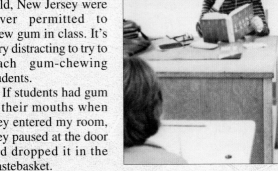

MY LATIN and French students at Garfield High School in Garfield, New Jersey were never permitted to chew gum in class. It's very distracting to try to teach gum-chewing students.

If students had gum in their mouths when they entered my room, they paused at the door and dropped it in the wastebasket.

They knew if I saw them chewing, I'd say, "Deposit the gum, please." I was so known for that remark, it appeared over my photo (above) in the school yearbook one year.

—*Ruth Overwyk, Polk City, Florida*

Teenage Teacher No Bigger Than Her Young Charges

AFTER WORLD WAR II, I taught at the Banner School, a picturesque little white schoolhouse in Adair County, Missouri.

I was paid $115 a month for 8 months of teaching. I lived with my Aunt Mabel and Uncle Jess and paid them $20 a month for room and board.

Uncle Jess, who was on the school board, would hand me my check, which came to $99.90 after deductions, and then give me a dime from his own pocket. "Never say you didn't get $100," he'd say.

Banner School had eight pupils my first year, all boys. I was 18 and weighed 100 pounds, and the three eighth graders were as big as I was. At recess, we played baseball and "Andy Over", but I begged off when they played football. We all left the schoolhouse together to walk home, and people who drove past said they couldn't tell me from my pupils.

My only first grader had a crush on me and gave me a nice makeup set at Christmas. He was jealous of my boyfriend, who had a new red 1946 Ford and sometimes picked me up on Fridays as we were all walking home. My little admirer

TINY TEACHER. Marjorie Eitel was barely taller than her students in 1946 (above right). She'd play games with them at recess, but not football (right).

was so jealous that he refused to accept a ride!

We had a pie supper that year, with the single girls bringing box lunches to auction off to the boys. When my lunch was held up, the first grader's father made sure no one outbid his son. He and I shared a box lunch that night.

—Marjorie Eitel, Kansas City, Missouri

Sticky Situation Only Got Stickier

ONE Saturday afternoon in the '20s, I was enrolling students about to start the fall term in the Glenella, Manitoba school where I taught. On that day, mothers brought their children in to meet the teacher and record the child's name, address and date of birth.

The second mother who came to my desk said, "I'm Mrs. Smith and this is Gooey. His birthday was August 3." I wrote down the date, then asked the little boy what his name was.

"Gooey," he replied shyly.

Wondering if maybe I'd heard wrong, I asked him to repeat it, but his mother, who by that time was wondering whether I was deaf, replied loudly,

"HIS NAME IS GOOEY!"

"Oh," I said, "that must be a nickname. What's on his birth certificate?"

"His name is on it. What else?" replied Mrs. Smith, clearly irritated with me.

By now, everyone else in the room was "listening in". Realizing that she had a very interested audience, Mrs. Smith proudly explained to us all that it was *not* a nickname and that she had been reading a story about a very smart man named Gooey. She knew that her baby would be just as smart, so she named him Gooey, too.

"Well, Mrs. Smith," I said, "Just how do you spell your son's last name?"

Well, that was the straw that broke the camel's back! The lady was now totally disgusted with me. Giving me a withering look, she turned to the others as if to say, "Are we going to turn our kids over to a woman who can't even spell?"

Then, out loud, she said, "The teacher wants *me* to tell *her* how to spell!"

Standing tall with her head held high, Mrs. Smith spoke very slowly, very distinctly, as if she were winning a spelling bee.

"The name is Gooey—I shall spell Gooey: **G...U...Y.**"

I've always wondered what the famous bandleader Guy Lombardo would have thought of this story.

—Margaret Taylor, Marble Falls, Texas

This Graduate Chose a Teaching Career

WHEN I graduated from Central City High School in Central City, Nebraska in 1922, there seemed to be three choices for the girl graduate—go to college, get married or teach rural school.

Most rural schools did not hire married women. I didn't have money for college or a serious beau, so

LOVED TEACHING. Dorothy Rains stands with her elementary school students in 1933 in Merrick County, Nebraska.

I chose to teach school. As an 18-year-old, I took on the task of instructing 21 pupils, grades one through eight, in Merrick County.

I walked 1-1/2 miles from my boarding place to school, sometimes wading through snowdrifts up to my knees.

I did my own janitorial work, including building the fire in the stove, carrying in the coal from the outside shed and all of the cleaning.

I was paid $75 a month for a 9-month period. How did I feel about this? I felt very lucky. I loved teaching, and just having some money of my own was great.

—Dorothy Rains
Central City, Nebraska

Weather Tested Teen Teacher's Mettle

By Virginia Becker
McHenry, North Dakota

TOUGH TRIP. Going home to visit could be difficult for teachers in the days of poor roads. Bad weather made things worse, as Virginia Becker found out.

I BEGAN TEACHING in 1947 at age 18, straight out of high school. I was assigned to a rural school about 30 miles from my North Dakota home and was paid $150—a good wage at the time.

I stayed with a young family, and on the coldest mornings, the man took me the 1-1/2 miles to school, both of us standing on a stone boat hitched to two horses with chains.

The boat skittered all over when the horses trotted. The man had the reins to hold onto, but I had nothing. I was too shy to hold onto him, so I learned to balance myself. What a ride!

That winter was so cold and stormy that I usually had only three pupils, all from a family living nearby.

The following year, I taught at a different school. One winter morning

"I made sandwiches for over an hour..."

when I walked the half mile to school, it was 33° below zero, and I found snow piled high against the door.

After kicking the snow away and rushing inside to stir the fire and add coal, I started shoveling a path to the two outhouses. When I finally moved enough snow to open the doors, I found the little houses were packed with snow right to the top.

I was shoveling out the second house when one of the parents dropped off his daughter. He was so agitated when he saw my frozen face that he sent me inside while he finished the shoveling.

Rural electrification arrived that year, and we got a two-burner hot plate. How we enjoyed having something warm each noon! The school lunch program provided free cheese, so the children brought buttered bread once a week and I made grilled cheese sandwiches.

The first time I did that, I ended up making sandwiches for over an hour. I had 10 students, and it seemed every one of them brought an entire loaf of bread. There wasn't a crust left.

My third year of teaching was in the tiny town of Hamar, about 10 miles from home. One weekend while out with my brother and a friend, we stopped by the school to start a fire. You needed to get a good fire going to burn off the gas from the coal, then close the draft and damper to keep the fire alive.

On this particular night, the fire just wouldn't get going, and we needed to leave to get to the movie, so we left the damper open a bit. When we returned 2 hours later, a blast of heat slammed into us as we opened the door.

Crayons Had Melted

The children's crayons had melted in piles under their desks, the water in the cooler was hot and I couldn't touch the bell on my desk. The thermometer had skyrocketed to 120°, and then broken. Why that schoolhouse didn't burn down, I'll never know.

The Thursday before Easter, I desperately wanted to go home, but the spring thaw had left our gravel high-

ways a mess. I found a family who could drive me within walking distance of home, so I quickly packed a suitcase, borrowed hip waders and rode off with them.

They dropped me off 4 miles from home, and I started walking. The first 2 miles weren't bad—just deep mud to plow through. Then I found the entire highway under water, with a current so fast it made me dizzy. I put on the hip boots and started to wade.

Home Was in Sight

I turned off the highway to walk the last mile uphill, trudging out of the water and into knee-high snow. At last I reached the crest, where I could see our home in the distance—but the sight made my heart sink. Everything in between was covered with water.

Our neighbors at the top of the hill came to my rescue. Their 10-year-old took me across the water on his horse. I'd never ridden a swimming horse before (and I haven't since). Was my family ever surprised to see me walk through the door!

That was my last year of teaching until after I was married. Then I lived at the "teacherage", so my battles with snow and cold were over. We even had indoor toilets and an oil furnace. With those luxuries, I earned my $235 salary just for *teaching*!

First-Year Teacher Sympathized with Student's First-Day Jitters

By Marilyn Byerley, Nevada City, California

MY FAMILY had produced three generations of teachers before I came along, but it wasn't tradition that made me want to teach. It was my second-grade teacher, Miss Evelyn Wagner. Miss Wagner was perfect, so I assumed teaching would be perfect, too.

In 1959, when I was hired for my first teaching job after college, I requested any grade except first. But first grade was what I got—and in a school with no kindergarten. My joy at starting my career dimmed a bit, but if Miss Wagner could do it, so could I.

When I reported for the first day of classes at Shoregate School in Willowick, Ohio, I'd just turned 21. As I sat in Room 3, nervously waiting for the bell to ring, I saw a man dragging his extremely reluctant son down the sidewalk outside my window. Hmm, I thought to myself, I wonder whose room he's in?

The bell rang, and the students began arriving in their first-day finery. I greeted each of them with what I hoped was a confident smile.

Suddenly I became aware of pathetic sobbing outside my door. As I walked toward the door, I realized the source of this commotion was the reluctant boy I'd seen a few minutes earlier. Oh, no, I thought—he's my student!

They didn't tell us about things like this in college. What would I do? This never happened to Miss Wagner! Could I quit right now? What other career might I enjoy?

When I reached the door, the child's father looked at me with pleading eyes. He explained that "Steven" didn't want to come to school today. I knew just how Steven felt.

The frustrated man had been trying to push Steven through the door, but the sobbing child had straightened both arms and locked them against the doorjamb, then braced his feet the same way. Steven wouldn't budge.

Steven's father and I looked helplessly at each other, then at Steven. Finally the man said, "I'll tell you what. I'll push on his arms, you push on his legs, and when he lets go, we'll push him in the door and I'll run."

Four years of teacher training never prepared me for this, but I didn't have a better idea, so I agreed. I pushed on Steven's legs, his father pushed on his arms, we got him through the doorway and Steven's father left. It took all the fortitude I had not to run out the door behind him.

But Steven stayed, and so did I, and eventually we both calmed down.

When I left that school 3 years later, Steven was a happy third grader, so I assume that traumatic first day didn't scar him for life. It didn't scar me either, nor did it scare me away from my chosen profession.

Looking back, I can laugh about that day—and only hope Steven and his father can, too.

UNEXPECTED PROBLEM. As a fourth-generation teacher, the author (back row, far right) thought she was well-prepared for her first day of teaching. A terrified child wasn't in her lesson plan.

Schoolmarm's Education Included Dust Storms

By June Drebing, Minnetonka, Minnesota

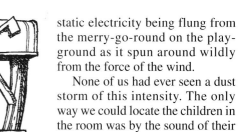

"SHEP", the family collie, accompanied me to the road from the farmhouse in Roberts County, South Dakota during the 1933-34 school year.

Standing in the gateway, he saw me turn as usual to walk my daily mile to Enterprise No. 4, the one-room country school where I was about to finish my first year as a teacher. I was 19 years old. Shep lifted his nose into the dusty air, gave a short bark as if to say, "There, that's done", then took his post by the kitchen door.

Normally, there'd have been green grass growing in the roadside ditches, spring flowers brightening the landscape and trees donning their spring finery, but not much was happening in mid-May of 1934.

Dust had drifted up along the fences, just as snow would have done the preceding winter—had there been any snow. My first task upon arrival at the schoolhouse was to remove the film of dust that had accumulated overnight on desks, windowsills and floors.

Experience had taught me there was little to be gained from doing the daily chores at the close of the school day—it all had to be done again in the morning anyway.

Although the schoolhouse was well built, dust still seeped in. It almost seemed as if the walls had pores designed for dust to enter. Its location in the middle of four plowed fields didn't help.

Parents Were Invited

That day was to be special, for I'd set it aside as one for the parents to come visit. Among my 28 pupils, nine families were represented. Not many parents were able to come, but I thought a few might make it.

In the afternoon, two mothers did make it to school to observe our classes. It was about 3 p.m. and I was giving a science test. Somewhere in the time between the first and second questions, our world suddenly changed from light gray to pitch black!

The wind became furious and brought with it such clouds of dust that we could barely see. The windows looked as if a giant hand had splashed wide swaths of black paint across them.

Peering out of them, all we could see were the sparks of static electricity being flung from the merry-go-round on the playground as it spun around wildly from the force of the wind.

None of us had ever seen a dust storm of this intensity. The only way we could locate the children in the room was by the sound of their voices. I tried to be very grown-up and "in charge" so the parents would have confidence in me, but to tell the truth, I was frightened.

Stories of country schoolteachers marooned with their pupils during blizzards ran through my head. Mentally, I went over our resources. We had no food because the lunch buckets had been emptied at noon. But there was plenty of water in the basement cistern (although it was normally only used for washing).

Not Even a Candle

Our coal was inside, so we'd have no problem if the temperature fell, but we had no lamp, no lantern and no flashlight—not even a candle. Thank heavens for our chemical toilets! How long would this awful thing last?

Fortunately, the worst of it was over in an hour or so. As the sky became a lighter gray, parents could see well enough to drive and began arriving to take their children home.

After they'd all gone, there was enough light for me to finish my paperwork for the day. Then I walked back to my boarding place, more convinced than ever that my first year as a country schoolteacher would be my last. But for now, my world was back to normal—a medium wind with light dust—and Shep waiting for me at the end of the driveway.

Housing Shortage Prompted Teacher to Build His Own Home

WHEN I ACCEPTED a teaching position in a remote area of South Dakota in 1941, at age 19, it was impossible to find a place to live. So I had an 8- by 12-foot cabin built and delivered to the school grounds.

The cabin was heated with a wood-burning stove, although in emergencies it was fueled with corncobs, coal and even "cow chips". Water was carried in a 3-gallon bucket from an outdoor pump. A few times, I went outside in the morning and found the dipper frozen in the bucket.

My trusty Montgomery Ward battery-operated radio provided my nightly entertainment, and my transportation was a

HOME SWEET HOME. Dan Duffy lived right on the school grounds in this tiny cabin he had built.

1930 Model A Ford coupe with a rumble seat, which cost $85. That car was my link to the rest of the world, carrying me the 37 miles home on weekends and to the grocery store 5 miles away.

—*Dan Duffy, Bella Vista, Arkansas*

Young Teacher Did Her Job Despite Primitive Conditions

By Nancy Little, Cambridge, Ontario

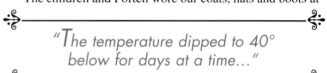

SPRING ARRIVED LATE at my school 13 miles from St. Georges-de-Bauce in northern Quebec in 1960. I could forgive its tardiness if only I could feel warm again. Since fall, I'd been teaching 13 French-Canadian children in grades one through six in a small school.

When I'd arrived the previous August, I'd been thrilled by the secluded setting. The school was surrounded by fir trees and backed by a gentle brook where the children and I often sat to eat lunch or toss pebbles.

Blue jays and other colorful birds often perched on the wire fence that enclosed the schoolyard. Inside the fence was our winter fuel, a huge pile of wood slabs. Before the first snowfall, the children and I had carried it all into the woodshed.

The father of two of my students drove all of us to school in an old station wagon fitted with benches for seats. As the teacher, I got to ride in the comfortable front seat.

A neighbor started a fire in the woodstove each morning so the schoolhouse was warm when we arrived. It was my duty to keep the fire going.

Fire Was a Mystery

Having come directly from a modern college dormitory in Chicago, I didn't have the slightest inkling about keeping a fire. I found that some wood burned better than others, so I kept using it every day.

One morning, I found a message from the caretaker scrawled on the blackboard: "Please stop using the soft wood. Use the hard wood."

Soft wood? Hard wood? Was there a difference? Apparently I'd been burning the cedar kindling used to start a fire, instead of the hardwood that kept it burning steadily.

That winter was bitterly cold. Sometimes the temperature dipped to 40° below zero for days at a time. Our firewood was only partially dry and gave off minimal heat.

The children and I often wore our coats, hats and boots at

CAPS ALLOWED. Chilly temperatures forced students to wear hats and coats in the classroom (above) when Nancy Little (top right) was teaching at this small school in rural Quebec (below).

"The temperature dipped to 40° below for days at a time..."

our desks to stay warm. The children's water bottles iced over in the cloakroom, and, to top off our trials, the chemical toilet frequently froze.

By spring, the struggle of working with limited supplies and no electricity in extreme cold had taken its toll. When the school inspector arrived to observe and rate my performance, I was apprehensive. He came with an associate and an older woman who'd taught at the school in the early 1900s.

Were Shortcomings Discussed?

I was seated at my desk at the front of the room as the former teacher talked to the inspector's assistant in the back. I was depressed—surely they were discussing my ignorance of woodstoves and chemical toilets.

Just then, the inspector, a kind middle-aged man, leaned over my desk, put his mouth close to my ear, and said softly, "Between you and me, you did just fine."

I could have hugged him. The inspector saw the school's primitive conditions and must have guessed what a struggle the year had been for me. His simple words of encouragement came at exactly the right moment.

It's been 39 years since I passed that inspection, but I'll never forget the idyllic setting, the students who became lifelong friends, the cold-weather challenges and, most of all, that kindly school inspector.

As a teacher, I'd give him an A+.

Chapter 5

We Couldn't Wait for Lunch and Recess

We Couldn't Wait for Lunch and Recess

My first great discovery at school had nothing whatsoever to do with intellectual things. The great wonder of the world that was unveiled to me was...*chocolate milk*!

I was raised on a farm. The creamy, delicious, unpasteurized milk we drank came from our own cows. And contrary to what we told city kids, the milk produced by brown cows was *not* chocolate.

Note, please, I wasn't a total rube. I did know about chocolate ice cream. But not chocolate milk.

I think a half-pint of milk at school cost 3¢ then. Nevertheless, Mom and Dad were determined that my sister and I should enjoy the finer things in life, so we got the money for store-bought milk, even though our cows produced at least 50 gallons every day.

That little bottle of chocolate milk was all the incentive I needed to go to school. Like most farm kids, we carried our lunches. For some reason, Dad took on the responsibility of packing our lunches every morning. This was a mixed blessing.

The up side was his raging sweet tooth and a belief that no kid should face lunch without a Hostess Twinkie, chocolate cupcake, coconut-covered pink or white Sno Ball, or a slab of home-baked chocolate cake with cooked fudge frosting. Just as long as it was sweet.

So we were two lucky kids. Except for one thing: Dad also was a crazed inventor of sandwich fillings. Any leftover that could be run through the meat grinder was a candidate for his creativity. His bologna/sweet pickle/radish sandwich spread wasn't too bad. And his egg salad was delicious. But it took time to develop a taste for his banana/orange juice/peanut butter spread.

Yesterday's beef roast, pork chop, liver or chicken meat could hide in the icebox, but it couldn't run. Eventually Dad would spot it. Into the grinder it would go.

I'm sure you remember the daily lunchroom swap session, where you tried to trade a Bermuda onion sandwich for a tasty turkey creation. As you can imagine, my sister and I weren't ever invited to swap sandwiches—at least after the first sample of what we had to offer.

Even our best friends would stare out the window when we offered to trade. Oh, sure, we could swap an apple for a banana, or a Hostess Twinkie for a Little Debbie. But no one would take a chance on one of our sandwiches. Whenever my sister and I reminisce about our childhoods, the one topic that's sure to come up is Dad's "lunchbox mystery spreads."

The tragic truth is that his eccentricity appears to be a genetic thing. Just ask my kids, who grew up in perpetual terror of my own sandwich creations. The little heathens just didn't know a good thing when they tasted it.

—*Clancy Strock*

Dishwashing Tykes Earned More Than Dad

By Terry Curtis, Austin, Texas

WET WORK. Terry Curtis (first row, third from left) has a typical red-haired, freckle-faced grin in this class picture from 1951-52 in Jacksonville, Texas. He may be shoeless because he got his tennis shoes wet during lunchtime work in the cafeteria.

IN THE LATE 1940s, our family lived on a small farm in the sandhills of Cherokee County, Texas. Papa was a railroad telegrapher, making almost a dollar an hour. We didn't have any idea we were poor. As far as we knew, the only thing out of our reach was the expensive school lunches.

At Joe Wright Elementary in Jacksonville, lunches cost the outrageous price of a quarter. Our family had one child in each of the five grades, so it would've cost $6.25 a week for all of us—far too much when we could easily carry a sandwich and a thermos of fresh milk.

We had no problem with this plan, but the school must have felt sorry for us. The principal offered my older brother and me a job in the cafeteria, washing trays and silverware. In exchange for working an hour each day, all five of us could eat lunch for free. This was the cat's pajamas!

The work was fun, and we were the envy of all our classmates. None of us realized we had these jobs because we were poor. When our friends asked how much we were paid, we told them $1.25, which was true—but we didn't explain that the five of us had already eaten it up.

Scraped and Sprayed

Every day, my brother and I left our fourth- and fifth-grade classrooms 15 minutes before lunch so we could eat before the other students arrived.

The washroom where we worked was separated from the serving line, so we had our own little den of operations, without interference from the adult cafeteria workers. The trays were handed to us through an opening in the wall, and we sprayed them with a high-pressured stream of water from a nozzle that hung from the ceiling.

Food scraps went down the drain to a giant disposal. Then we put the trays and silverware in a large commercial dishwasher and added detergent that looked like cherry-flavored Kool-Aid. Sometimes we had to climb up on the drain table and use a small log to pound the doors so they'd close properly.

Our tennis shoes slipped and slid constantly on the wet tiles, causing many near misses. We were usually pretty wet before the lunch period was over, but this was refreshing during the hotter months.

Naturally, things are bound to get out of hand when you put two red-haired, freckle-faced boys alone in a cafeteria washroom. We couldn't resist spraying some people through the little window—accidentally, of course. Others we just tried to pop outright with our towels.

Scorpion Caper a Washout

One day I set a rubber scorpion in the window, hoping to scare some girls. The first girl who saw it threw her tray in the air and screamed. She wouldn't quit hollering until I'd "killed" the scorpion and thrown it down the disposal.

I had to do it quickly, too, before some 20 teachers and cafeteria employees could get to her and find out why she was hysterical. Of course, I was a hero for killing the scorpion, as she explained to the adults. (I didn't mention that it was rubber.)

The worst part was, that scorpion had cost me the whole 25¢ I'd earned picking dried black-eyed peas for our neighbor. "Better the scorpion down the drain than our jobs," my brother said. He was right about that.

Played a "Clean" Joke

Another of my tricks was filling an empty cherry Kool-Aid package with some of the dishwasher detergent, then walking around the grounds at recess, pretending to eat it. When another kid begged for some, I'd pour a small amount in his palm, and from there it went right into his mouth. When he gave me an anguished look, I'd say, "You didn't tell me you were going to eat it! I thought you wanted to wash your hands."

Working there was a wonderful experience, although I've yet to find another person who ever worked in a school cafeteria for meals, or did what we did at such a young age.

My wife and I have raised six children of our own, and I still enjoy washing dishes with the family. I just wish I had one of those pressure nozzles hanging from the ceiling. ✧

Careful Budgeting Left 5¢ A Week for Drugstore Sodas

MONEY WAS SCARCE when I was in middle school during the 1930s. My father had little or no work because of the Depression, so Mom had to budget carefully.

At the beginning of the week, she gave me 50¢ for my school lunch—a dime for each day. A nickel would buy a bowl of soup, a half-pint of milk with a cookie, or tuna salad with a big soft pretzel.

For 4¢, I could buy a vegetable or a salad. Two slices of bread with brown gravy cost 2¢. I never bought meat—that cost a whole 8¢.

My friend Marjorie and I planned our daily menus very carefully, spending only 9¢ on each day's lunch.

Every Friday after school, we took the five pennies we'd each saved to a nearby drugstore soda fountain, hopped up on the stools and ordered sodas. Marjorie always chose strawberry, while I alternated between lime and chocolate.

We drank our sodas slowly, savoring every sip. After finishing hers, Marjorie always sighed contentedly and said, "Gee, that was good. I wish I had another nickel."

I've never tasted anything since that could compare with those delicious nickel sodas.　　*—Irma Schuster*
Norwood, Ohio

She Looked Forward to Fruit and Cookie Shortage

IN JUNIOR HIGH, I had to carry my lunch. I lived too far from school to walk home at noon.

Some days when my mother had no cookies or fruit to put in my lunch, she'd give me a nickel to buy something.

With my 5¢, I could walk across the street to Gus the grocer's and get a large banana and a large glazed doughnut. It was such a treat that I was glad when we ran out of cookies and fruit at home.

—Josephine Bolerjack
Green Valley, Arizona

Brown Brothers

STOVE WARMED TWICE. Students gathered around their stoves and furnaces in early one-room schools for warmth, but they also were used to heat some delicious lunches.

Everyone Contributed To Communal Soup Pot

THE AROMA that filled our one-room country schoolhouse was enough to make anyone eager to get to school.

Once a week during the cold winters, the teacher asked each of us to bring a potato, carrot, turnip or onion to school. She'd cut up the vegetables along with a big piece of meat she'd brought herself, put them in a heavy black pot with water and seasonings, then set the pot on the potbellied stove.

As the pot simmered throughout the morning, a delicious aroma filled the room. We could hardly wait for lunch.

The taste of the soup and the warm atmosphere in our little schoolhouse made us all feel closer. Any disagreements just melted away.

Our teacher must have added a secret ingredient, because I've never been able to duplicate the wonderful taste of that soup.　　*—Lillian Rozanski*
Crystal Lake, Illinois

Lunch Meant Biscuits—and Sometimes Rabbit or Squirrel

BLACK'S SCHOOL was the last one-room schoolhouse in Mercer County, Kentucky when I began attending class-

POTBELLIED STOVE. A flat top on a stove offered the potential for cooking, as well as heating the schoolroom.

Ewing Galloway

es there in 1946.

There was no lunchroom, of course, so we brought our lunches. Mine always included a fresh biscuit with homemade jam, jelly or preserves. Occasionally I had peanut butter and crackers, or boiled eggs.

Sometimes our mothers would get up early enough to fry a piece of chicken, squirrel or rabbit on the wood-burning stove for us to take. Some of the children even liked opossum and groundhog.

Our mothers also made sure we had a good breakfast before we left—usually eggs, biscuits and hot chocolate.

One year the government allotted the school some dried beans and potatoes. The teacher cooked them on the potbellied stove in our classroom for lunch. It sure tasted good on a cold day.

—Dorothy Mae Tyler
Harrodsburg, Kentucky

Pupils Helped Make Soup Several Times a Week

SOME OF my classmates in a remote area of Osceola County, Michigan had to walk 2-1/2 miles to our one-room school in 1931. Very few missed a day, even in the worst winter weather.

One stormy, blustery day, one of the students said, "Wouldn't some real hot soup taste good on a day like this?" It sounded like a good idea, so we talked about it.

By the next day, we'd borrowed a cast-iron kettle that fit perfectly on our potbellied stove. The parents furnished nutritious vegetables stored from their gardens. The kids eagerly helped prepare the vegetables, and the soup cooked while we learned.

This became a ritual, and we enjoyed a hot, wholesome soup or stew two or three times a week. The parents took turns donating meat to add to the pot. (I'm sure some of it was venison, but nobody mentioned it at the time.)

Many times there was enough left over for a hot bowl of soup before we started the long trek home on snow-covered roads.

This cooperative project involving both kids and their parents is one that we'll always value. It gave us great memories, and we learned a lesson that wasn't printed in any book.

—*Bernice Boven, LeRoy, Michigan*

Versatile Lunch Bucket Handy for Self-Defense

WHEN I started first grade, my grandmother bought me a light blue metal dinner bucket to carry on the 2-mile walk to our one-room school in northern Missouri. In the 1930s and '40s, most of the other pupils carried their lunches in half-gallon pails that had once held sorghum molasses. I was very proud to have a genuine lunch bucket.

My bucket carried many a peanut butter sandwich, along with apples from Grandpa's trees, and slices of homemade bread with butter and sugar.

I used it to carry home big blue plums from a tree we passed at a deserted house, as well as hickory nuts and hazel-

nuts, and pretty rocks we found along the road. I found so many uses for the bucket that the metal handles broke and had to be replaced with baling wire.

The bucket was also handy for self-defense. One day I took the shortcut home from school, which involved crossing the creek on a log. A big boy stood guard on the log, refusing to let us little kids cross. I hit him with my dinner bucket and he fell into the creek.

On another occasion, I used the bucket to fend off a buck sheep that tried to butt my sister and me as we crossed a pasture. One good hit turned him, giving us time to run for the gate.

Then there was the day my little sister and I found an opossum hanging upside down in a small hedge. I climbed up, grabbed it by the tail and started walking home with it. My sister stayed close to me so she could hit it with the bucket if it curled up and tried to bite. Fortunately, she didn't have to use it. You should've seen the look on Dad's face when we walked into the yard.

Grandma knew what I needed for school, but I doubt she knew how many uses I found for that little blue dinner bucket. —*Marjorie Eitel*
Kansas City, Missouri

Lunches Carried in Lard Buckets and Newspaper

AT Mount Vernon School in Blount County, Tennessee, we brought our lunches wrapped in newspaper, or carried them in 1-gallon lard buckets.

When weather permitted, we sat outside under a tree to eat. If it was raining, we ate at our desks. The school didn't have running water in 1927, so our only drink was well water.

I usually brought salty ham biscuits for lunch. My mother made biscuits fresh each morning in her wood-burning stove, and we always had pork in the smokehouse. Sometimes I had fried eggs on biscuits. Boiled eggs were common, too, and there were peaches and apples from our orchard in season.

Citrus fruits were rarely seen. One year I got an orange in my Christmas sock and brought it for lunch. There was one little boy who'd never seen an orange and asked if he could have the peelings. I gave him a section instead.

—*John Russell, Clearwater, Florida*

BUCKET O' FUN. The venerable lunch pail or bucket allowed children to bring lunch to school and bring back treasures they found on the way home. It also could come in handy as a weapon, as Marjorie Eitel explains above.

She Bypassed Grandma's Bounty for Onion Sandwiches

IN THE mid-1940s, I stayed with my grandparents in Dowagiac, Michigan for about a year. While attending the grade school there, I'm sure I embarrassed my dear grandmother at lunchtime every day.

My grandparents were farmers, and while they didn't have much money, they had all the food anyone could want. They butchered cows, pigs, chickens and lambs. Milk, butter and eggs were plentiful, and Grandma baked breads and desserts daily. Her huge garden provided enough food to last the whole year, as she canned everything.

I know we had more than most families, because my grandparents often shared their abundance with their friends and neighbors.

In spite of all the good food available to me, I insisted on taking two mustard-and-onion sandwiches to school for my lunch every single day. You can imagine my grandmother's frustration.

"Catherine, your teacher and friends will think I'm not feeding you well," she protested. "And can you imagine how awful your breath smells?"

But I insisted on those mustard-and-onion sandwiches and nothing else. I still love them. —*Cathy Reits*
Grand Rapids, Michigan

Coach Gave Him a Dime For His Extra Meal

I NEVER carried a lunch to school or ate in the cafeteria. In all the years of my childhood, my family was accustomed to eating only a good breakfast and a big supper. We never had a meal at noon.

One of my fondest school memories is from 1939, when I was an eighth grader in Morrow, Ohio. My homeroom teacher, who was also my track and basketball coach, put a dime on my desk for lunch every day that year. His name was Harold Schnell, and he was only 24 at the time—that dime had to be a sacrifice for him.

We had track and basketball practice every day after school, and Mr. Schnell wanted me to be healthy, so I bought lunch every day with the dime. I later learned that he didn't know I simply wasn't accustomed to eating lunch.

—*Bill Turner, Lebanon, Ohio*

Boiled Corn on the Cob Was Her Lunchtime Favorite

I BEGAN attending the one-room Miller's Valley School in Todd County, Kentucky in July 1921. Everyone brought his or her own lunch, which we sometimes traded. We ate outside, sitting at the edge of the woods.

I loved boiled corn on the cob and took some every day for lunch. When I was finished, I always threw the cob over my left shoulder into the woods. I loved corn so much that some of my relatives nicknamed me "Pig".

—*Reathy Stokes, Oak Grove, Kentucky*

Boys Roasted Potatoes In Furnace's Ash Pan

THE ONE-ROOM country school I attended in North Dakota in the 1920s had 12 pupils.

In winter, the five of us boys would each bring a good-sized potato from home. At morning recess, they'd go to the basement, pull the ash pan out of the old coal furnace, brush back some of the ashes and put the potatoes into the pan.

By noon, the potatoes were roasted. We'd bring out butter, salt and pepper from home and enjoy a welcome hot lunch.

—*Max Priebe, Edmonds, Washington*

MARCH MISSY. Author in 1927, a year before she played the Victrola as students marched out of school to music.

Students Walked Home For Lunch Every Day

MY ALMA MATER, the No. 6 School in Kingston, New York, was built in 1898. We had no auditorium, no gymnasium and no cafeteria.

We went home for lunch every day and were allowed to carry a lunch to school only if there was some emergency at home. In those cases, one of the classrooms was designated as the lunchroom, and the teachers took turns supervising the students.

I lived 1-1/2 miles from school, and since I had to go home for lunch every day, I did a lot of walking. School started at 9 a.m. Then I walked home for lunch at 11:30, returned to school at 1 p.m., and walked back home when school let out at 3:30.

We were often a block away when the warning bell rang 5 minutes before the start of morning and afternoon classes, and we had to run to be in our seats in time.

If we were late, we had to stay after school, but that was no punishment for me. I enjoyed helping the teacher empty the wastebaskets, wash the blackboards and clap the erasers to get the chalk out of them.

—*Marjorie Le Borgne*
Laguna Hills, California

ARE WE DONE? Mary Caretto (far left) took good care of her first graders at Woodbury School in Grundy County, Illinois. But the author (back row, second from right) feared for her sandwich's fate when the teacher grabbed it and opened the furnace door.

Shoveling Down Grilled Cheese

By Judith Pfeifer, Hartsville, South Carolina

DURING the winter of my first year in school in northern Illinois in the late 1940s, my mother had to go to the hospital for surgery.

That left my dad, who was not familiar with the kitchen or my mom's creativity when it came to cooking, to pack lunches for me and my sister every day.

When I opened my lunch that first day, I had a simple cheese sandwich and began to complain. It was just one more sad reminder that my mother would be gone for a whole week.

The teacher jumped up and took my sandwich. As she rushed to the furnace in the corner of the room and pulled open the door, exposing the roaring fire inside, I was overwhelmed with remorse for having whined. My teacher, Mrs. Caretto, was a determined woman who was not only my first teacher, but had been my dad's first teacher and was a Sunday school teacher in our little rural church. In short, I couldn't get away with anything.

Teacher Was Cookin'

I thought she was going to throw the sandwich inside and tell me that, if I didn't appreciate the food, I could do without! I immediately realized eating a dry sandwich was better than spending the afternoon hungry.

But that was not the teacher's plan. She grabbed the coal shovel, placed my sandwich on it and thrust it inside the furnace. A few moments later, I had a hot, toasted cheese sandwich, then she toasted my sister's cheese sandwich, too.

The next day, Mrs. Caretto was confronted with 10 students, all with plain cheese sandwiches ready for toasting. Of course, she couldn't go on forever toasting sandwiches, but the incident opened up the possibility that the furnace could be used for hot dinners.

Soon, one mother sent a potato wrapped in foil to be placed on the stove and then the idea took hold. In addition to potatoes, we had little baking dishes of leftovers of all kinds, and the air was heavy with the aroma of hot, home-cooked meals by lunchtime.

Over the years, my four children have complained about the poor quality of school lunches. I believe that no matter what a child is served, there will be complaints, and that feeding many children every day is a challenge.

But I can never resist noting, "If you think that's bad, my first hot lunch was a cheese sandwich toasted on a dirty coal shovel!"

Every Boy Had a "Flip" on the Hip

IN 1927, when I was attending Mount Vernon School in Blount County, Tennessee, almost every boy had a flip (some used the term "slingshot").

It wasn't unusual for us to stand in a line and shoot at a tin can placed on a fence post. Then, when classes started again, the flip would be in the hip pocket of our overalls or around our necks.

Some of us had a hoop and what we called "the scotch" to roll it with. We often rolled them on the way to school and at recess. We'd even have contests to see who could roll the hoop the farthest on a railroad track before it fell off.
                                        —*John Russell, Clearwater, Florida*

SCHOOL SUPPLIES. Author considered a slingshot essential equipment.

CHRISTMAS FUN. A special treat probably followed this December 1957 Christmas program at Victoria (Kansas) Grade School. Karen Ann Bland (back row, third from left, and inset) recalls treats from another season below.

After we licked our plates clean, we wiped our plates and forks and returned them to our desks, ready for the next day's lunch.

I don't remember whether or not I ever thanked the teacher for that little act of kindness, but I've never forgotten it. Over 50 years later, I can still taste those delicious potatoes that she baked for us.
—*Cathy Reits*
Grand Rapids, Michigan

Sweet Feast Awaited After Lenten Mass

I ATTENDED parochial school in Victoria, Kansas in the late 1950s and early '60s. Each Friday during Lent, we could buy breakfast in our school cafeteria after Mass.

For 15¢, we were served a piping-hot mug of hot chocolate dipped from a huge kettle with a soup ladle, and a large, gooey cinnamon roll made by the lunchroom cooks. What a treat! —*Karen Ann Bland, Gove, Kansas*

Meals in Cafeteria Made Easy Mark for Comedians

WHEN I WAS in high school, my nickname was "Jud".

One day a classmate asked another, "Where's Jud?"

Another student replied, "He's over eating in the cafeteria."

"Ha, ha," the first replied. "Who ever heard of anyone overeating at the cafeteria?"

I learned about this exchange for the first time when I read it in our school publication later that year.
—*Albert Judkins, Inverness, Florida*

She's Never Forgotten Lard-and-Rhubarb Lunch

I CAME FROM a large family, and our folks didn't have much money during the 1940s. I remember racing home from school for lunch and facing some pretty bleak menus.

The memory of one meal in particular has stuck with me all these years. It didn't seem too bad at the time, but I realized when I grew up that a meal of bread spread with lard, sugar and rhubarb sauce wasn't very nutritious.
—*Gloria Albrecht, Duluth, Minnesota*

School Furnace Yielded Perfect Baked Potatoes

BACK IN THE 1940s, my nine siblings and I walked a mile to our one-room school in Celery Center, Michigan. Every morning, each of us carried a sandwich wrapped in newspaper plus the biggest potato we'd been able to find in our garden the evening before.

When we arrived at school, our teacher would have a big fire going in the basement furnace. She put all the children's potatoes in coffee cans, then set the cans on a ridge around the furnace's firepot.

At noon, the teacher retrieved the potatoes. She always remembered which potato belonged to which child. On the rare occasion when she didn't remember, believe me, we knew.

The teacher brought a big crock of homemade butter from her parents' farm, and we marched single file to her desk for a spoonful. The potatoes were always done, piping-hot with crispy skin, and the butter melted into them deliciously.

Doggone! Lunch Didn't Live Up to Expectations

STORE-BOUGHT MEATS were a real treat for a farm girl growing up during the Depression. When we were lucky enough to have wieners, I chose to have mine fried for my school lunch.

One day in 1929, when I was in second grade, I spent the whole morning thinking about the wiener sandwich I'd brought for lunch. It seemed like an eternity.

When I finally bit into the sandwich, I was so disappointed. Someone had stolen my wieners!

Every bite seemed to stick in my throat. I fought back tears and choked down the bread so my teacher wouldn't find out and punish one of my classmates for the theft.
—*Mrs. Edward Rinehart, Dover, Ohio*

Cook's Job Meant Mom
Rode Bus to School, Too

A HOT LUNCH PROGRAM was started at Jackson Township School in Wells County, Indiana in 1941, and my mother was asked to be one of the cooks.

When Mom protested that she didn't have a car, she was told to ride the school bus. When she pointed out that I was only 5, and there was no one to care for me, there was an answer for that problem, too: "Put her in first grade."

So I entered first grade at age 5, riding the bus to school with my mother. The first bus had a long bench seat along each side, with a row of seats down the middle.

Meals were prepared in the home economics room. The students came there to pick up their lunch trays, then carried them back to their desks to eat.

One day a friend was carrying a tray with a bowl of hot chicken noodle soup when a boy came running around the corner and ran into her. For a time, she had red worm-shaped marks where the hot noodles had struck her.

—*Velma Souers, Warren, Indiana*

"Milk Break" Became a Treat
For Disadvantaged Child

ONE DAY when I was in the second grade, I saw a milk truck pull up to the steps leading to my classroom. A man dressed in white hopped out and brought in a basket containing small red and white boxes of milk.

"Class, it's milk break," said our teacher, Mrs. Welchman. "Have your money ready when the milk is passed out."

I watched the little boy next to me stuff his hand in his pockets and pull out a fistful of items—a stick, a small chain, a rock, a pencil. He opened his hand wider to reveal two shiny pennies.

My eyes followed the pennies as he dropped them into the milk-money box. All the children put their pennies in the box and received a box of milk in turn.

"Sharron, come and get yours," Mrs. Welchman told me.

"I don't have any money," I replied, tears rolling down my face.

"Well, it seems we have one extra box of milk here," she replied. "You take it. You can bring your money another day."

She motioned for me to come get the milk. It felt so cold in my small hands.

I opened the box as I'd seen the other children do, then lifted it to my lips. The milk was cold and sweet. I'd never tasted anything so good.

From that day on, I watched eagerly for the milkman, because every day there seemed to be an extra box of milk just for me.

—*Sharron McDonald*
Springdale, Arkansas

Surplus Peanut Butter
Stuck to Them Like Glue

DURING World War II, surplus food was sent to schools throughout the country. Our one-room school in Buffalo County, Wisconsin received very large quantities of things like soup, crackers and peanut butter. It was the teacher's job to feed the stuff to us.

I'll never forget the peanut butter. Back in those days, it wasn't mixed as it is now. There was a film of oil on top, and someone had to mix it up. But this peanut butter just didn't seem to mix, no matter what you did to it.

That didn't stop the teacher from making us eat it. She'd give each of us a big spoonful of the stuff, and we'd try to get peanut butter off the roof of our mouth the rest of the day.

—*Ronald Baertsch, Huber Heights, Ohio*

"Kick the Can" Nearly
Became "Kick the Bucket"!

AFTER World War II ended, my family moved to a farm near the small town of Wilsey, Kansas. When I was 9, I attended the fourth grade at Sunflower, a little one-room country school.

At recess, one of my favorite games was "kick the can". You stood in the middle of the playground in a circle where a tin can had been placed. Then you closed your eyes and counted to 100 while everyone hid.

After that, you had to go find the others before they came and kicked the can away. One day when it was my turn to hide, I climbed up onto the rafters in an old stable nearby that was no longer used.

Through a crack in the wall, I could see everything that went on out on the playground. When everyone but me had been found, I heard all the children yelling and saw them running toward the schoolhouse as the teacher held the door open for them.

Through the crack, I spied the biggest, meanest-looking bull I'd ever seen. He'd broken through the fence next to the school and was butting anything in his way. Next, he came into the stable where I was hiding!

I could look down through the rafters and see him directly below me, stomping and snorting. Thank goodness he couldn't see me!

Petrified, I wondered how I'd ever get down the ladder and into the school. Finally, the bull sauntered out of the stable and back to the swings. I crept quietly down the ladder and peeked around the door.

The bull's back was to me, so, thinking "now or never", I started running like a streak for the schoolhouse door. Nearing the school, I was terrified because I could hear that bull hot on my heels!

The kids were yelling as I shot through the door, and the teacher slammed it quickly behind me. We watched from the window as the bull stood there dumbfounded. Then the teacher called the owner, and he came and caught the bull and mended the fence.

It wasn't until all the excitement was over that I realized something that might not have helped the situation—I was wearing a red coat! —*Norma Woodson*
Jefferson City, Missouri

Students Looked Forward to Daily Ritual of Beans and Cocoa

By Haskel "Hack" McInturf, Oroville, California

IN AUGUST 1936, the height of the Great Depression, our family moved to a small mining community north of Oroville in northern California. Three weeks later, my brother Leo and I enrolled in Morris Ravine School, a one-room school built shortly after the Gold Rush.

I was a student there for only 5 years, starting at age 8. Yet to this day, I am blessed with a profusion of cherished memories each time I drive along the winding gravel road where the school once stood.

One of the most pleasant memories is of cold winter days, when oak logs fueled the long cast-iron heater, warming a pot of pinto beans for that day's lunch. There were

"It would've been agony to smell the beans and not get to taste them..."

very few winter days when we didn't have a pot of beans, and no one ever passed them up. But Leo and I came close.

The beans were one of the agricultural commodities the federal government distributed to the schools at that time. We also received raisins, prunes, apples and oranges. One favorite commodity was cocoa, which our teacher prepared each morning with milk from her own cows.

Students Weren't the Only Ones Attending School

EVERY DAY was field trip day in our school. It was a wonderful one-room school in Stonington, Michigan surrounded by woods and swampland.

We would spend our recess time exploring around the school.

One day when the superintendent visited our school, he was not only surprised but shocked when one of the boys walked in with a horned owl sitting on his shoulder!

Another memorable visit from the superintendent helped us finally get a well and running water. Although it was the first day of school, we weren't able to use the outdoor toilets. Porcupines had gnawed the seats, and the holes were so rough and so large that we'd have fallen in! —*Lee Deneau Lansing, Michigan*

There was no welfare program then, although there was a form of general relief for the most needy. Our father had found a steady job a few days after we moved, but he never would've accepted a handout in any case—and he considered the commodities a handout.

Few people were ever able to change our father's mind about anything, but our teacher, Essie Mooney, was among the rare ones who did. It took a lot of persuasiveness, but she finally convinced him the commodities were meant for all children, and that they were not a form of relief.

Leo and I were very grateful for her intervention. It would have been agony to spend every morning smelling those savory beans and that delicious cocoa, only to have been denied the pleasure of tasting them.

BELOVED SCHOOL. Author (front row, second from right) and his brother Leo (front row, center), shown in this 1938 photo, built a historical marker with the above plaque after their beloved school was closed and later torn down.

Chapter 6

How We Celebrated Holidays

How We Celebrated Holidays

Teachers refer to the period from New Year's Day until Easter as "the tunnel months"—a long dark spell to be endured until willows bud, robins return and you can tramp around in mud puddles.

The brief bright spots are Valentine's Day and Presidents' Day.

Most teachers mourn blending together the birthdays of Lincoln and Washington. Individually they created two excuses to get kids excited about redecorating the classroom. And excitement was much to be desired in those slow-crawling winter months.

Lincoln was a cinch, because even the most untalented could cut out a stovepipe hat from black art paper. Washington took a little more skill.

I dreaded Thanksgiving because my turkey renditions inevitably looked like buzzards that had been run through a weed-blower.

Why, oh why, hadn't the Pilgrims been content to feast on pigs or rabbits or a few tasty Atlantic codfish? Or was their first Thanksgiving a potluck ("bring your own silverware and a covered hot dish!") with the Indians contributing the meat?

Of all the holidays, none could top Valentine's Day and May Day for sheer gut-wrenching trauma. Both gave you a pretty clear reading as to where you stood in school, popularity-wise, by the number of valentines or May baskets you received. And not just how many, but also *who* they were from.

Quantity counted, but quality was critical. Who wanted a card from that dumb Stinky Schwartz, anyhow? On the other hand, did someone lose the card you were sure was coming from Mysterious Marjorie?

Halloween, Thanksgiving, Columbus Day, Easter… each was an excuse to create a break in the monotony of the school year. And bless the teachers who dipped into their own meager personal funds to provide the necessary, but unbudgeted, art supplies for the classroom decorations.

Alas, those traditional school holidays we recall with such nostalgia are far and few between these days, sacrificed on the altar of political considerations and the narrow special agendas of adults.

I'm sorry no one ever asked the kids.

Better still, I wish I could transport the handwringers back to my childhood school. I'd have them stand in the central three-story stairwell among 200 or more kids and listen to those young voices fill the building with *Adeste Fidelis*, *O Little Town of Bethlehem* and, finally, *Silent Night*.

And then I'd ask the dissenters to explain, please, how the world was worse off for this celebration of goodness and hope and togetherness.

—*Clancy Strock*

Christmas 'Grand March' a Lifetime Memory

By Dorothy Foss
St. Paul, Minnesota

WHEN WE MOVED to Duluth, Minnesota in 1931, and I was enrolled in third grade at Merritt School, I heard excited accounts from my classmates of the annual Christmas Grand March. I was eager to find out what it was all about.

After months of waiting, the holiday season was upon us. We'd trimmed our class tree with chains of colored construction paper and topped it off with a cardboard star.

Handmade gifts for our families were on our desks. I made two: a button box and a multi-colored oilcloth cover that could be slipped over a cleanser can to make it more attractive.

I was especially proud of the button box. Our teacher, Miss Jennings, had helped me sew the buttons on the top.

GRAND MEMORIES. When Dorothy Foss entered third grade at Merritt School in Duluth, Minnesota, she heard wonderful stories about the school's Christmas festivities.

"Hurry, everyone," Miss Jennings announced. The big day had arrived! "Check to be sure your gifts are neatly displayed on your desks. The Grand March is about to begin!"

I put the cleanser can cover on the left side of my desk and the button box on the right to cover the inkwell. Anticipation mounted as I heard voices singing *Jingle Bells*.

"To review," Miss Jennings said, "we will remain seated until three classes—kindergarten, first and second grades—walk the perimeter of our room. Then we'll get up and orderly follow, all the time singing our song."

The 5-year-old kindergartners filed in. Some were shy and didn't sing. A few forgot what they were supposed to do and stopped to look at something until their teacher gently guided them back in line.

Some sang the correct words, while others didn't care what they sang, just as long as it was loud.

They had barely left the room when the first graders came in singing *Away in the Manger*. They were less enthusiastic about singing and seemed more interested in studying our decorations and gifts.

Decorations and Gifts Were Fascinating

The second graders came and went to the strains of *O Little Town of Bethlehem*, and then it was our turn. We followed them out singing our carol, *Wind Through the Olive Trees*.

What fun it was to walk through all the classrooms and see the fascinating decorations and interesting gifts, especially in the sixth-grade room, where the students' advanced age allowed them more creativity.

The march ended in the gymnasium, where the principal, Miss Wolfe, greeted us. Each class was invited to sing the first verse of its song. Then the lights were turned off and the room hushed, as we all joined in the singing of *Silent Night*. It felt as though I was actually present on that wondrous night.

"Merry Christmas, everyone," said Miss Wolfe when the singing ended. "Enjoy your holiday, and come back ready to learn with enthusiasm!"

I didn't realize it at the time, but the Grand March had given me a poignant memory that returns every Christmas like a beautiful gift bringing the blessing of great joy. ❖

Remembering Last Veteran

MEMORIAL DAY assemblies at Duluth East Junior High School in the late '30s and early '40s consisted of patriotic songs and readings.

The highlight of the program was a visit by Duluth's last remaining Civil War veteran, Albert Woolson. He lived near the school and was accompanied by his daughter. Mr. Woolson lived long enough to be the very last Union veteran of the Civil War. There is a statue of him in Duluth, as well as in Gettysburg.

We kids were probably not as impressed as we should have been with our noteworthy visitor.
—*Joyce Heisserer, Detroit Lakes, Minnesota*

Teacher Was a Good Egg at Easter

By Myrtle Beavers, Destin, Florida

THERE WEREN'T many occasions for fun at our little one-room school in Hix, Oklahoma during the Depression. But the Easter egg hunt on Good Friday was one of them.

Not only was the Easter egg hunt fun, but when it was over, school was dismissed for the day!

Our teacher, Mr. John Bateman, encouraged all the mothers to boil and color eggs for the hunt. Each mother was to donate three eggs for each child in the school, then hide them on some land near the school during the noon hour.

Mama boiled our eggs on Thursday night. My two brothers, two sisters and I would help color them. We made the dye by dipping crepe paper in water. If we were lucky, we'd have a crayon to draw pictures on the eggs.

Mothers Had Job of Hiding

Around noon on Good Friday, the mothers would gather a short distance from the school on a little triangular finger of land that ran from the road for about 300 yards into a point.

The land was perfect for the hunt. One side was bordered by a river, and the other by a high, steep cliff. The land was flat, with very little vegetation, except for some nice shade trees and mayapples, which made good places to hide eggs. Patches of tiny lavender flowers also dotted the area, giving it the first lovely color of spring.

Once the mothers were gathered just beyond the school,

EASTER FUN. Myrtle Beavers, the smallest child in this photograph taken about 1940 in front of the family's barn at Hix, Oklahoma, loved the school egg hunt.

on a little rise, one of them came to tell Mr. Bateman they were ready to hide the eggs.

The hidden eggs included one that had been beautifully decorated by Mr. Bateman. He called it the "lucky egg" and said that whoever found it would get something special. It was usually a bag of Easter candy, a yo-yo or some other treat.

When Mr. Bateman was given the signal, we drew the curtains and waited for our mothers to hide the eggs. It seemed to take forever, until we heard a yell from outside—the signal that the eggs had been hidden.

Searched High and Low

Out the door we raced, through the school yard, across the road and into the land where the eggs were hidden. We scattered all over, looking under dead branches, around stumps, under rocks, in tree forks, in clumps of grass—everywhere!

It wasn't long before someone cried triumphantly, "Lucky egg!" But we kept looking until no more eggs could be found and the hunt was over.

The eggs were counted to make sure all had been found. Most of the time they were. Sometimes the mothers did too good of a job and a few eggs remained hidden.

But everyone was happy. We had our Easter eggs, and school was over for the weekend. It was the end of a wonderful day, as we walked home along the dusty road, eating some of our eggs. ✲

EGGS-CELLENT ADVENTURE. Children like these love the excitement of dyeing and decorating Easter eggs.

J.C. Allen and Son

J.C. Allen and Son

April Foolers Ended up Feeling Foolish

By Bernice Haliburton
Guymon, Oklahoma

WE OBSERVED all the holidays at Round Prairie, our two-room, two-teacher country school near Allen, Oklahoma. Every school day had its special attraction for my brother, two sisters and me, but the holidays were truly exceptional.

Christmas was the best, although we made special days of them all.

But the one that ranked near the top was April Fools' Day. And it was one April 1, back in 1926, that we decided to celebrate the day in a big way.

Grades one through four were taught by a married lady who was very competent. Grades five through eight were taught by a man who was well educated, an accomplished musician and an excellent athlete. They both lived in town and drove to school together.

April 1 that year was temperate. There was no need for a fire in the school's wood-burning stove. Most of the students arrived early, before the teachers, and were outside, thinking about April Fools' Day jokes.

Why not make the teachers think we'd played hooky? We could hide awhile in the nearby woods, then sur-

prise them by all walking in together.

We younger pupils were flattered to be included in the plan and willingly followed the older "pied pipers" down the hill and into the woods.

We amused ourselves with exploring, playing and just generally relishing our freedom. We collected rocks and bird feathers and noted the tiny plants that were just starting to show green.

But after some time passed, we began wondering if we had been missed

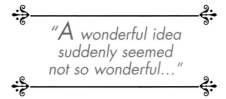

"A wonderful idea suddenly seemed not so wonderful..."

yet. What were the teachers thinking? What would they do?

Then someone reminded us that a whipping at school meant another at home. How could we have forgotten that? The thought struck terror in us.

The day was wearing on. What seemed such a wonderful idea only a short time ago suddenly seemed not so wonderful at all. We must return, it was decided, or we really would be in trouble.

Slowly, we trudged back up the hill, through the now-deserted school yard

APRIL ANTICS. When the author played hooky, like the kids above might be doing, on April Fools' Day, she found she wasn't the only one who enjoyed a joke.

and entered the classrooms. The canvas curtains that usually separated the school into two rooms had been rolled up as they were when we had programs.

Silently, we took our seats. The few students who had arrived after we executed our plan were quietly studying or reciting their lessons.

The head teacher, the man, ordered us miscreants to line up in front of the stage. My heart pounded. There was a lump in my throat. I could hardly suppress the sobs I felt rising.

When we lined up, oldest to youngest—I was the very last—the teacher went to his desk and picked up his sturdy wooden paddle.

He ran his hand over the paddle. Apparently satisfied it would do the job, he asked the first student, my brother, to step forward.

The teacher then drew the paddle back for the first blow. Not a sound could be heard, not even breathing.

Then the teacher shouted, "April Fool!" What a relief—even if the joke was on us! ❧

Kissing the Witch
On Halloween

By Dianne Bahn, Yankton, South Dakota

HALLOWEEN was the one time of the year the storm cellar in the school yard at our rural school in Stanton County, Nebraska was cleaned and actually used. It was the setting for our annual Halloween Spook House.

The teacher would select several students to plan and carry out the activities. Then, on the big day, the rest of us anxiously awaited our turns to be blindfolded and led down the wooden steps into the "Witch's House".

Once in the horror house, we were forced to eat a witch's "eyeball" (a peeled grape), touch the witch's "brains" (cooked cold spaghetti) and had our hands thrust into the witch's "blood" (ice-cold water colored with ketchup).

One year, one of the girls thought it would be great fun to have the witch kiss each boy. A pair of lips was drawn on a piece of paper with bright red lipstick and the paper pressed against each boy's cheek.

Even though the boys realized they hadn't really been kissed, they were not very pleased about having a bright red lip print on their cheeks and immediately washed it off.

After all the tricks, everyone was given a treat, such as a candy bar. This was in the '50s and '60s, when a good-size candy bar was still only a nickel.

As we grew older, the Spook House became less frightening. But it was still exciting to be led down the stairs and experience all the tricks.

For trick-or-treating, or the school Halloween party, we wore costumes made from whatever was around the house or could be borrowed from relatives.

I don't ever recall anyone having a Halloween costume bought from a store. Our parents would have thought it wasteful to buy something we'd wear only once or twice.

Old clothes formed the basis for most of our costumes. We were cowboys, Indians, gypsies, hoboes, ghosts, witches, clowns, kings, queen and soldiers.

Witches' hats were made from cardboard and black construction paper, sometimes covered with aluminum foil.

No one cared if your witch's cape was really a black and gold apron, or if your Martian antennae were your sister's hair band with two green pipe cleaners attached.

Our costumes, like our fun, had no boundaries, because we had lots of imagination. ♣

Teacher Was the Real Queen

ONLY ONE TEACHER, Miss Gusta Moritz, made May 1 a special day at the country school I attended in Stanton County, Nebraska. Miss Moritz was my teacher from kindergarten through fifth grade.

We drew names to determine which of our classmates we'd bring a May basket for. Although ready-made May baskets were available at Woolworth's or Hestead's dime store, my mother always made my May basket.

Every family also made a May basket for Miss Moritz. How she managed to maintain her slim figure after receiving all that candy is a mystery.

We also elected a May Day Queen. Miss Moritz nominated the candidates, choosing those who hadn't already been a queen at a previous May Day or Valentine's Day.

The May Day Queen wore a crown and cape of crepe paper, and, of course, was the first to get her May basket.

We also marched around a maypole holding colored streamers. Miss Moritz held the heavy pole. It must have been a chore for her. But she never complained, nor asked one of the older boys to do it. —*Dianne Bahn*
Yankton, South Dakota

MAYPOLE DANCE. In the '50s, May Day celebrations such as this one thrilled children, including the author. A May Day Queen was elected, but she thought the teacher was the unsung heroine.

Jim Shippee/Unicorn Stock Photos

Valentine's Day Was a Kansas Winter Respite

SPECIAL DAY. The author, shown on her front porch in 1952 (left), wore a "dream dress" on Valentine's Day that year and was chosen to hand out the valentines at her school in Frankfort, Kansas (above).

By Charlene McCoy, Lincoln, Nebraska

WINTERS WERE LONG in Kansas, with few breaks in our grade-school routine between Christmas and Easter.

But when the calendar proclaimed the first of February, the heart-shaped candy began to appear in the Ben Franklin store in downtown Frankfort.

The candy was a mint-like confection, in pink, white, yellow and green. The flavor and the colors didn't matter as much as the all-important words on them. They ranged from the traditional "I Love You", through the platonic "You're Nice", to the slightly racy "Hubba Hubba".

My best friend, Karla Shaffer, and I spent many important minutes sorting through our candy collections. One needed to be selective in the messages given to the boys in class. No wrong signals should be sent.

I'm sure now that the boys just ate the candy, noticing, if anything, only the quantity given, not the intended messages.

I thought Valentine's Day was the one date that should always fall on a school day. I was so disappointed when it came on a weekend. It just didn't seem the same. We got a break from the three R's to work on our valentine boxes. And our class was especially blessed because one of our own, Clayton Miller, had his birthday on Valentine's Day.

That meant cupcakes from Clayton's mother, as well as cookies and Kool-Aid from the teacher. Along with our personal supply of candy, that made for a great afternoon.

I recall a special Valentine's Day in 1952, when I was in fifth grade. My aunts in California sent me a dream dress. It was red-and-white checked, with puffy white sleeves, and had two pockets, each covered with a red heart.

I felt like a princess, even as I trudged to school in ankle-deep snow, clutching my books, lunch box and valentines.

My day was made complete and perfect when it came time to vote for the boy and girl who would pass out the valentines. When the votes were in, our teacher, Miss Katz, announced that Clayton and I would do the honors.

The special day continued after school when our Girl Scout leader, Mrs. Shedden, made beautifully decorated heart-shaped cookies for us.

My heart still remembers and treasures those fleeting times of innocence and beauty.

Opening of Valentine's Box Brought Fear and Excitement

IN THE 1920s, I loved the holiday celebrations at our rural Minnesota school, but all pale in comparison to Valentine's Day and the Valentine Box.

At the start of February, our class got a sturdy cardboard box from the grocer that we covered with white paper, then cut a slot in the top.

Every time someone dropped a valentine in, I was filled with apprehension in those days before children were told to have valentines for everyone. Would there be some for me, and what would happen if there wasn't even one?

The labor of making our valentines carried over to our homes, where we pored over wallpaper books and catalogs to create and inspire our masterpieces.

With help from the seed catalogs, our messages could say: "If we cantaloupe, peas lettuce marry anyway"…"Don't turnip your nose, be my valentine"…or "You beet a path to my heart, valentine."

The long-awaited day arrived and I was breathless with anticipation. One valentine I remember, probably because it was not homemade, was a red heart with a Dutch shoe. Inside it read, "Wooden shoe be my valentine?"

I treasured that for a long time and I am happy to say that everyone received at least one memento, if only from the teacher. But I can still close my eyes and feel the excitement of that long-ago opening of the Valentine Box.

—*Ruth Taylor, Dixon, California*

The Social Event Of the Year

By Oliver Glanzman, Mondovi, Wisconsin

OUR ONE-ROOM country school celebrated all of the holidays. For me, the most special was Christmas. One particular Christmas remains so firmly in my memory that I must share it.

The scene was the Gilman Valley white-frame school in the township of Gilmanton, nestled between the high bluffs of Buffalo County in western Wisconsin. The time was December 1932, and I was in the seventh grade.

Presiding over the Christmas program was our long-suffering underpaid teacher, Florence Marquardt. Miss Marquardt also served as janitor, child psychologist, playground supervisor, nurse and educator who had to make do with outdated textbooks and lack of materials.

Besides all this, she was in charge of the actors and actresses in grades one through eight who would be entertaining the entire community on the night of all nights.

"I got the biggest laugh of the evening..."

Preparations for the Christmas program started before Thanksgiving when Miss Marquardt chose plays, recitations, stage crews and other helpers. It was great to be in the seventh or eighth grade because we set up the stage, which was stored in an abandoned cheese factory a quarter mile away.

Weeks later, the big night finally arrived. Miss Marquardt came early to light the kerosene lamps hanging from the ceiling, fire up the furnace and check the tree decorations.

When farm chores were done, all the parents, hired men and girls, children, grandmas and grandpas piled into sleds pulled by horses to go to the school.

Our sled was a double-duty one—just that morning it'd been used to haul the contents of the stable out to the field. Although straw was strategically placed and the occupants covered with blankets, we all hoped that our body heat wouldn't melt the substance on the planks!

Upon our arrival at school, you could hardly tell that it was open (the frosted windows cast a yellowish hint of light). But inside it was as warm as our hearts were that season.

Soon the show was ready to begin. Little girls in dresses, white stockings and patent leather shoes, and boys in knickers twisted and squirmed through their recitations.

A special treat occurred when the preschoolers lisped through a short song and a "Merry Christmas to all". The audience always clapped in appreciation.

Interspersed with the recitations were short plays. In one, I was behind a folding screen in a "haberdashery" shop. The lead player was singing and ironing my trousers while I waited behind the screen. The script called for another cast member to "accidentally" go behind the screen.

Startled, we both then ran out from behind it. I was dressed only in my underwear—quite daring in those days! I did get the biggest laugh of the evening, a good reward for my embarrassment.

The last number on the program had the whole school, all 26 of us, singing *Silent Night* around the manger scene. Soon it was over and time for Santa Claus to make his appearance. He distributed the teacher's gifts to us and also gifts from the children who'd exchanged names (15¢ was the gift limit).

Then, after Santa made his noisy "Merry Christmas, Ho-ho-ho" exit, it was time for the school clerk to pass out the apples. Delicious brand apples were rare and costly during the Depression and, even today, when I take a bite of one, I'm taken back in time.

Our teacher was given a big hand for her efforts and said she hoped everyone had a good time. Next we all put on our wraps and boots and headed to the waiting horses and sleds.

With bells tied between the hames, we jingled our way home. So ended the social event of the year—Christmas at the one-room country school.

YOUNG THESPIANS. Author (see arrow) and classmates at his Gilman Valley (Wisconsin) school put on a memorable Christmas program in 1932.

In 1949, Santa Came to School by Plane

By Donald Bins
Green Bay, Wisconsin

WHEN I TOOK my first flight on my 16th birthday, I never thought that 3 years later I'd be the pilot for Santa Claus.

In 1946, a schoolmate, Emery Bins (no relation), and I formed a two-piece band called The Swing Kids. I played the accordion and Emery played the drums.

We started playing at a small club on the east side of Green Bay, across the road from the grass airstrip where three or four airplanes were kept. I became acquainted with the pilots who hung out there.

We were playing at the club on Saturday, April 7. I remember the date because the next day I would be 16. One of the pilots, Gene Bertrand, was there and asked me if I would like to take an airplane ride for my birthday.

After my first flight, I was hooked. The next step was to convince my parents that a 16-year-old should take flying lessons.

Well I did, and I soloed that same year, on Dec. 14. I also started a long friendship with Gene. It was Gene and his girlfriend who introduced me, on a blind date, to the girl who would become my wife.

By the spring of 1949, I was able to buy my own plane. It was Gene's and just like the one I'd soloed in, a 1941 Piper Cub Cruiser. I was all of 19 and an airplane owner.

In November of that year, I got an idea about how to make Christmas special for the kids at my old grade school, Sum-

SANTA'S PILOT. At Christmas 1949, author used his first plane (top) to take Santa to grade schools where Mary Kennedy (above left) and Agnes Bins (right) taught. His pal Emery Bins played Santa then... and also years later, when the two of them posed (left).

mit School. I contacted Mrs. Mary Kennedy, who was my teacher from first through fourth grade. I made arrangements with her to land my plane next to the school and have Santa deliver the presents at the school's Christmas program.

There was plenty of snow that Christmas, so I had the plane equipped with skis. I called on my old classmate and fellow musician, Emery, to play Santa.

Only Mrs. Kennedy knew about the plan. But the whole school knew Santa was coming in by airplane after I made a low pass over the school before landing.

I can still see the looks on the children's faces as I taxied up to the school and when Santa got out with his bag of toys that the teacher had given us beforehand. I'm sure it was the first time many of the kids had a close look at a plane.

After that delivery, we took off and flew 5 miles north to the school at Bay Settlement where Emery's mother, Mrs. Agnes Bins, was the teacher and surprised the kids there. ❖

Turkey Tale Takes the Prize

JUST BEFORE Thanksgiving 1943, when I was in sixth grade at the elementary school in Gretna, Virginia, our teacher, Miss Myrtle Haden, had us all write a composition on our Thanksgiving turkey. She said a prize would be given for the best one.

We wrote our stories, they were read to the class, then handed in for grading and judging.

Nothing more was said about the compositions until the last day of school before Christmas vacation.

On that day, Miss Haden asked one of the boys to go to her car and bring in a box she had there. The box was brought in and placed on Miss Haden's desk.

What a surprise when I heard my named called as the winner! I got another surprise when I went up the desk and Miss Haden opened the box.

In it was a great big white leghorn rooster! —*Atha Bailey*
Gretna, Virginia

Plain Valentines Came from the Heart

By Madonna Dries Christensen, Sarasota, Florida

VALENTINE'S DAY helped relieve the monotony between the seemingly endless Iowa winters and the arrival of spring.

When I was a child in the '40s, my younger sister, Shirley, and I hurried into the local Ben Franklin store as soon as the valentines appeared. We'd sort through the cards, selecting the appropriate verse for each classmate and the teacher. We were very careful about the messages on the cards we intended to give the boys.

"Valentine's Greetings" was always safe. But "Please Be Mine" might give a geeky boy the impression we liked him!

The year I was in fifth grade, the selection was taken out of our hands. I came home from school to be greeted by this announcement from Ma, "I got a bargain on valentines—this whole package for a dollar."

Frills Weren't in the Cards

That Ma had chosen our cards was bad enough. But when I saw them, I knew this Valentine's Day was ruined.

The cards had no lacy frills, no lollipops stuck in slots, no crinkly hearts that unfolded, no cupids aiming arrows at unsuspecting targets and no amusing or thoughtful messages.

Instead, Ma's bargain package contained plain red hearts, made out of construction paper. They were each 3 inches in diameter, and there must have been a hundred of them.

"They're so simple and nice, aren't they?" Ma said.

I thought they were dreadful. But I knew economy came first. This package had enough valentines for me and all my siblings.

At first, I threatened not to take any of those plain old hearts to school. But then

I realized that not taking valentines would be even more humiliating. I was stuck with what I had.

Ma suggested pasting the hearts onto lacy paper doilies, or adding pictures of flowers or birds cut from magazines. I wrinkled my nose and said, "That would make them look even more homemade."

No Ambition to Be Postman

So I addressed the plain hearts, sulked off to school and deposited my pitiful offerings in the beautifully decorated box at the front of the room. When we had our class party, I didn't volunteer when our teacher, Miss Klein, asked who'd like to be the "postmen"—one boy and one girl who'd hand out the cards. I didn't want to hand-deliver my lowly declarations of friendship.

The plain red hearts began showing up on desks along with the fancy ones—those with verses and messages that caused a lot of chatter and laughter as my classmates teased one another about secret boyfriends and girlfriends.

When the dismissal bell rang, I gathered up my cards, anxious to leave my plain red hearts behind. But as I walked to the door, Fred, a red-haired, freckle-faced boy, stopped me and said, "Your valentine was the best I got."

I thanked him, but on the way home, I wondered if he was just being polite or if he liked me.

I hurried home, eager to read my cards and to see what the message on the valentine from Fred would reveal. ✤

CHOSEN CAREFULLY. Like the card below says, "Valentine Greetings" was considered a safe message for grade-school classmates (especially certain boys!) you didn't want to get the wrong impression, according to the author. She's on the right in the 1945 photo at left with her sister Shirley.

Chapter 7

Cherished Photos

1. Oakland Mills Country School

1. *BEST FOOT FORWARD.* Max Philpott (front row, on left) of Fort Madison, Iowa and his buddy wondered who'd feel the "discipline stick" first. He did after he was caught fighting. This picture of the 1850s log school, later covered with siding, was taken in 1922.

2. *AMISH LUNCH BREAK.* Paul Hershey (second row, left) of Columbus, Ohio was 10 when this picture was taken in 1946 at the Intercourse (Pennsylvania) Secondary School. Paul said Amos Fisher, seated next to him and wearing his cap, was trying to get something from Paul's lunch box when the picture was taken.

3. *BASKETBALL BEAUTIES.* The Emlenton (Pennsylvania) High School girls' basketball team posed in 1915 in their game attire. Ruth Nuhfer, Warren, Pennsylvania, says her mother, Blanche (Grieff) Barnes, is on the right.

2. Wanna Trade?

3. Distaff Dunksters

4. Posed Posse

4. *SHOOTING BLANKS.* Willard Bailey and his friends at Inglewood High School in 1926 had a "senior skip" day with a Western flavor as they dressed up like cowboys and rode a wagon around town. Willard, of El Segundo, California, is at top right.

5. *WAY TO GO, SIS.* After 6 months of kindergarten at Armour Public School in Chicago, Illinois, proud graduate Marilyn Prunchunas, 5, got her diploma and a hearty handshake from her brother, Edward. After the ceremony and cookies and milk, Marilyn told her father, Casey, of Chatsworth, California, who took the picture, "I'm ready for first grade."

6. *KISS WAS AWFUL.* As part of the third-grade play at State Road Elementary School, Parma, Ohio, in 1948, the peasant girl (kneeling) had to kiss the scarecrow. All the girls said, "Yuck, kissing a boy, how awful." The costumes were mostly homemade, remembers Gail Stevens of Largo, Florida (the gypsy at far right).

5. Pomp and Circumstance

6. Dance, Gypsy, Dance

7. 1923 Car Pool?

7. *ALL HERE?* This could have been the 1923 class picture for the Lucas School, a few miles southwest of Satanta, Kansas, according to Edmund Wright of Satanta. It shows all the students, including Edmund (left), in their teacher's car.

8. *SOUND START.* Robert Kurt (front row, fourth from left) was a 10-year-old saxophonist when he posed for this 1939 picture of the Elmwood Park (Illinois) Elementary School Band. Five years later, he began playing professionally and performed with Kate Smith, Victor Borge, Nat King Cole, Lena Horne, Sophie Tucker and others before becoming a commercial artist and photographer. Robert lives in Warrenton, Missouri.

8. Big Band Sound

9. Tempting Scissors

9. MAINE EVENT. Using the scissors was what these children obviously were waiting for in this 1922 photograph at the Presumpscot School in Portland, Maine. Ken Cole (last row, on the right) of Riverview, Florida shared the photo.

10. SMALL CLASS. These 15 students graduated from Maxwell (Indiana) High School on April 24, 1936, with apple blossoms decorating the stage, remembers Betty King (Eloise Leary in photo) of Pennington Gap, Virginia. The school year ran from September to the last week of April.

10. Happy Grads

11. "Religion" Made It Four R's

12. Go, Platter!

11. *WORE TWO HATS.* Renata (Paetz) Nelesen, and her brother, Harold, attended this one-room parochial school near Marshfield, Wisconsin, and their father was the teacher, says Renata's daughter Janet Duebner of Sturgeon Bay. Rev. August Paetz was also pastor of the church, St. Peter's Ev. Lutheran, from 1907 to 1927 and posed with his students for this photo in 1913. Renata is the littlest girl in the white dress. Harold, now 91 and living in Westlake, Ohio, remembers getting wood from the woodpile behind the school and helping light the stove on cold days.

12. *SOCKS OPTIONAL.* The high school basketball team in Platter, Oklahoma won several games and tournaments in 1938. Note the trophies, the leather basketball and its laces, as well as some players without socks. Team members were (left to right) Melvin Washer, Howard Crawford, Alvin Bell, Jesse Davis, Lee Syler, Dewey Lewis and Bill Bell with coach Bunion Reed.

13. *TWIST OF FATE.* The stage crew for the 1952-53 school year at Point Loma High School in San Diego, California saw no major disasters during performances. Junior Wesley Phillippi (with broom to the right of ladder) came up with the idea to snuff out an onstage electric candle noiselessly by unscrewing a fuse.

14. *DIMES FOR VICTORY.* In 1942 in Edmonds, Washington, first graders and their families saved cooking fat, string, scrap metal and even hair for gun sights to support the war effort. Doris Pollack (second row, third from left) of Concrete remembers bringing dimes to school to buy savings stamps that became bonds.

13. Quiet Backstage!

14. Patriotism Abounded

15. FLOWERS UP. Elise Johnson (far left) was practicing a "lily drill" when this picture was taken in 1911, according to her daughter-in-law, Marilyn Wade, of Bainbridge Island, Washington. The girls, connected by a ribbon and holding paper lilies, performed for a school program at Centreville, Alberta. The photo was taken by their teacher, who developed and printed it in the Johnson home, where she was living.

16. FOOTBALL EXCITEMENT. The Rome (Georgia) High School "Hilltoppers" band paraded down the town's main street before football games, says Johnny Davis of Rome. If the football team won, the band would march back up the street. Barbara Ann Bruner, later Johnny's wife, played trumpet in the band in 1951, when this picture was taken.

15. Lily Drill

16. Victory March

17. Bentonville's Brightest

18. Bar-Belles

17. *ALL-GIRL GRADS.* The 1931 graduating class of Bentonville (Indiana) High School consisted of these seven young women. Frances Petersen Curtis from Connersville, Indiana, who sent the picture, is in the back row in the center.

18. *HEALTHFUL EXERCISE.* At least as early as 1907, female students at Western Union College (later Westmar College) in Le Mars, Iowa took part in athletics. One of the women, Carrie (Hahn) Zeuhl, is the aunt of Mary Vogt, Lincoln, Nebraska, who provided the photograph.

19. Gridiron Grammar Schoolers

20. Sadie Would Be Proud

19. *CYO TEAM.* These seventh and eighth graders formed the St. Helena of the Cross team that competed in the CYO grammar school league in Chicago in 1963. The photo's from Casey Prunchunas, Chatsworth, California, whose son Edward is at front left.

20. *GOT HER MAN.* "Queen" Dottie (Jones) Dunkleberger and "King" Fred Basehore were the happy couple at the Sadie Hawkins Dance in 1948 at Mechanicsburg (Pennsylvania) High School. Dottie now lives in Carlisle.

21. *TEAMWORK.* The 1931 girls' basketball team at Bourbon (Indiana) High School worked a simple plan —six players were divided into three sections of the floor and they couldn't leave their sections, so passing was more important than running the ball, says Melita Poulson Kester, Elkhart, Indiana (front left).

21. Neat High-Tops

22. *WHO'S MISSING?* Not shown in this 1939-40 third-grade class photo in Etna, Pennsylvania is one girl who had been in the hospital after an apendectomy, remembers Anna Mae Michalowski (front row, second from right) of Gibsonia. The girl got to watch the May Day ceremony but couldn't perform, which made her cry.

23. *HILLS OF WEST VIRGINIA.* This photograph of teachers and students at a West Virginia school was taken before 1915, says Edwin Meador, Oxford, Ohio. His aunt, Amy Howard (back row, second teacher from right in white blouse), taught in several West Virginia schools between 1904 and 1941.

22. Smiling Faces

23. Pastoral Setting

24. "The Wishing Well"

25. Corsages for the Ladies

24. *FULL HOUSE.* The Art and Drama Department of Howell (Michigan) High School put on a production of *The Wishing Well* for 2 nights to a packed house in March 1928, relates Viola Stoddard (back row, sixth from right), Polk City, Florida. She was in the chorus.

25. *POLITICALLY ACTIVE.* At least two members of this 1941 eighth-grade graduating class at South School in North Chicago, Illinois went into politics, reports Elaine (Manzke) Eagon (front row, third from left) of Waukegan. One served as a North Chicago alderman and another in the Illinois General Assembly.

Chapter 8

My Most Embarrassing Moment in School

My Most Embarrassing Moment in School

If ever there was a perfect environment for humiliating moments, you couldn't construct a better place than elementary school.

New social skills were tentatively being tried. For boys, there was the inevitable jostling and shoving to establish the leader of the pack. There also was the slow realization that girls were, well, *interesting*.

At about the same time, girls discovered that not all boys were as loathsome as their bratty brothers.

All of which led to a lot of awkwardness and stumbling on both sides.

Fads in clothing didn't dominate as they do today, mostly because we were lucky to afford *any* new clothes. Nevertheless, you didn't want to be too different from your classmates.

I learned that the hard way, making a bum decision when choosing a new winter jacket. What the clerk talked me into was not just the only one of its kind in our town, but probably the only one like it in the entire state of Illinois. I looked like a zebra in a flock of sheep.

Yet I was stuck with it well into my high school years.

The ultimate embarrassment years ago was to be "held back" from advancing to the next grade with your class. You instantly became an alien in two worlds. Your former classmates shunned you as though you had

a dreaded disease. To your new mates, you were "the slow one".

I don't know if it was a good system or not, but it was powerful incentive to earn passing marks. Today, you just get handed along. A frightful number of kids graduate from high school unable to read, write or make change...and are not embarrassed about it.

Another major source of red faces was in the area of dating, as some of the true stories in this chapter attest. Those were the days when boys were expected to be the pursuers and young ladies waited to be pursued.

Any man who claims he wasn't terrified the first time he asked the object of his affection for a date has a severe memory problem. And any girl who claims she wasn't knock-kneed when she came down the stairs, all prettied up for her first date, must have had a lot more aplomb than any of *my* daughters.

Many of our tales of humiliation have to do with the calls of nature. On the one hand, you dreaded having to raise your hand and let the whole class know where you needed to go. But on the other hand, things could be infinitely worse if you tried to tough it out.

What with all the breathlessness and uncertainty and fumbling and bumbling and stumbling, you faced dire social peril at every turn. Or so you thought.

Somehow, we survived.

—*Clancy Strock*

She Majored in Embarrassment

By Eula McGee, Dowling Park, Florida

MY FIRST YEAR of kindergarten in 1926 was a total fiasco. The teacher finally told my parents, "Keep this child home!" I was too immature and cried constantly. Guess who repeated kindergarten?

My basic problem throughout school was shyness and lack of confidence. One incorrect response or disapproving look and my cheeks would flush and tears would flow. I belonged to that group of kids never chosen to represent the school in contests, compete in athletic events or be on the Safety Patrol.

After eighth grade in small-town Fairton, New Jersey, I knew something would have to change. Soon I'd be attending the consolidated high school in Bridgeton. A ninth grader wouldn't cry no matter what, would she?

I decided to adopt an air of self-confidence and enter high school with the best of them.

After 4 years, hardly anyone knew I was there—except when I masterfully performed great feats of stupidity. Our high school was a multi-story edifice with one wing used for junior high students.

GRADUATION AND BEYOND. Eula McGee graduated from high school in 1939 (above) after a tumultuous school career. Then things started getting better, as her smile (right) attests.

My freshman English class was located on the first floor, on the corner where you entered that wing. It was probably Thanksgiving before I was able to leave class and turn in the right direction to my next class on the second floor.

Usually, I'd have to ask someone how to get to class (late, of course). And, because I was small and immature-looking, I was terribly embarrassed at being mistaken for a lost junior high student.

The "Mixed-Up-Shoe" Incident?

I was even more embarrassed at the "mixed-up-shoe incident". On a morning when I was especially late, I grabbed my black oxfords on the run, lacing them up at the bus stop with eyes half open.

Sometime during my first class it hit me—one shoe (the one with the rounded toe) was mine, and the shoe with the pointed toe was my younger brother's. The only

thing I learned that long, long day was the art of hiding feet under an open-bottomed chair and walking unnoticed among hall traffic.

Another lowlight occurred the day I almost became a field hockey hero. I had the ball and was running toward the goal, far ahead of the pack. When I made my shot, the ball rose swift and sure—right into the goalpost. The ricochet struck me square in the head and knocked me out!

Lying on the sideline, I awoke to shouts of the team continuing the game without me. Another time, I was headed for the winning goal when the ball somehow got caught in a clump of grass and wouldn't come loose!

That was school life for me—a series of catastrophies. Space doesn't allow for further examples, but I must share my final act of stupidity with you.

Final Faux Pas

It happened on graduation day (when I bought my baccalaureate dress, the saleslady mistook me for an eighth grader). At the time, my brother-in-law was the caretaker of a country estate.

A few days before, I was showing off my cap and gown to the family when the chauffeur there expressed an interest in attending the ceremony. So I invited him and gave him instructions on where to sit. The ceremonies were to be held outside on the steps at the school entrance.

Marching with my class down the hall to the exit on the big day, I was surprised to see the chauffeur sitting in the hallway.

Thinking he'd become separated from my family, I whispered to him, "Didn't you get your ticket? You're supposed to sit outside."

He seemed totally ignorant on the subject and asked me to repeat myself, which I did. Since I had to move on, we never settled the matter, but during the ceremony, I was concerned about the possibility that he hadn't been able to get a ticket.

You can imagine my chagrin when I discovered later that I'd mistaken a teacher for the chauffeur (they were dead ringers for each other)!

I determined then that I would adopt a second air of self-confidence and this time make it real. Eventually, I got it right. ✦

Science Project Due

Huge Mistake on Display For Him to See

BACK IN 1937, our new junior high in Teaneck, New Jersey had just opened. Looking down the hallways, you could see all the showcases that had been built into the wall. Unknown to me, these showcases would soon cause me plenty of grief.

As the year got under way, we were studying energy. We could pick any energy source and do a project on it. I'd seen a mill with a waterwheel a few years back, so I decided I'd make a waterwheel.

I gathered wood from an orange crate and really got into the project. I must say it turned out great!

Then the day came to turn in our projects, so I brought mine to school in a bag. In my homeroom, my best pal asked me what I had in the bag. "Don't you remember today we turn in our projects?" I asked.

He said he'd forgotten all about it and didn't know what to do. I came up with a scheme that I thought was foolproof. My pal had his first-period class with a different teacher than me, so I gave him my waterwheel to take to class, and then he would return it to me at lunch and I'd turn it in that afternoon.

Project Was *Too* Good

When he came to lunch empty-handed, I was in shock, and he was upset, too. His teacher was so impressed with the waterwheel that he'd kept it for the showcase display!

I was beside myself, but it had been my plan and I was stuck with it. For my class, I quickly drew a picture of a windmill (which was awful). The teacher told me I'd have to do a lot of extra credit to make up for not doing a real project like my classmates.

The worst part was seeing my waterwheel in the hall showcase with my pal's name on it. That really hurt, but I learned a valuable lesson that day.

—*Robert Stefanow, Maywood, New Jersey*

And Now...an Important Announcement

WE LIVED on a farm near Fordsville, Kentucky, and it was in the early '20s when I attended first grade. In our lunch pails, we usually carried something good our mother cooked for us.

For example, we might take fried chicken, a biscuit, a piece of fruit from one of our fruit trees and a slice of home-made cake.

HUNGER PANGS. Author wanted to speak out in first grade before her stomach did.

I especially remember one day near noon when every student was studying and the room was very quiet. Suddenly (forgetting that I was in school), I spoke out loud, saying, "I'm hungry!"

Of course, everyone started laughing. My feelings were hurt, and when they continued giggling, I even shed a few tears.

Then the teacher came over, put her arm around me and said, "No wonder she's hungry, it's practically lunchtime. No more laughing—we'll have lunch in 5 minutes."

—*Mary Craig Brite*
Davenport, Florida

"Flap Down" Flight Caused Bit of a Fright

MY PARENTS started me in a country school in Valley Brook, Oklahoma in September of 1927. My usual way of dressing for school was to wear something like coveralls. These were difficult to get in and out of and had a seat that buttoned up at the waist and dropped down for "necessary functions".

As the weather got cooler, I'd just put on two pair of coveralls and then remove the top pair as the day grew warm. One day I was visiting the outdoor toilet during recess when the bell rang to let us know it was time to line up and return to class.

In my hurry to get in line, I inadvertently buttoned the bottom rear flap of the inner coveralls to the button of the top pair of the outer coveralls. That left the bottom flap of the outside pair unsecured and flapping behind as I ran to the school building.

Since the kids already in line could only see me from the front (with the flap waving behind me as I ran), some were laughing, some hid their faces and others looked like they were about to cry.

Although it must have seemed like I was totally exposed, I really wasn't. The

BUTTONED UP. Author (right) and cousin modeled coveralls similar to the ones that caused a "flap" in 1927.

teacher got me buttoned properly.

—*Bob Lay, Choctaw, Oklahoma*

One Good Lick Was All She Got

By Julia Reifel, Seattle, Washington

ALTHOUGH first grade was a long time ago, my most embarrassing moment was so awful that I'll always remember it as if it happened yesterday.

The steps of our school building had handrails made out of big iron pipes that were great for sliding down when the weather was warm, but when the temperature dropped to the freezing point, they stayed frosty with cold until the afternoon sun hit them.

HEALED. Julia Reifel had recovered from her frozen "treat" by the time this picture was taken.

In the first grade, we had a 15-minute recess—rain or shine. When the bell rang, we'd all line up on the steps until the second bell rang, then go quietly into the building and to our classroom (where it would often take another 15 minutes to get out of our warm clothing and back to our desks).

On one very cold day, I got in line behind my cousin Johnny when the bell rang. He and his friends were up to their usual tricks and, with the ice on the handrails, Johnny had a whole new game to play.

Teased into Tasting

He told me that the ice on the pipe tasted just like ice cream and that if you got a real good lick of it, the taste would stay in your mouth clear up to lunchtime. Well, I may have lived only across the street, but I had never had ice on a pipe that tasted like vanilla ice cream. And, if my own cousin would tell me that, it must be true.

So, I took a big lick and, just like Brer Rabbit, I was stuck fast...to an icy pipe by my tongue!

Just then, the bell rang and the whole class went inside, took off their coats and sat quietly for roll call. Then the teacher, seeing I was not at my desk,

asked where I was (everyone had seen me on the steps, but no one had seen me come into the building).

Johnny finally spoke up to say, "She can't come in. She's stuck!" The teacher then took Johnny by the hand and had him lead her to the back door, where I stood silently crying crocodile tears that were only making things worse because the tears were freezing as fast as they hit the pipes.

When she saw me, the teacher let out a squeal. Then she ordered Johnny to run and get the janitor. I was so embarrassed that I had let Johnny talk me into something so stupid that I just wanted to melt into the steps.

But there I was. I couldn't talk, I couldn't help myself and I couldn't stop crying. Finally, the janitor arrived and assessed the situation, shaking his head. Johnny was sent back to class while the janitor ran to the tool shop in the basement, quickly returning with a blanket and a blow torch.

Janitor to the Rescue

After the teacher wrapped me in the blanket, she hurried into the building and soon returned wearing her coat. The janitor heated the pipe close to my mouth until the teacher felt it getting hot.

In a few minutes, ice was dripping into my shoe and soon I was free. Then the janitor carried me across the street and helped my mother put me to bed.

SNOW JOB. Boisterous youngsters like these can create all sorts of shenanigans on a cold winter day.

They piled blankets on top of me without saying a word. When I stopped shivering, the two of them went into the kitchen, where the janitor told my mother what he'd done to free me.

Soon the doctor arrived, and the threat of pneumonia kept me home from school the rest of the week. But for 2 weeks after that awful day, I'd cry and pretend to be sick because I was afraid the other kids would laugh at me for being so dumb.

Not until years later did I learn that Cousin Johnny had a whole week of discipline to serve for his part in the "Great Ice Cream Caper".

She Was Bloomin' Embarrassed

THIS INCIDENT took place while I was a third grader at Madison School in Butte, Montana in 1935. Whenever we went into a classroom or restroom or had a fire drill, the girls would line up in one line and the boys in another.

One very cold winter day, after my mother had washed our clothes and they'd frozen on the line, I didn't have any clean underwear to wear to school. Since my mother was quite tiny, she offered me her black bloomers instead.

Later, while we were all standing in line to make our morning trip to the restrooms, there was a "SNAP!" as the elastic around my waist broke and those bloomers slipped down to my ankles!

I was so embarrassed. All I could do was pull them up, run to the restroom and cry. Soon after, the teacher came inside to console me. For the next several days I had to endure some kidding, but it taught me a valuable lesson: Never wear your mother's black bloomers! —*Gloria Martin Westminster, Colorado*

Outdoor Graduation Had Its Risks

OUR ninth-grade graduation at Bret Harte Junior High in Los Angeles was held outdoors in February of 1940. My hair was very dark then, so the bird's deposit on my head showed up extremely well.

At the time, I had no clue as to why my classmates were laughing so hard.

—Lorraine Jobst
Watsonville, California

She Escaped "Solitary Confinement"

IN 1954, I attended first grade in a small country school in New Port, Arkansas. The one-room building sat in the middle of a cotton field. A scratched blackboard covered one wall, and a wooden button with a nail driven through it locked the slab door at the end of the day.

One day the teacher took us to a larger school in a nearby town. We'd been invited to a special Christmas program. When we got there, I went with several

FEARFUL CAPTIVE. Sharron McDonald visited a more modern school with indoor plumbing and had an unforgettable experience.

other girls to the fancy "indoor" restroom marked "Girls".

Once inside the small cubicle, I prepared to sit on the sparkling white stool. Then the door came open. I pushed it closed. It swung open again. What was I to do? Sit down with the door open?

Then I noticed the silver metal on the door and the inside frame. While inspecting it, a little bar slid neatly into the slot and the door stayed closed. Straightening my clothes afterward, I prepared to return to the program and my classmates.

I pushed on the door, but it wouldn't open. I pulled on the door, but it wouldn't move. I tried to get the little silver bar to slide like it had before. The door still wouldn't open.

Now my heart began to race, and I gasped for air. The class would leave without me; everyone would leave the school and turn out the lights; no one would ever know I was locked in here.

I had nowhere to sit but on the toilet, and nowhere to lie down but the floor. The floor!

Looking down, I realized that the walls and door didn't reach all the way to the floor. I got down on my stomach, and fresh cool air caressed my burning face. Then I slid out under the door toward freedom.

Afraid my teacher had already left, I ran frantically out of the restroom and down the unfamiliar hallway. Soon I heard children's laughing voices. Entering the gym, I sat as close to my teacher as possible.

As I recall, it was several years before I felt comfortable going into a modern restroom alone again.

—Sharron McDonald
Springdale, Arkansas

Innocent Invitation Was Revealing

A RAINSTORM one day in 1940 left me at Glendale (California) High School without a raincoat, umbrella or boots. A male friend, knowing where I lived and seeing my dilemma, chivalrously offered to drive me home.

When I got home, I thanked him and invited him in for a soda. We walked in the front door but stopped abruptly at the living room.

To my horror, my mother had done the wash that morning and hung my underwear on a temporary line in front of the fireplace to dry.

To this day, I blush when I remember the incident.

—Dorothy Curtis
Bishop, California

Mom's Timing Couldn't Have Been Worse

WHEN I was in the fourth grade at Horace Mann School in Kansas City, Missouri, our class put on a Christmas play in front of the whole school. The play was in the form of a trial in which a judge and jury would decide the favorite holiday of the year—which, of course, was Christmas.

The teacher chose me to be "The First of May". I was to hold a bunch of artificial flowers in my arms, sway

MAYDAY! Ruth Woolfolk was younger here, but changing into a costume for a fourth-grade May Day program was more revealing than she'd wished.

them back and forth and sing: *Oh, I am the first of May, I'm merry and bright and gay. With flowers I come from my fairy home to bring you this glorious day.*

It was a bad case of miscasting. I was big for my age, a klutz and couldn't sing. I had a lavender print sleeveless dress to wear, but my biggest problem was that my mother made me wear heavy underwear to school.

We girls were using one of the classrooms for dressing. Because I had to strip down to bare skin to get rid of my underwear, I got way back in the furthest corner of the classroom. Just as I was stark naked, there was a knock on the door.

My mother had come to help me dress. Naturally, everyone then looked around to see where I was. I was so embarrassed! I'm 84 now, but I can still remember the feeling. —Ruth Woolfolk
Nashville, Tennessee

DESK TRAP. Desks with folding chairs, such as the ones in this photograph, caught many a child unaware. Martha Hall Burtt recalls what happened to one little girl in her first-grade classroom.

'Janitorial Surgery' Frightened Wide-Eyed First Graders

By Martha Hall Burtt, Baton Rouge, Louisiana

THAT SPRING MORNING started like any other at Central School in New Iberia, Louisiana in 1926…with children playing happily. We were waiting for the bell to ring, which it did all too soon.

Our first-grade classroom was downstairs on the first floor. The desks were made of iron and wood, and the seats folded so that the janitor could easily clean under them. How we loved to sit and kneel on those folded-up seats! They gave us extra height—and with it, importance.

However, our teacher, Miss Sealy, warned us not to kneel on the seat because our legs might get caught. But what first grader could remember that in the excitement of answering a question?

That's exactly what happened that morning. Miss Sealy asked a question, and all the children who knew the answer waved excitedly, hoping she'd call on them.

In her enthusiasm, a little blond-haired girl folded the seat of her desk and knelt on it. Before anyone noticed, we heard a scream. When we turned to look, we saw the cute blond girl with her leg caught tight. No matter how she tried, she couldn't budge it.

Miss Sealy reassured her with kind words. "I'll get it loose," she said. She tried pushing and pulling. She even soaped the leg, but nothing happened.

When all else failed, Miss Sealy sent for the principal. Since the principal was my mother, I knew everything would be fine. Mamma could fix anything. But even though she brought in Vaseline and they greased the leg, it still wouldn't slip out.

Finally, the rest of us were sent out on the playground, and the janitor, Mr. Dugas, came into the room with a saw. We couldn't believe they were going to saw off her leg!

There was little playing during our extra recess. We all stood under the classroom window waiting for that little girl's screams, but none came. Could you saw off someone's leg without a sound?

At last, after what seemed like hours, out came the blond haired girl on two legs—limping, but on two legs. As we watched, Mr. Dugas came out with the saw in one hand and the seat of the desk, in two pieces, in the other.

That's when we finally realized what had happened. What a relief! ❧

Not the Ride They Had in Mind

BACK IN the early '40s, our small northern-Wisconsin high school held its sporting events on Friday afternoons. One day my girlfriend and I made plans to skip out of school early (the only time I ever did that) and hitchhike to the game in a town about 7 miles away.

We got away without any problems and thought we had it made—especially after a car slowed down to give us a ride. Our enthusiasm faded quickly when we saw the driver was our school principal!

Although he gave us a ride to the game, he gave us a warning first, "Next time you want to go to the game, ask first." But I'll bet he and his wife (our shorthand teacher) had a great laugh later on. —*Amy Jump Alexander, Iowa*

THUMBS DOWN. Author, in earlier photo, skipped high school to hitchhike to a game. Guess who picked her up?

Ewing Galloway

She Took Her 'Business' Elsewhere!

By Irma Schwantes, Fulda, Minnesota

RECENTLY my big sister described an incident from her school days in 1925 that gave us all a chuckle. Anita began her education in a little country schoolhouse near Gibbon, Minnesota.

That tiny one-room school was on land owned by our aunt and uncle. With the help of migrant farm workers, our dad was raising sugar beets there. The school's single classroom was typical of those seen on television shows like *Little House on the Prairie*, and the "restroom" was a small building out back with a cutout half-moon high up in the door.

Since the school was on the same acreage as our little farmhouse, it was a short walk across the yard from home to school. And, if the little building with the half-moon in the door was occupied (or if there were boys standing

OUTDATED. When Irma Schwantes' sister moved to a new city and a school with indoor plumbing, her sense of direction—and decorum— led her back home.

around waiting to tease), it was a simple matter to run home to use a similar facility over near the granary.

However, before Anita's first school year ended, the family moved to New Ulm, Minnesota, and she and our older brothers were enrolled in St. Paul's Lutheran School on State Street.

This was an enormous change for a little girl. Where before there had been acres of fields to play in, now there were rows of houses along a well-traveled street. Her backyard now was much smaller, although there was still a little building with the half-moon in the door back there.

Where Was the Rest Room?

The two-story brick school with many more children and separate classrooms for each grade was an imposing sight for someone from the country. All this space and splendor impressed Anita, but still, there was something missing: She could find no little building with the moon-shaped cutout anywhere in the school yard.

Soon she learned that in the city, those little outdoor facilities were in-

doors. And, oh my, how grand they were! All white and shiny, they were even fancier than Great-Grandma's white porcelain commode tucked away in her bedroom.

When the time came for Anita to use the facilities, she had no idea what to do. Surely she couldn't risk dirtying the sparkling white chambers!

So, without a second thought, she took off for home as fast as her short legs could carry her. She ran down the hill to Broadway, raced around the corner and then scurried the three blocks to home, cutting across the neighbor's backyard on the way to the little outhouse in our backyard.

Finishing her business, Anita didn't even notice Ma's surprised look at the kitchen window as she hurried out to return to school before the noon hour bell rang. But when she returned later that afternoon, Ma asked her why she'd run home to use the outhouse during the noon hour.

She explained that the school facilities were so clean and beautiful that she couldn't bring herself to actually use them—so what else could she do but hurry home?

Anita says she has never heard our mother laugh as long or as hard as she did on that day. ✄

"Tardy Slip" Was Showing

ONE of my most embarrassing moments came when I was in 10th grade at Patterson (California) High School. I was hurrying because I was late for class.

In those days, we wore cotton-gathered skirts with full slips. I'd made my slip out of cotton with rows and rows of ruffles, which I'd starch and iron.

The slip was fitted around the stomach with a zipper in the back. As I neared the classroom, my zipper broke and the slip dropped to the floor like a brick!

Of course, the teacher picked that very moment to look down the hall. I was so embarrassed that I reached down, picked up my slip and ran back to the restroom.

All I can say is that it was very

HER SLIP SLIPPED. Marla von Moos (center) wasn't embarrassed on graduation day in 1954.

hard walking back into the classroom after that. —*Marla von Moos Patterson, California*

Name Was to Blame

I GREW UP in the farm region of northwest Missouri and attended a one-room school near Pickering in the '30s. Naturally, with no indoor plumbing, the bathrooms were two outhouses located in the far corners of the school yard.

Only a few days into my year as a first grader, I experienced a most embarrassing moment. In order to lessen confusion and not take her attention away from the class, Miss Lanning had instructed us to write our name on the blackboard in the back of the room if we needed to go to one of the corner houses.

Sadly, I hadn't quite mastered the art of writing my name yet. When the urge came, I searched frantically through my jumbled desk trying to find a piece of paper that had my name on it.

Unfortunately, the paper I finally found had my full name on it, and writing out "Wilma Jean Rickabaugh" turned out to be a long and tedious task. Well, as they say, you can't fool Mother Nature—a puddle began to form around my shoes.

SHORT IS BETTER. Wilma Godsey (front row, second from right) wished for a shorter name in first grade. She's shown with her schoolmates in 1936.

With me in tears and the other kids snickering, my beloved Miss Lanning took me behind the big old wood-burning stove and dried me off as best she could. I doubt she's still with us today, but if she were and we met on the street, I think she'd say "Do you remember…?

—*Wilma Godsey, Palatine, Illinois*

Schoolmate Got Himself Into a Sticky Situation

By Leon Scarbrough, Lakeland, Florida

THE YEAR was 1942 and it was fall. In fact, the date was December 10. It'd been cold in south-central Alabama—really, really cold—for several days now.

The thermometer couldn't seem to get above 16°, and we weren't ready for this kind of weather—just as we hadn't been ready for the World War that had broken out only a year previous.

A little group of friends and I were all about 12 and in the sixth grade. We met every morning before class on the south side of the Thomasville (Alabama) Grammar School. During our get-togethers, we talked about many things.

On this morning, the topic of conversation was the weather and its effects of cold on things. Ted started the conversation by asserting, "When metal objects are frozen solid for many hours or even days, things stick to them and you can't get them apart until the metal object warms up."

When Wilson spoke up, saying he didn't believe that, he was quickly supported by Alex and Willie. I didn't want to comment because I wasn't sure (we'd hardly ever had weather this cold before).

Then Ted suggested we try it out and see. I agreed, but what metal object could we use? We all knew it had to be something that had been cold for a long time. Then Willie suggested the flagpole in front of the school.

We walked to the front of the building and, sure enough, that old flagpole looked as if it was frozen. We looked at each

other, but no one looked like he wanted to touch that pole. For several minutes, we stood around it in a semicircle.

Then Ted spoke up. "We better get on with it—school's going to start soon."

"I'm not afraid to touch it," Alex said in a loud voice, "In fact, I'll lick the pole with my tongue to prove I'm right!"

We moved in close to make sure we could see. Alex put his book case on the ground, then put his right knee on the book case and got real close to the flagpole.

Then he opened his mouth, stuck out his tongue and touched the pole. Suddenly, he let out a loud howl and turned white as a sheet. He couldn't take his tongue off the pole!

We found out fast that you can make noises without using your tongue. Alex let us and everyone passing know he couldn't get loose!

Help Came Quickly

Willie ran in the front door of the school and around the corner to the principal's office. He came back almost at once with Mr. Harris right behind him. Mr. Harris took one good look and told Alex, "Don't move—I'll be right back."

We found out later that Mr. Harris had a hot plate that he used to brew coffee sometimes, and now was a real good time to use it. In a few minutes, he was back with a soda straw and a cup of warm water.

Slowly, he dribbled warm water on Alex's tongue and, after what seemed like an eternity, Alex was freed. Mr. Harris sent Alex home and told him to come back when he got a little smarter. The rest of us were marked as late.

We learned a good lesson that very cold day. Later in life, we also learned that Alex became a slick-tongued radio announcer. I wonder if he ever told anyone about December 10, 1942?

Life as a "Lord" Was Unsuitable to Little Lady

DURING the '30s, I attended a consolidated school in Unionville, Pennsylvania. Most of the time there I was quite comfortable and happy—except for one unforgettable day!

In fall of 1931, I was in the first grade (being small for my age, I'd been held back a year by my parents). On that day, my father insisted I wear a beautiful brown velvet Little Lord Fauntleroy suit with a lacy collar.

It had been brought back from England a few years before by my father's sister, and I was the only one of my siblings who could possibly fit into it. But it was a boy's suit—on a girl! What an awful day!

The other children teased me, telling me, among other things, that I should use the lavatory downstairs (the boys' room) rather than the one upstairs. I was upset all

LORD WAS LADY. Author (second from right, wearing dark hat) was hanging her head on this day, too.

day, crying and gloomy and I wished I could have found somewhere to hide.

Either my sister in the same class said something or Miss Kelly, our young teacher, wrote a note home, because after that horrible day, I never saw the suit again.

—*Mary Beale Wright, New Port Richey, Florida*

Friend Left Her to Face the Music Alone

WHEN I was a youngster, we lived in the very small rural community of Knowlesville, New York. I attended Knowlesville Union School, a two-story rural school with the first four grades on the first floor and grades five through eight on the second floor.

About once a week, we had an assembly program, when the whole school gathered on the second floor. One day in 1941, we had an amateur show, and anyone who wanted to could participate.

My friend and I decided we'd sing a little song that was in a songbook my brother had sent me. He was in the Army then, and it was a cute song called *I've Been Working in the Cow Barn* (sung to the tune of *I've Been Working on the Railroad*).

I was 12, and it was the first time I'd ever been on stage, so I was nervous. When we got up there, the two judges told us two people could not perform together. My girlfriend then ran off the stage, taking the songbook with her and leaving me standing there alone!

I knew I had to think of something quick, but the only thing that popped into my mind was *The Star-Spangled Banner*. So that's what I sang, squeaking and squawking the whole time—kind of like Alfalfa of the *Little Rascals*.

To make matters worse, when I started singing, all the children patriotically stood up. Boy, did I feel stupid! When I finished, I ran off stage as fast as I could…to my one and only standing ovation!

By the way, my friend, who then sang "my" song, finished first in the competition. I don't recall, but I'm sure I came in last.

—*Betty Dunn Medina, New York*

Response Not Quite What He'd Hoped for

IF WE NEEDED to be excused from class to use the bathroom when I was in second grade, we had to go up to the teacher and ask permission.

I did so one day and, as the teacher said, "Certainly you may," she reached out and hugged me and gave me a kiss on the cheek—right in front of the whole class!

I don't think anything she could have done would have been more embarrassing.

—*Will Kindberg Huntington Beach, California*

Dad Took a Shine to Daughter's Date

ALTHOUGH it was 50 years ago that I attended the Junior Prom at Sacred Heart High School in Waterbury, Connecticut, I can remember it as if it was yesterday.

I'd borrowed a white linen jacket from one of my friends and dug out a pair of old black woolen pants from the closet. With a corsage in hand, I'd arrived at my date's house, thinking I looked like a million bucks.

But my knees were shaking as I rang the doorbell because I knew her father was a very strict man. When I entered the living room, the whole family was there and I had to pass in review.

Then I heard a few snickers, which made me even more nervous than I already was. It turned out that the moths had had a family picnic on one leg of my pants, and there were places where you could see my lily-white leg showing through.

Then the father, whom I'd thought was so strict, said, "Come with me, son." He took me into the bathroom and got out his shoe-shine kit. With a can of black shoe polish, he painted the offending portions of my leg black.

Because of his ingenuity, his daughter and I went off to the prom with no one else being the wiser. —*Donald Barth Naugatuck, Connecticut*

Sweet Peas Sabotaged His Dream Date

By Bill Bowen
Chapin, South Carolina

IN 1945, while I was in the seventh grade in Charleston, South Carolina, the light of my life was one of my classmates, the beautiful Mitzi. We were a real "item", and she seemed to return my feelings of affection—that is, until the big Junior-Senior Dance.

In those days, we had grammar school graduation ceremonies, baccalaureate services and the Junior-Senior Dance, which was the social highlight of the year.

Since my family lived in a modest five-room bungalow while Mitzi's lived in a two-story brick house with more than one bathroom, I felt as if I'd improved my social circle.

He Was Accepted

They were obviously well-off and quite able to offer a much better than average lifestyle for their little debutante. Still, in spite of the economic differences, I was accepted by her family.

That was no doubt due to the agony inflicted on me by my mama (who used the "ruler across the knuckles method" of teaching manners).

On the night of the fateful dance, despite my somewhat threadbare blue suit, I thought I looked pretty good. We (the suit and I) were so clean and shiny that we were able to project an aura that hid many of the fabric's shortcomings.

I went to pick up my date, and I shall never forget the vision of loveliness that answered the door. She was draped in crinoline and covered by a blue strapless gown.

The dress was beautiful and fit Mitzi perfectly—in spite of the fact that it was held up by something like cellophane tape to ensure her modesty.

My friends and I had decided that we'd give our dates either orchid or carnation corsages, and we all did. All, that is, except me.

Ever frugal and domineering, my Grandma Bowen convinced my dad (who'd inherited at least the first of these traits) that it was a waste of money to pay a florist for such a simple task.

So there I stood in the doorway of the home of the most beautiful creature on earth, in full view of parents, grandparents and assorted relatives who'd gathered to celebrate her entrance into the wonderful world of dating.

Yes, there I stood in a shiny blue suit bearing a sweet pea corsage the size of something you might drape over the winner of the Kentucky Derby!

At first I took the gasps and murmurs I heard to be in appreciation for Grandma's taste. In retrospect, they were probably expressions of horror followed by a discussion of whether to pin the sweet peas up like a corsage or drape them over Mitzi's shoulders as if she were Man O' War.

What to Do?

The stickability of the cellophane tape, the weight of the flowers and what to do with the half roll of waxed paper Grandma had used instead of a florist box also may well have been matters of concern.

The sweet peas eventually ended up draped over Mitzi's shoulder, pinned at both the front and back of her strapless gown. After the dance, I'm sure, the family saved a bale of hay by feeding them to their horse.

That night was the beginning of my lifelong quest to understand women. Mitzi was apparently so overcome by my appearance and the beauty and volume of her flowers that she was struck speechless.

As a matter of fact, I don't believe she ever spoke to me again. ❧

PEAS REIGNED. At an elegant school dance, such as this one, appearance is everything. Unfortunately for Bill Bowen (at left), his frugal family created a corsage for his date that may have cleaned out the garden.

H. Armstrong Roberts

It Must Have Been Near Lunchtime!

DURING the '40s, I attended Turtle Butte School in rural South Dakota. I wasn't used to standing in front of a class, and my most embarrassing moment came on the day I was told to go to the blackboard during math class and write "pie"—or at least that's what I thought I'd been instructed to do.

Was I ever red-faced when I found out the teacher wanted the math symbol!
—Faye Bertram
Winner, South Dakota

PIE-PLEXED. Faye Bertram (front, left) got her math and her meals mixed up in the story above.

18...19...20... Con-*grad*-ulations!

I'LL NEVER forget how my graduation day began in 1947. I found myself in the gym with Miss Schaefer, my physical education teacher, because I still had to meet one more requirement for graduation—20 pull-ups!

It was do or die. My graduation dress was limp, sweat rolled off my face, my hair was damp and my arms felt like rubber...but I finally did it.

Miss Schaefer congratulated me, saying I wouldn't have to do another pull-up until college.

But I fooled her. My college phys ed class involved nothing more than games and I haven't done a pull-up since that hot June day.
—Elaine Ponton
Holtville, California

Baseball Foe Hid in Locker, But She Almost Got "Dugout"

MY MOST embarrassing moment never occurred, but if I had been found out, I'm sure I would have been mortified...and it was all because of sports.

My dislike of sports began in 1955 in Peterborough, Ontario, when I was in the eighth grade. I became fearful that a ball might break my new glasses and I would no longer be able to see well.

In high school, our physical education in the warmer months was playing baseball in the school yard. How I detested it! I felt so inadequate and helpless and I was not good at catching a ball.

The teacher always took roll call in the gym, then we'd exit through the locker room to go outside. One day I had a brilliant idea—I would lag behind and let my classmates go outside, then hide in a locker until the teacher passed through. When the coast was clear, I'd exit from my hiding spot, change into street clothes and sit in a corner of the locker room and read until the class was finished.

I don't know why, but one day the teacher decided to check the lockers. I could hear the metal doors clang open and slam shut, closer and closer to me.

My heart pounded hard in my chest and skipped some beats, and my stomach did somersaults. I almost passed out with fright that the teacher would discover me, but, fortunately, she passed my hiding spot.

I continued to hide in a locker during the baseball season, and the teacher never checked lockers again. How lucky I was to have not gotten caught.
—Shirley O'Brine
San Leandro, California

Impromptu Concert Played to Mixed Reviews

DURING my first year in high school in Middleport, New York in 1936, I took an art class that required me to go to the art room during a free period and work on my assignment.

One day when the art teacher was instructing students in another classroom at the time, I decided to show off in front of a fellow student (a girl, of course). So I played a little tune with a ruler on the steam pipes behind my desk.

What I didn't realize was that the sound followed the metal pipes all through the school and was audible in every room. After a few minutes, I glanced up to see the principal, looking very stern, staring in at me through the window in the door—I'd been caught red-handed!

He came into the room, grabbed me by the collar and escorted me to a nearby study hall, saying in a voice loud enough for everyone to hear, "Don't you ever go into the art room again when no teacher is there!"

You can imagine my embarrassment.
—Robert Chandler
Naples, Florida

MUSICAL PIPES. Robert Chandler's musical talent went farther than he expected it would.

Chapter 9

The 'Happy, Extras'

The 'Happy Extras'

The three R's were the meat and potatoes of our educational system, but most schools also offered extracurriculars, a variety of desserts to suit many tastes. During the cash-strapped Depression days, it required teachers willing to give of both their time and their own money. School boards then couldn't afford many frills, nor were taxpayers eager to fund them.

One teacher of that time recalls how he was given $300 a year to form and conduct a choir—but only if he made sure all the lights had been turned off.

After-school activities were like little magnets, each attracting its own constituency.

Future attorneys and politicians tended to join the debating club.

Outgoing types with big dreams joined the Drama Club for their first whiffs of spotlights and applause.

Future collegians joined the Latin Club. I'll never forget my misery when I was appointed gladiator and had to stand around in a short skirt, holding a wooden sword, at the annual Roman Banquet.

Those who intended to become farmers joined the Future Farmers of America. Young women with domestic leanings were drawn to the Home Economics Club.

As happens today, those who could run fast, jump long or high, catch or throw a ball were destined to be the school heroes. They could swagger down the corridor, six wide, proudly wearing their letter sweaters and dating the prettiest girls.

Fortunately for me, there were better things to do than stand around in a short skirt at a banquet where the other kids were prone on couches, eating grapes—The Music Man came to town!

Yes, indeed, a regular Professor Harold Hill! Sterling, Illinois was going to have a band if Gunnar Benson had his way. Boys *and* girls. Parents somehow managed to come up with the money for instruments. It wasn't until years later that I learned Dad had borrowed the $45 for my cornet, needing 3 years to pay off the loan.

Thinking back, I can't begin to imagine the despair of the teacher who led that first band. All I remember is that we made terrible noises and had not the foggiest sense of rhythm. But Mr. Benson, full-time teacher, spare-time Arthur Fiedler, carried on.

A Band Mothers group raised money through endless fudge, doughnut and bake sales to make dashing blue capes lined with gold.

And there we were one day, proudly marching down the street just like a regular band, the pride and joy of parents, aunts, uncles and the city fathers.

Yes, those Happy Extras nourished the spirit while classroom work nourished the brain. All in all, it worked pretty well.

—*Clancy Strock*

First Track Meet Was Consolidated Confusion

By Carol Sue Brodbeck, Ypsilanti, Michigan

SPUD PUT. Carol Sue Brodbeck holds a potato from her family's bumper crop in 1949, 5 years before she entered junior high school and participated in track events.

SINCE our newly consolidated school building in Ottawa Lake, Michigan was not yet ready for occupancy in 1954, our local Sportsmen's Club was used as a temporary junior high school.

That first year, the big dance floor was divided in half by movable blackboards and student box lockers. The next year, the dance floor was divided into thirds, and the club barroom area was designated as a fourth classroom.

I was 10 that year and can still recall how strange it felt to be taught geography by a teacher standing behind a bar!

Our first track meet was another memorable introduction to the consolidated school system. When our little country school was invited to participate in the big meet at Ottawa Lake, we received a list of the events to be held.

Since we had no idea what many of the sports were, we looked up the information in an encyclopedia. Then two sports-minded boys came up with the equipment we needed.

For the high jump and pole vault, they sunk posts in the ground and laid a cane pole (the kind used to roll up rugs) on top to form a crossbeam. Another cane pole served as the pole we used for vaulting.

A heavy rock was painted black to use as a shot put. We had several weeks to practice our new sports. On one occasion, one of our oversized classmates broke our vaulting pole—it was a miracle she didn't break her neck! It was tough to scrounge up another pole, but we finally did.

Then the day came to have our own meet so we could pick those who'd compete in the township meet.

I'm not sure why, but girls won most of the events. On the day of the big meet, we went off dressed in the recommended uniform, but the meet was bigger than we ever imagined—there were so many athletes.

Somehow we found our way to the starting point of each event. That's when we learned that our representatives in

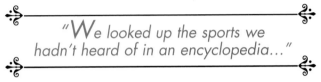

"We looked up the sports we hadn't heard of in an encyclopedia..."

the pole vault, shot put, high jump and broad jump were disqualified because they were girls competing in a "boys only" event! We couldn't believe we hadn't learned that requirement from our research.

It was a big disappointment, but we still watched the meet with interest. We asked someone why there were wood shavings under the structures used in the jumping events and were told that it was to "soften the fall".

We all agreed that was a good idea (another thing not mentioned in our research). Looking back on all our weeks of practice, it was a miracle none of us ever got hurt falling on that rock-hard clay! ⚘

Four Years of Cheers (And Half-Covered Knees)

WHAT a thrill it was to be chosen for the cheerleading squad from 1950 to '54 at Perry High School in Pittsburgh, Pennsylvania. By my senior year, I was named captain, which meant nothing more than standing in the middle and yelling before each cheer, "Are you ready? Let's go!"

Our colors were blue and white. Our skirts had to hit exactly the middle of our knees, which was regularly checked by our physical education teacher and coach. We practiced each day before school for an hour on the auditorium stage.

That meant I had to get out of bed at 5:15 a.m. and travel 45 minutes from the country into the city. Each morning on his way to work, my dad dutifully dropped me off.

We practiced our moves, jumps and splits over and over. To this day, I can recite some of the cheers, but those high jumps with arched back, legs together and toes pointed are just cherished memories.
　　　　　　　　　　　　—Janet Houghton Loughran
　　　　　　　　　　　　The Woodlands, Texas

COVER THOSE KNEES! Author, in her cheerleading outfit in '52, practiced hard and early!

DREAM TEAM. In 1952, the Raymond High School Seagulls basketball team completed the school's first undefeated season, winning 20 consecutive games and placing third in the final AP statewide poll, notes John Betrozoff (back row, fourth from left) of Redmond, Washington, who furnished the photo. The small school won its first district tournament game but lost the second one and was eliminated. The proud people of Raymond collected funds so that the team could go to Seattle to watch the tournament.

Couldn't Keep Her Eyes On the Ball

ABOUT 1940, when bloomer-legged, one-piece, sickly green gym suits were the rule of day in our area of southern Indiana, I wore the smallest size made for high school girls.

Not only was I small, but decidedly *un*-athletic. When sides were chosen for baseball, volleyball or basketball, I was always the last one picked. Well, to be honest, I wasn't exactly picked—it was more like I was sort of forced onto a team.

My gym teacher, Miss Goff, caught on to my dilemma almost as quickly as I did. She started suggesting that, since there seemed to be an uneven number of us, I should act as the referee, umpire or timer—whatever was needed that day.

I knew the rules well and, with Miss Goff to back me up, I made the tough calls. You might think the story would end there, but it didn't. While officiating a basketball game, I got hit in the head with a passed basketball and ended up with a black eye.

For more than a week, I endured the teasing of the boys' coach, Mr. Johnson, who also taught my history class. But that was nothing compared to what he heaped on me the spring day I arrived in his class after a baseball game.

I'd been the third-base coach when a hard-hit line drive slammed me in the face hard enough to knock me out and give me *two* black eyes!

One consolation was I didn't have to go into the shower when I was hurt. So many of us country girls hated to uncover in a group that Miss Goff felt our hair to see if it was wet and our clothes to see if they were dry.

If there were any doubt, she'd lower our grade a letter for not showering.
—*Jo Carey, Homer, Alaska*

Homemakers Would Have Made Poor Hermits

LIKE MOST GIRLS at Stanton (Nebraska) High School in the '60s, I belonged to the Future Homemakers of America. Every spring we held FHA Week. Beforehand we'd vote on the special activities for that week.

There was a "dress-up" day, when we wore our nicest outfits. As if to protest, the boys generally made it a point to dress as slovenly as possible—without breaking the school dress code—on the same day!

We also had a "clash day", when we wore flowered blouses with plaid skirts or red blouses with purple skirts. My senior year, we asked the principal for permission to wear "nice slacks" as one of our FHA Week observation days. But, with the dress code still strictly skirts and dresses, we were flatly turned down.

Probably our most interesting FHA Week activity was "Silent Day". We all made buttons that professed our determination to be silent the entire school day. The only exceptions were that we could participate in class discussions or talk to a teacher about our schoolwork.

That day the school was certainly very quiet, with only the boys being able to chat between classes and during lunch. It's probably not surprising that this particular activity was never chosen again—most girls agreed it was the hardest activity we'd ever picked.   —*Dianne Bahn*
Yankton, South Dakota

The 398.2 Kid

By Dorothy Stanaitis
Gloucester, New Jersey

NOT ONLY was Shirley Singer the first kid in our fourth-grade class to raise her hand when a question was asked, she had more A's on her report card than MaryBelle Peece or John Morrow.

She also was the first of us at the Rhoades School in Philadelphia to get her own library card from the city in 1943. It seemed as if Shirley usually finished her schoolwork first, too (we'd watch enviously as she took out a storybook to read while we still had arithmetic problems to do).

But Shirley knew more than arithmetic—she knew her way around the city. Most of us were only allowed to go to the local stores or to the movies. Shirley, on the other hand, went all by herself to the local branch of the Free Library of Philadelphia.

One day at recess, Shirley showed me her library card and invited me to go with her to the library on Friday. I couldn't imagine my mother letting me go, but Shirley was up to the challenge.

She brought an application card to the house and asked my mother to let me join. Impressed by her confidence, Mother signed the application and said I could go with Shirley on Friday.

Big Day Arrived

I was wild with excitement. On Friday we left school together, then made a stop at Shirley's house. Her family owned a grocery store several blocks away and lived in the room behind it. I felt special being allowed behind the curtain that separated the store from their kitchen.

There, on an upturned barrel, was mail delivered earlier that day. Shirley was expecting a reply to a letter she'd written, and she wasn't disappointed. A letter from Washington, D.C. was there—and it was signed by Franklin Delano Roosevelt!

I was astonished. It had never occurred to me to write to anyone but my grandmother, yet here was one of my classmates corresponding with the President of the United States!

I didn't know that the White House automatically replied to all letters. I thought that Shirley was advising the President the way she was advising me. Reading the letter without comment, she put it aside, as if getting official mail was nothing to get excited about, so I stifled my curiosity.

Still, on our way to the library, all I could think of was that Shirley was writing to FDR. I was overwhelmed. But then the library was overwhelming, too.

My parents got their books and magazines in the mail, and it was exciting when *The Saturday Evening Post, Collier's* or the Book-of-the-Month-Club selection arrived. But that paled in comparison to signing up for my very own library card.

After we were directed to the children's section, Shirley was ahead of me, as usual. We respected the "Silence Please" signs and didn't speak. I wasn't sure what I was supposed to do, so I just plunged into the first shelf and began looking through the books.

She Selected Three Books

When Shirley beckoned me to leave, I'd collected three that appealed to me: *Thimble Summer* by Elizabeth Enright, *Roller Skates* by Ruth Sawyer and a book of fairy tales.

As we checked out, I was surprised to hear the librarian break her own rule, "Well," she said, smiling at me, "you certainly made good selections for your first visit—two Newberry winners and a three ninety-eight point two."

I had no idea what she was talking about. I didn't know that the Newberry Award was given to the best children's book of the year or that fairy tales were

HEAD OF THE CLASS. There's always one student in class like this whose hand goes up first and gets straight A's, but Dorothy Stanaitis found out that she had her own triumphs.

numbered 398.2 in the Dewey Decimal System.

But she seemed pleased with my selections and that made me pleased, too. My parents didn't own a grocery store, I seldom raised my hand first in class and I hadn't even known how to get a library card without help. Yet, here I'd been singled out and complimented by an important adult!

Elated, I smiled broadly at Shirley as we silently left the library. I was filled with happiness and self-worth. Although I didn't correspond with the President, I was a valued reader of prize-winning books and three ninety-eighty point twos! ✄

GAVE TEACHER AN "A". Author treasured the creativity of her teacher.

Field Trip Was a Stone's Throw Away

WHEN I WAS in fifth grade, in 1929, in Nelson, Minnesota, field trips by bus and especially for lower grades were not common.

Our teacher was rather clever. She took our geography class to the cow pasture across the street from the school. We learned that the high humps and low spots left by the cow's feet resembled mountains and valleys.

We learned that flowers and bushes, such as violets, cowslips, sumac and highbush cranberries grew there. In connection with our study of the land, we learned about cultivating of the soil— the teacher removed the pencil from her hair bun and stirred the soil around the plants in the windowsill.

—*Viola Iverson*
Sarasota, Florida

After Rocky Start, Rookie Debaters Did Well

DEBATING couldn't compete with sports in popularity at our high school in Farmington, Michigan in 1929—but it certainly ranked high in the interests of the debating team.

Dean Parker and Louise Perry were seniors that year, and I was a junior. Our coach, Dorothy Ingalls, was in her first year of teaching.

None of us was experienced, but we were motivated and serious. At least one other person tried out for the team that year. Philo McCully was a classmate of mine and one of the school's sports' heroes.

He enthusiastically attended our meetings before the team was selected and was the undisputed star of the first debate. He not only had charisma and facts, but he spouted plenty of statistics to support his arguments.

At the second practice session, we all wanted Philo on our side. Alas! Like politicians I've known since, Philo was more show than substance—it turned out he'd invented the statistics he'd quoted so glibly!

Since the other three of us were convinced one needed to shore up one's arguments with more than imagination, Philo, a charmer, then decided to give all his considerable talents to sports.

Dean's father owned a cow and chicken farm, so he had obligations after school. In his free time, Dean entertained us with tales of how he practiced his debates while milking—he said the cows never interrupted him.

None of us had cars, so we rode buses or streetcars to all our debates. I remember one streetcar trip during which we spotted a sign that said, "Pleasant Ridge—Keep Off!" We thought that was hilarious.

I can also recall the day this photo (below) was taken. I'm on the left. Notice how nicely Louise, Dean and Mrs. Ingalls are dressed. I wasn't proud of that pongee dress at the time (you'll notice the neckline doesn't fit too well).

Louise and I followed the photographer's instructions to cross our legs "just so". Dean's knees are just far enough apart so you can glimpse Miss Ingalls' lovely strapped shoes.

All three of us earned bachelor's degrees and later used the skills we acquired in debating. Dean became a Methodist minister, while Louise and I went on to become schoolteachers.
—*Virla Jean Lynk, Saginaw, Michigan*

GREAT DEBATE! Virla Jean Lynk (seated at left) was proud of her accomplishments as part of the Farmington (Michigan) High School debate team.

Friday Ordeals Paid Off In the End

BEGINNING my freshman year in high school in Goodman, Wisconsin and on through my senior year, we had a physical education teacher who was an excellent dancer and wanted his students to learn how to dance.

This was in the '50s, when dancing with a boy or girl was not an experience any of us looked forward to. Despite that, our physical education classes every Friday were set aside for dancing lessons.

Oh, how we disliked those Fridays! The boys would stand on one side of the gym and the girls on the other. And although the boys were required to ask the girls to dance, they were apprehensive about it.

The girls were equally apprehensive about which boy would ask them. Of course, there were popular boys and girls...and not-so-popular ones. So there would be a mad dash to ask the popular girls for the next dance.

Those of us who weren't asked after the rush were required to dance with each other.

Our instructor told us that someday we'd appreciate knowing how to dance. At the time, we didn't believe him—it was just something we had to do to pass physical education class.

Since then, I've spent many an enjoyable evening dancing, and I even seek out ballrooms, dance fests and new places to go dancing.

Looking back now, I have to thank that physical education teacher for taking the time to show us how to foxtrot, jitterbug, waltz and polka.
—*Betty Wywial, Beloit, Wisconsin*

Scary Santa Was Culmination of 'One-Room Christmas'

By Sarah Wealti, Belleville, Wisconsin

WHEN I was in grade school in the '30s, I attended a one-room school in western Dane County, Wisconsin. At the Lyle School, there were 2 special days that made it all worthwhile.

One was "Playday", when all the rural schools in the township met for a picnic, races and games. We competed for a red and white township banner that the winning school got to keep for a year. Our school won it five times in a row.

The other special day, of course, was the day of the Christmas program. The day before Thanksgiving, a time was set aside to exchange names for gift-giving during the program. None of the gifts could exceed 25¢ in price. Naturally, all the girls hoped to get their best friend's name; the boys fervently hoped they wouldn't have to buy something for a girl.

Also on that day, we were assigned the poems or parts in the dialogues we had to learn to present at the program. The little ones had short poems, while the older ones either had longer poems or parts in one of several plays.

After Thanksgiving, we practiced every day. Nobody wanted to shame their family by not knowing their lines. Finally the big day came (usually the Friday night before Christmas). What excitement that was!

Bedsheets Served as Curtains

A couple of bedsheets were hung on a wire stretched across the front of the room to serve as curtains. Another part of the stage was blocked off by another curtain so the casts of the plays would have a place to stay out of sight until it was their turn to go on stage.

Some of our school desks were pushed together, while others were carried out to the woodshed. Extra seats were made by placing heavy planks across nail kegs or blocks of wood. A tree had been decorated with homemade ornaments and tinsel, while the whole room sparkled with colored pictures and more tinsel.

The program began with all us kids standing together to sing Christmas carols without music (except for a pitch pipe). We weren't good—but we were loud!

Then we recited our parts. At the end, we sang again and while we were singing, we heard jingling bells and somebody hollering "Whoa!" Next a big fellow in a red suit and white beard came stomping in, yelling "Merry Christmas!"

He would ask the little ones if they'd been good, but most of them were too scared to answer. Then he gave each one (even the little ones who hadn't started school yet) a bag of candy and peanuts. Some years there'd be an orange or a popcorn ball, too.

Handed Out Exchange Gifts

After that, Santa passed out the gifts we had for each other and left, saying that he would be seeing us again in a few days. I can still see the wide-eyed look of mingled fear and delight on those small faces.

The gifts we exchanged were mostly storybooks or coloring books, paint sets, puzzles, pocketknives or whistles. Sometimes the older girls were given autograph books.

And, of course, each family gave the teacher a gift. Sometimes it was homemade cookies or candy, but most of the time it was a box of pretty handkerchiefs—Kleenex had not been invented yet, so teachers appreciated those hankies.

We kids were so excited we didn't think we would ever sleep that night, but walking a half mile or more through the snow tired us out quickly. Ah yes, those were the days. How I wish children today could enjoy times like that! ✦

A League of Their Own

BACK IN the mid-'40s in Augusta, Arkansas, my mother, Mary Routh Helms, was part of the all-girl football team at Laura High School. The girls were allowed to participate in football as part of the physical education program.

Mother, who played during her sophomore and junior years, smiles when she recalls competing with the small surrounding towns in their bid for fame as the best all-girl team.

Many of these tough little ladies (including my mother) worked in the fields picking cotton. Yet somehow they managed to find the energy to go to school and play football, too!
                                    —Linda Helms Stodola
                                       Lawton, Oklahoma

FEMALE FOOTBALLERS. The author's mother, Mary Routh Helms (No. 22), and her teammates had the energy to go to school, do chores and play all-girl football in the '40s.

Broomstick Twirlers Made It into the Band

A YOUNG MAN from California spent the summer of 1934 with his cousins in our small town of Manti, Utah. He was a drum major in his high school. That summer, he taught my girlfriend and me how to twirl a baton.

When we started school that fall, we taught some of our friends what we had learned. One day the school band director saw us showing off, then told us we could all march in his band if we could provide our own batons and uniforms. We were delighted!

It was the middle of the Depression and, although we had no money, we began planning our uniforms. First we persuaded the industrial arts teacher and students to make our batons, which they created out of broomsticks.

We wore white duck slacks and white shoes. With our mothers' help, we made our own blouses from red satin. Five girls marched at the rear and wore small hats, while two of us were at each side of the front of the band. In order to make those two hats, one of the mothers covered "Mother's Oats" cartons with satin and gold braid.

We marched several times that fall and, after practicing throughout the winter, competed in all the band concerts held in our region. We even got to perform at Brigham Young University.
—*Betty Keller Anderson, Manti, Utah*

Lessons Tapped Hidden Talent

FROM 1942 to 1948, while I was attending first through sixth grades at Morgan School in Clarksburg, West Virginia, we had tap-dancing lessons regularly during the school week. We were dismissed from the classroom and paid 15¢ per session at the school gym. My mother was the accompanist, and a man called Louie was our instructor.

We gave special programs on the auditorium stage and also traveled around town entertaining other groups, mostly in the evenings. Our outfits were light blue drawstring skirts with starched white blouses.

Since I was the tallest, I always danced in the middle. We really thought we were special and loved the loud applause we got. I still remember the steps we danced to *A Bicycle Built for Two* and have even taught them to my granddaughters.
—*Janet Houghton Loughran, The Woodlands, Texas*

TAP LINE. Janet Houghton Loughran (fourth from right) took tap-dancing lessons while in elementary school in Clarksburg, West Virginia in the 1940s.

Dance-Goers Got a Sandy Surprise

AT OUR small high school in Jewell, Kansas, we didn't have prom during the '40s. Instead, we had a formal junior-senior banquet and dance. The junior class was the host to the senior class and faculty, with our mothers cooking the meal and sophomores acting as table servers.

During my junior year (1946), we chose the theme "Arabian Nights". A lot of work went into the plans and preparations, and it was all kept secret from the other students.

JEWELLS OF THE NILE. "Arabian Nights" was the theme of Donna Schindler's Jewell (Kansas) High School dance.

We hung crepe paper streamers to form a tent in the gym, where dinner would be served. Table decorations and programs followed the theme. But the biggest surprise—never duplicated before or since—was walking through a "desert" to reach the oasis.

We spread a large tarpaulin over a section of the gym floor and then the junior boys brought several pickup loads of sand to spread out.

Where they got the sand was always a mystery, although some mention was made of an area along the highway where construction was going on (all the sand went back the next day).

The crowning touch was the addition of three camel cutouts, borrowed from a local church's Nativity scene. The surprise on our guests' faces and the compliments we received were worth all the hard work.
—*Donna Schindler Arasmith, Philipsburg, Kansas*

Radio Show Brought Breath of Fresh Air

I WAS very fortunate to attend a little rural school between Cambridge and London, Wisconsin between 1933 and 1936 —fortunate because the school had a table-model radio.

At 9 a.m. on Wednesdays, we enjoyed a half-hour radio show from Madison radio station WHA called *Ranger Mac*. It was about birds, animals, plants, trees, weather, seasons and the environment. At lunchtime, we'd have on the *Capitol Times* noon news, direct from the newspaper's publishing building and read over station WIBA.

Once every other year, our teacher would escort the seventh- and eighth-grade classes to the State Capitol in Madison, only 25 miles away. There, we would witness state lawmakers in action as part of our citizenship curriculum.

At noon, we would stop at the *Capitol Times* news office, where we were seated in front of a microphone next to the broadcaster and had our names read over the air.

What a never-to-be-forgotten thrill that was for a bunch of country kids, 64 years ago.
—*Gordon Gottschalk*
McAllen, Texas

"Pole Patrol" Had an Important Mission

IN December of 1946, I was in the fifth grade at Loma Portal Elementary School in San Diego, California and asked if I'd like to join the Junior Traffic Patrol.

I suppose I readily accepted because it was a job that required great responsibility. Being able to get out of class every now and then may have had a little something to do with my decision.

Our uniform consisted of white pants and shirt, a red knit sweater with a badge and a yellow cap with red piping. The boy who held the highest rank (third from left in the front row of the picture) wore a different-colored hat with a star on it.

Morning, noon and afternoon, we'd go out to help students cross a fairly busy street two blocks from school. For the morning and afternoon, three boys were required.

The senior member of the group led us in formation carrying a pole about 4 feet long. Held horizontally, this pole prevented kids from crossing the street until the proper time.

Meanwhile, the other two boys carried poles that seemed 8 to 10 feet tall but were probably only 6. On one end was a stop sign mounted at an angle. These boys stood about 30 feet down each side of the street.

Whistle Directed Them

With a whistle blast from the senior member, the other two boys braced their poles and held them out at arm's length. Twisting the pole 90° put the stop sign in the proper upright position facing traffic and, of course, one hand was held up in the "stop" position.

When it was safe, the children were allowed to cross the street. Once they were safely across, two blasts from the whistle would signal it was time to return the stop signs to their original position.

Though being in the Junior Traffic Patrol had a certain amount of prestige about it (at least for a 10- or 11-year-old), standing on the street holding a

ATTEN-TION! **When Wesley Phillippi (back row, on the left) completed his stint in Junior Traffic Patrol at his elementary school in San Diego, California, he got an honorable discharge certificate.**

pole didn't promise much excitement or glamour. This was especially true at noon when you were all alone with no one to talk to.

But the lack of excitement was actually good news. I can't recall that we ever had an accident or even any close calls. In spite of the bad rap about "California drivers", they were a lot more courteous than what I see today.

I'm sure many who read this can recall similar days of standing on a street helping kids cross safely. Today the job is often given to adults who, at times, have to step out into hostile traffic with nothing to protect them except a whistle and a handheld stop sign.

I guess, as kids, we were doing a lot more than we realized.

—*Wesley Phillippi, Des Moines, Iowa*

Field Trips to Capital, Fair Were Thrilling

By Freda Jeffreys, Wake Forest, North Carolina

IN THE EARLY 1930s, we lived on a farm in Wake County near Rolesville, North Carolina.

My three sisters, one of my brothers and I attended Rolesville Elementary School and walked through the woods and farms, gathering other students as we went along.

Some of the boys gathered sticks and pine straw. When we reached the little three-room schoolhouse, they used them to quickly make a fire in the potbellied stove to warm our chilled faces, near-frostbitten feet and aching hands.

Our three teachers boarded with families in the community. They taught us well and did what they could to expose us to things happening outside our small world.

Two field trips stand out in my mind. Our transportation was a big, open Chevrolet truck. A landowner let a farm laborer drive his truck for such occasions. It was common practice then, and people went to conventions and association meetings on those trucks. The fare was 5¢ each.

Museum Exhibits Were Wondrous

Once we went to Raleigh, North Carolina, our state capital, about 15 miles away and visited the capitol building, with its domed ceiling, and the museum of natural history. Seeing those giant whale skeletons, flying fish in the air and huge turtles made our eyes bulge.

We saw other things we'd never seen before, including a homemade liquor still and a replica of the electric chair.

SCHOOL BUILDING REMAINS. The author (left) attended this school during the Depression. The building remained a school until 1952, when it was turned into apartments.

After leaving the museum, we went to a park, ate our bologna sandwiches and had the greatest treat—a ride on a beautiful carousel.

The same teachers took us to the state fair in Raleigh. Most of us had never been to a fair of any kind, and money was scarce during the Depression. I had one nickel to spend and rode the Ferris wheel. My sister gave me half of the hot dog she bought with her nickel.

The organ grinder and his monkey were entertaining, and the monkey held out a cup to collect coins. We saw elephants and watched a man spin cotton candy. We all went home with great stories to tell! ✤

Turkeys and Touchdowns

THANKSGIVING DAY was the most exciting day of the school year in Scranton, Pennsylvania, because that's when the four major high school football teams played each other. In 1960, it was really exciting for me—I represented Central High School as "Miss Golden Eagle".

Central and Scranton Technical High School always met in the big stadium in the center of town. The other two schools, Dunmore and West Scranton, met at another stadium.

That day was perfectly gorgeous football weather, and the stands were packed with returning alumni as well as current students and their families. During the game, the stands rocked with cheers, songs and stamping feet.

Halftime was great, too. Although some of the routines may have been lacking in precision, we made up for it with great enthusiasm. Central lost the game that day, but you couldn't fault the team—they gave it their all.

"And," we consoled each other, "there's always next year."
—*Suzanne Bevan, Fredericksburg, Virginia*

MISS GOLDEN EAGLE. Suzanne Bevan represented Central High School in Scranton, Pennsylvania as a baton twirler in 1960 during the school's big Thanksgiving football game.

Fifth Grader's First Dance Was Magical

IN 1927, I was a fifth grader attending a three-room school in the very small town of Tabernash, Colorado. As a treat, the teachers decided to hold an afternoon dance for all eight grades in the big hall above Boden's Mercantile Store—the same place the grown-ups danced every Saturday night.

This would be my very first dance and I was excited, for I loved nothing better than dancing around the house to the music of our phonograph's cylindrical records.

But first, I needed a new pair of shoes. So my mother took me to Boden's store, where we purchased the most beautiful shoes I was ever to own. They were high-tops, of course, with the upper part a soft, dove-gray leather and the lower part a lovely, shiny black.

On the day of the dance, after my mother took me up to sit with my friends on the sidelines, we enviously watched the girls who'd been fortunate enough to be asked to dance.

Suddenly, I looked up to find a big, handsome eighth-grade boy asking me to dance! Away I "floated".

I don't remember if either of us danced very well, but out of all the dances I went to later in my life, this first dance will always have a very special place of its own.

And it was all because of the kindness of an eighth grader named Edward Smith, who asked a little fifth-grade wallflower to dance—a fifth grader who happened to have on a beautiful new pair of shoes, which didn't happen often in those days!

—*Flora Smith Crowner*
Yampa, Colorado

Curtain Was Down, But Show Continued

WE ALWAYS had a Christmas play at our school in Surgoinsville, Tennessee in the late '40s. Since I could never remember my lines too well, I was put in charge of making sure the furniture was in place and pulling the curtain open and closed.

That curtain was actually a white sheet on a wire and was easy to operate—at least, it usually was!

One year, as the last part of the play was taking place, the wire came loose and the sheet collapsed on top of the actors. There were arms and heads flying as kids scrambled to get out from underneath.

Meanwhile, over in the corner, a little girl kept on saying her lines as if nothing had happened. The whole time we were working to get the stage cleared, she kept on with her piece.

It was probably the funniest Christmas play we ever did—at least the audience seemed to think so!

—*Cecile Chmelik*
Watersmeet, Michigan

Gap-Toothed Kids Got Royal Treatment

IN THE FALL of 1963, I entered Mrs. Lucas' second-grade class at Pleasant View Elementary School in Branchland, West Virginia. Anxious about having the principal's wife as a teacher, I came to class promptly and prepared to do my best for fear I'd end up in the principal's office.

But as the days passed, I became more comfortable in class. In fact, I came to look forward to Mrs. Lucas' class. She was patient, kind and good to all her students.

It was during the fall of that year that a fellow classmate and I decided we would run for carnival queen. Selection for this royal honor was based on the amount of money one could raise for planned and future school projects.

We aimed to work hard and hope for the best since we were not only competing against each other, but we also had to defeat candidates from grades one to eight. Our mothers baked cupcakes and goodies every night, and we sold them during lunch and recess every day.

I sold chances on a stuffed animal of some sort in an effort to better my chance to win. Mrs. Lucas got in on the act and helped us peddle our wares. She even brought in a box of trinkets for us to sell.

All that hard work paid off, because I was crowned carnival queen, and my classmate Sheila Baker was named princess. We both were so excited!

For our crowning and the trip we won, my mother bought me a beautiful gray wool skirt with a matching vest and a white blouse with a Peter Pan collar. A pair of Mary Janes (black, of course) rounded out the ensemble. Sheila's mom dressed her in an equally attractive outfit.

Then our beloved teacher drove us to the county seat, Hamlin, to have our picture made in our tinfoil crowns. We were so excited that we beamed. As you can see in the photo (below), our missing two front teeth—a common affliction for kids in the second grade—didn't hamper us from smiling profusely for the photographer.

Afterward, Mrs. Lucas treated us to soft-serve custard cones at a nearby restaurant. I often think about that year in second grade. We all shared so many experiences.

And, despite the daily goings-on of school and the routine of practicing reading and struggling with math, I still remember that wonderful teacher who loved and supported us. I'm so glad I had a teacher who cared enough to make me feel like a queen.

—*Paula Midkiff Nelson*
Hamlin, West Virginia

TOOTHY THMILES. Paula Midkiff (left) was crowned carnival queen for raising the most money for her school in 1963. Her classmate Sheila Baker was named princess, and both traveled to the county seat to have this picture taken.

FLAPPERS GALORE. The author (front row, fourth from left) found that her knowledge of the Charleston helped ease her transition into junior high school life.

The Charleston Came To Her Rescue

By Suzanne Bevan, Fredericksburg, Virginia

MY STOMACH was churning, my head was spinning and my knees were knocking that day in the fall of 1955. It was the first day of junior high school in North Scranton, Pennsylvania, and I was a nervous wreck.

For the past 7 years, I'd been happily cocooned in a small, friendly family-like atmosphere at Longfellow No. 28 Grade School, located only three blocks from my home.

We'd all walked to and from school every day and home for lunch, but now I was going to have to walk 3 miles uphill, sometimes in the snow, to a multi-storied monster-like castle named North Scranton Junior High School.

We'd also been given a lecture informing us of the many rules and regulations to be followed—and woe to the one caught going up the down staircase! Easily intimidated, I just knew I'd forget something and be sent to the dungeon (the principal's office), where I'd be beaten and chastened and maybe even locked up. I had a vivid imagination!

The Days Did Get Easier

Somehow I made it through the first day and then the second. After a few weeks, I was familiar enough with the layout and rules not to go into a panic every time a bell rang. Still, my schedule card, glued to the inside of my big notebook, was checked every 15 minutes for reassurance.

Making friends was difficult for me. I felt intimidated by those in my classes who seemed to fit right in and go about the day as if they had a handle on life and weren't scared a bit.

I also worried that the clothes I wore weren't suitable or in style. Afraid to be laughed at, I was sure I'd be ridiculed if I opened my mouth. I seemed to be on the outside looking in, while trying desperately to be just like everyone else.

Gym class was a first for many of us. Now, instead of recess on the playground, we changed into gym clothes and trooped into a big gymnasium, where we learned to play girls' basketball, volleyball and gymnastics. Not good at any of them, I wondered if I'd ever fit in.

Then one day the gym teacher announced that the spring play was coming up and she needed girls to dance the Charleston. I'd been taking ballet and loved to dance. The previous summer, I'd learned the Charleston. It was so much fun and so outrageous compared to formal ballet steps.

She Jumped at the Chance

Heart pounding, I volunteered. The teacher gave me a schedule of practices. I was thrilled—here was something I knew how to do. Maybe I'd find some friends after all.

At our first rehearsal, it was obvious that the teacher didn't know many Charleston steps. When it ended, I timidly approached her and told her that I knew how to do the Charleston and asked whether I could help with the choreography.

She watched as I demonstrated and was gracious enough to let me help. After that, I was called on to demonstrate the steps and help lead the group. Even the "big girls" asked me for instructions, which I was thrilled to supply!

We'd been asked to come up with authentic costumes if possible. My grandmother had a beautiful black velvet two-piece outfit hidden away in her closet that she let me wear. Some of the other girls borrowed stunning beaded or lacy dresses and authentic costumes from their friends and relatives.

At last the big day arrived. We were a smash hit! Hearing applause for the first time from your peers is one of the most thrilling sounds in the world. My self-esteem got a big boost and I'd made new friends as well.

"Gee!" I thought to myself, "This junior high school's not bad at all—maybe I'll try out for the Drama Club!" ✦

Chapter 10

Hijinks and Discipline

Hijinks and Discipline

E ven as I write this, my grandson Brian is serving a detention at his junior high school in Minnesota. It's not a big surprise, because he comes from a long line of males with a history of letting their imagination overwhelm their common sense.

It seems the lad who sits next to Brian in study hall drops into a deep coma the instant he sits down. It is a learned reflex that is totally beyond his control.

Last week, Brian borrowed some flaming-red nail polish from one of his sisters and proceeded to give the sleeping lad a manicure. Mid-crime, an alert teacher nabbed my grandson. Instant justice was dispensed, without benefit of due process or legal representation.

Brian protests that habitual sleeping through study hall should be at least as heinous an offense as administering a manicure. So why was *he* punished? I'll never admit it to him, but I think the young man has a point.

And even if he doesn't, practical jokes have been going on in school since the days when Greek youths tried to set fire to Plato's toga.

Some pranks that I recall involved little effort or cleverness. For example, it was no big trick to make blowguns out of the slender bamboo stakes used to brace up greenhouse plants. A 6-inch section worked quite nicely with grains of rice for ammunition.

But other mischief required lots of planning and ef-

fort. In the '30s, a midget car called the Crosley was introduced. The richest kid in town had one. It was a happy day when we discovered that eight of us could lift his car and carry it to the top of the high school front steps. The only way to reclaim it was to find seven kids who would help carry it back down…and most rich kids didn't have seven friends in those Depression days.

Eventually every youthful criminal met his downfall, growing bolder and bolder until he was collared by teachers who had seen it all and knew every evil trick.

Justice was swift and pitiless. "Young man, go to the principal's office this minute," the teacher would order.

At Lincoln School, that involved a foot-dragging "last mile" walk down an echoing, empty hall to where the principal lurked behind a ponderous golden oak door. Inside was a small anteroom with a wooden bench.

Minutes passed. Hours passed. Weeks passed. Birthdays passed. All the bluff, bluster and bravery slowly ebbed out of you, replaced by sheer pants-wetting terror.

Everything was magnified by your awareness of the standard parental threat of the day: "If you get a whipping at school, you'll get a worse one when you come home!"

A lady sitting beside me in the doctor's waiting room recently recalled those moments all too well. We plea-bargained on just one point—"Please don't tell my parents and I'll never be bad again!"   —*Clancy Strock*

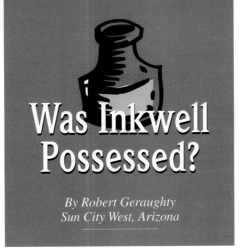

Was Inkwell Possessed?

By Robert Geraughty
Sun City West, Arizona

THE parochial school I attended in Kansas City, Missouri in 1930 was close enough to home that I could walk to school and come home for lunch. There was even time for an occasional foray to the trash bin behind Smith's grocery store.

That bin was a real delight for a 10-year-old boy. Discarded orange crates could be made into birdhouses, and overripe fruits and vegetables were great for bird feed.

After school one day, I stopped by the trash bin and saw something I'd never seen before—a small white slab with a wisp of white smoke coming from it.

It was very cold, and when I touched it, I felt a burning sensation. Curious, I picked it up with a handkerchief, took it home and started experimenting.

A small piece placed in a glass of water bubbled vigorously. The smoke increased and the water got very cold. A piece put on the table slowly disappeared and, unlike ice, left no water behind.

Brother Gave Science Lesson

Just before dinner, my brother came home from high school and told me I'd found dry ice. He explained how it was made, what it was used for and said the white smoke was only carbon dioxide.

My brother was okay, but he was really smart and I didn't care much for smart people—probably because I wasn't one!

A few weeks later, I stopped by the bin on the way back to school from lunch and spotted another piece of dry ice. Since I didn't have my book bag with me, I wrapped it in my handkerchief.

When I got to school, I went right to our classroom and directly to Mary Jo Connor's desk. Taking the cork top off her inkwell, I placed a small piece of dry ice inside and put the top back on.

I'd picked her desk because she was "nasty nice", very smart, the teacher's pet and she didn't like me. Then I returned

ICE-CAPADES. Author learned that mix of science and mischief could put a chill on an annoying classmate.

to the school yard and came back into class with everyone else.

Our first assignment after lunch every day was spelling, and it was done in ink. But before the nun could even utter the first spelling word, Mary Jo raised her hand and said, "Sister, there's ink in my inkwell, but I can't get any on my pen."

The nun picked up the inkwell and stated that it felt cold and that the ink was frozen! To this day, I don't know what that nun thought. The sisters in those days led a pretty cloistered life. It was only about 30 feet from the convent to the school, and they had no other contact with the outside world.

I suspect she may have believed she was witnessing a miracle or possibly the work of the devil. Had she been a little more suspicious, she would have seen 24 awestruck kids standing around Mary Jo's desk while one little boy sat in the back of the room laughing.

Fate Intervenes Again

The next semester, Mary Jo had been particularly nasty to me. Then, like some strange twist of fate, everything fell into place again. One day I found an even larger piece of dry ice in the bin.

Soon I was at Mary Jo's desk. Short on time, I was concerned that this piece might be too much for the job. I looked at the clock and had to choose—yes or no? Of course, I decided yes.

A few minutes later, as we sat at our desks getting ready for spelling, that large piece of dry ice built up so much pressure inside Mary Jo's inkwell that it blew the cork about 8 feet into the air!

This time I didn't think it'd be a good idea to remain at my desk laughing, so I was up with all the other wide-eyed kids who were looking at the mysterious inkwell.

After the excitement had died down a bit, I looked at the nun and said, "Sister, I have been thinking about this a lot, and I believe it's the work of the devil." ❧

Fate Worse Than Death

BACK IN the '30s, if a boy disrupted our fifth-grade class at U.S. Grant School No. 21 in Scranton, Pennsylvania, our teacher, Miss Morris, had a punishment that worked.

After school, she would make the boys walk the girls, hand in hand, outside to the front gate. What an embarrassment to be seen by all the other kids.
—*Serafino Tunis*
Cleveland, Ohio

PULL AT YOUR OWN RISK. This high-spirited youth was no doubt punished by the teacher, as Serafino Tunis sometimes was.

She "Got the Strap" for Fib About Score

THERE WERE six of us first graders at Saskatchewan's one-room Leather River School in 1939. My seat was at the back of the first-grade row.

One day all the first graders were given a sheet of 10 questions to answer. When we finished, the teacher gave us the answers and we marked our own papers. Then she asked us our scores, starting at the front of the row.

"Maurice, what was your score?"

"Ten," Maurice said proudly.

"Mabel?"

"Ten," Mabel answered.

Joan and Wilda answered all the questions correctly, too. Even little Allan had 10 correct answers.

When it was my turn, of course I claimed a perfect score, too. But when the teacher checked and saw I had only eight answers right, I was in trouble. She kept me after school and gave me "the strap"—three sharp smacks on each hand.

I felt I'd been unjustly punished and indignantly told my parents so.

"What did you get the strap

AD-LIBBED FIB. Angeline Kraft (second from right) learned two valuable lessons when she fibbed about a test score.

for?" Dad asked.

"For lying," I mumbled.

"Did you lie?"

"Yes," I said hesitantly.

"Well, then," Dad replied softly, "you got what you deserved, didn't you?"

I learned two valuable lessons from that incident. First, I learned to accept responsibility for my actions, regardless of the circumstances. Second, in all the years that I was a teacher—from 1952 until 1998—I was always careful never to embarrass my students.

—*Angeline Kraft*
Delta, British Columbia

was inside the school, why not play a trick on her and all of us hide?

We chose the coal shed that was now a storage shed. As we all piled into the windowless building and closed the door, the slide lock fell, locking us inside.

At first, it was very quiet and dark. Then voices were heard. "Whose idea was this anyway?" eventually escalated to "You know, this isn't so funny—we could be in deep trouble!"

"We'd better figure out what we're going to tell Mrs. Walker and get our stories straight," someone said. For a while we all practiced what we'd say, since surely we'd be interrogated.

I was a first grader then and was becoming frightened—it seemed like we'd been in the shed for an eternity! We started to scream and yell.

The older students assured me that Mrs. Walker would come looking for us soon. Finally, we heard the school bell ringing incessantly and after a few more minutes, the door to the coal shed opened, spilling in light and Mrs. Walkers image.

She didn't appear to be angry. In fact, I remember a slight smile on her face. I guess she figured it was a trick that had backfired and there was more of a lesson in experiencing it than any scolding she could have done.

—*Jean Nelson Frothinger*
East Grand Forks, Minnesota

Careful Rule Interpretation Saved Him from Paddling

FAST TALKING got me out of a paddling when I was in sixth grade. It was 1945, and I was attending Ross School in Nashville, Tennessee. I delivered papers after school, so I always hurried home first, then went back out to pick up my papers.

One day I was on my way to the pickup point when I met a group of schoolmates on their way home. It had snowed that day, and the boys started throwing snowballs at the girls. Naturally, I joined in the fun for a few minutes, then went on to pick up my papers.

The next morning, the girls reported us for throwing snowballs at them. The

principal lined all of us up for a paddling. Since we'd been on our way home when the incident occurred, she said, we were still under the school's jurisdiction.

When I heard that, I pointed out that I'd already gone home and was on my way to pick up my papers when the snowball fight started. The principal agreed, and I wasn't paddled—but the other boys were.

It was the closest I ever came to getting paddled at school.

—*Bob Martin, Livermore, California*

Vanishing Student Body Didn't Faze Teacher

ONE SPRING DAY during recess at White Swan No. 89 (a little one-room school near Lake Andes, South Dakota), one of the older students had a "bright" idea. While our teacher, Mrs. Walker,

Sister Philomena's Folly

THERE WAS PLENTY of discipline at Saints Phillip and James School in New Castle, Pennsylvania back in the '40s. The nuns constantly walked the aisles and cracked us on the knuckles with rulers for what would seem like no reason at all today.

One sister disciplined me many times for chewing gum. She made me go to the front of the class, sit on a stool, take the gum out of my mouth and stick it on my nose. I'd have to sit there for the rest of the day.

Well, Sister Philomena, wherever you are, it didn't work—I still chew at least a pack of gum a day!

—*Carrie Hink Pirkkala*
Medical Lake, Washington

He Ran Away to Join the Circus...But Not for Long

By Myron Brown, Aptos, California

AN IDEA formed in my mind as I ran out of the woodshed one day in 1932. I was holding my bottom with both hands and crying so loudly that the neighbors must have thought Dad was killing a pig.

I was 14, and I don't remember why I was being punished. But I do remember making up my mind to run away from home. The next morning, I grabbed my books and a sandwich and headed out the door.

But instead of going to Washington Junior High in Rexburg, Idaho, I hid my books in an empty culvert and started toward the fairgrounds. The circus had arrived that morning and was setting up for a 3-day stay. The whole county had been talking about it for weeks.

At the fairgrounds, people were hurrying and running everywhere, pulling ropes, pounding stakes and raising tents. Big black electrical cords were snaked all over the ground. In the distance, I could hear the roar of animals. The air was filled with the aromas of cooking food and strong coffee.

"Whaddya Want, Kid?"

Suddenly a gruff voice startled me out of my dream world. "Whaddya want, kid?" a man yelled at me. He was huge and frightening. A voice that sounded like mine yelled right back, "A job!"

The man didn't laugh or make fun of me. He pointed to a little house on wheels and said, "The office is over there. And stay out of everybody's way!"

As he pointed, I noticed what enormous muscles the man had in his arms. He reminded me of Charles Atlas holding the world on his shoulders.

I quickly walked to the office. "I want to join the circus," I told the woman there. I thought she might scream or chuckle, or maybe call the police. Instead, she asked quietly, "Do your parents know you're here?"

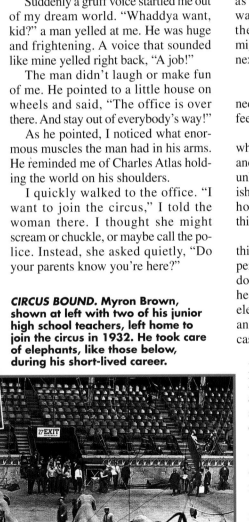

CIRCUS BOUND. Myron Brown, shown at left with two of his junior high school teachers, left home to join the circus in 1932. He took care of elephants, like those below, during his short-lived career.

I thought about the way my backside felt after my dad finished using the razor strop on it. "I'm an orphan," I said.

The woman didn't even bat an eye. Then she asked if I was afraid of elephants. I must have gulped loudly enough for her to hear, but what I said was, "Of course not."

She called someone over a loudspeaker, then asked my name, age and address (which I "forgot"). She said she'd hang onto my cap, to keep me from running away before my job was finished. That was strange —I was running away from home, not the circus!

The man with the Charles Atlas physique appeared. He was to supervise me while I fed and watered the elephants. I'd never seen anything as big as those six elephants. But my boss warned me not to be afraid. He said the elephants could sense fear and might pick me up and throw me into the next county.

It Couldn't Get Better

The boss showed me everything I needed to do, and I hustled to keep the feed and water plentiful.

At lunchtime, we went into a big tent, where we washed up, picked up a tray and helped ourselves at a smorgasbord unlike anything I'd ever seen. After finishing that wonderful meal, I thought, "I hope they hire me forever, because things can't get any better than this."

As I stepped out of the tent, something blocked out the sunlight. A large person stood right in my path. I stared down at the ground and saw a pair of heavy men's shoes. As my gaze traveled upward, I saw trousers...a woman's blouse...and a straw hat so big it cast the face in shadows.

But I didn't need to see the face. I knew who it was. Her name was Mrs. Barnes. On her left shoulder, above her blouse pocket, was a gold star stamped with the words "truant officer". She was holding my cap.

Mrs. Barnes moved aside, and there behind her stood both my parents. I was sure I'd be spending the rest of my life in jail.

My parents and Mrs. Barnes took me to school, where the principal reprimanded me and made me promise to never repeat what I'd done. Then Mrs. Barnes took me to my classroom. The other students glared at me as I sat down. Now that I think about it, I'll bet I smelled a lot like those elephants. ❧

Payback Time for a Paddlin' Principal

DURING the 36 years I worked in the public school system, an incident when I was principal of Central Elementary School in Beech Grove, Indiana still stands out in my mind.

It happened after one of my second-grade teachers asked me to investigate the boys' rest room. When I found a group of students involved in horseplay, I warned them sternly that if the behavior were ever repeated, they would feel my paddle.

Then I sent them back to their room. The next day, the teacher sent one of her students to my office with a note saying, "This boy did it again!"

Without investigating or asking any questions, I reminded the boy of what I'd promised the day before in the rest room. Then I used the paddle on him as I'd said I would.

He didn't protest or try to explain. Afterward, I wrote on the note what I'd done and sent him back to class. Before I could count to 10, the teacher had hurried back to my office and informed me that I'd paddled the wrong boy.

In fact, she said he was the best boy in the class! Realizing I'd made a terrible mistake, I asked her to bring him back to my office. When he arrived, I apologized, then proceeded to take my coat and glasses off.

"If I can give it, I can take it," I told him as I handed him the paddle and told him to let me have it. I'm certain he hit me much harder than I'd hit him!

When word got out about what had happened, his prestige among fellow students rose greatly, and I was well respected, too.
—*Delmer Rund*
Beech Grove, Indiana

Saved by the Beads!

MANY YEARS AGO, when I was a sixth-grade student at Elmwood Grade School in Springfield, Ohio, my friend Millard and I were caught talking by our teacher.

Miss Augusta Wiggle was also the school principal and had the reputation of being very strict. We all referred to her as "Gussy Wiggle"—but definitely not when she might hear!

I remember all too well the cold chills I felt running up my spine when she peered at me through her old-style glasses that pinched together on the bridge of her nose.

Millard had been showing me his brand-new Barlow knife when I got caught. "Okay, Thomas…out in the cloakroom," Miss Wiggle barked. On the way there, she reached to the top of a large bookcase to retrieve her paddle.

I was then ordered to put my hands in my pants pockets and bend over. But as Miss Wiggle wound up for her first swat, the dreaded paddle became entangled in a long string of beads she was wearing that day.

"Pop-a-dee-pop" was the next sound as her beads bounced all over the cloakroom floor.

Thinking quickly, I immediately dropped to my knees and began gathering every bead I could possibly find.

"Why thank you, Thomas," said Miss Wiggle. "Now do you think you can behave?"

Emphatically nodding my head, I said, "Yes, ma'am" and was told to return to my seat.
—*Tom Hummel*
Grove City, Ohio

J.C. Allen and Son

SHELL GAME. Stanley Yancis and his buddies thought it would be fun to fill the school with turtles they caught.

Pranksters Filled School with Turtles

IN THE 1920s, when I was in third or fourth grade, everyone in our school went outdoors to each lunch. One day my friends and I discovered several dozen turtles gathered along a creek, preparing for winter hibernation.

We filled our sweaters and jackets with as many of the lethargic turtles as we could carry. Then we slipped past the teacher and the other students and released the turtles in the one-room schoolhouse.

When the lunch hour ended, Miss Goldsmith told all the children to return to their seats. The students ran into the schoolhouse—and then ran right back out, yelling and screaming. The warmth from the coal-fired heater had revived the turtles, and they were crawling in every direction. Miss Goldsmith directed those of us who were responsible for this mayhem to gather up the turtles and return them to the creek bank.

That afternoon, we had a biology lesson and learned what the turtles were doing at the water's edge, and why. The whole class promised to never disturb turtles again.
—*Stanley Yancis*
Wilkes-Barre, Pennsylvania

Teacher Made Pupils Write Their Wrongs

LOVED HER STUDENTS. Magdalene Becker (left) started teaching in 1927 near Murry, Wisconsin. Her first class (above) had 21 students, but in her second school (below), she taught up to 47 students.

WHEN I STARTED teaching at Lone Pine School near Murry, Wisconsin in 1923, I had just turned 18. No one could've been more nervous. Luckily, it was a small school, with only 21 pupils in eight grades. My salary was $75 a month.

In 1929, I moved on to the Murry School, which was a real challenge—47 pupils in eight grades. Luckily, my students felt challenged and were eager to learn. Because they worked so hard, we had time to do many extra things, like form a harmonica band and square-dance at the county fair.

I never had to worry about discipline—the children were too busy. Besides, they didn't like the way I handled it!

Children who broke the rules had to write down what they did, why and what they intended to do about it. No poor sentence structure or misspelled words were allowed. The younger ones had to stand up and tell us, since they couldn't write it. One dose of that medicine was enough!

I retired from teaching in 1970, but many of my former students have stayed in touch with me. In 1999, several students I'd taught 70 years before visited me. I consider that real pay—and a measure of their gratitude.

—*Magdalene Becker*
Ladysmith, Wisconsin

Fear of Flying

MY FOURTH-GRADE CLASSROOM in 1940 was on the third floor of a three-story building. In the outside corner of the classroom was a library closed in by two partitions with shelves.

On the outside walls, there were windows, which were open in warm weather. The windows had no screens.

One day my friend John Michel and I were in the library making paper airplanes and sailing them out the windows. We'd watch them sail all the way to the ground.

After a while, we noticed the principal was standing be-

hind us. She was a large, tall woman and could scare any small boy.

She sent us down to pick up all the airplanes and bring them to her in her office. There she had us separate them. John only had a couple, but I had eight or 10.

She told me to go home and tell my mother that I was expelled. Well, I could imagine what would happen if I told my mother that, so I started crying.

I cried and cried, until finally the principal said she'd let it go this time. I think she just wanted to scare me.

It worked. I never did anything like that again.

—*Paul Ohlemacher, Sandusky, Ohio*

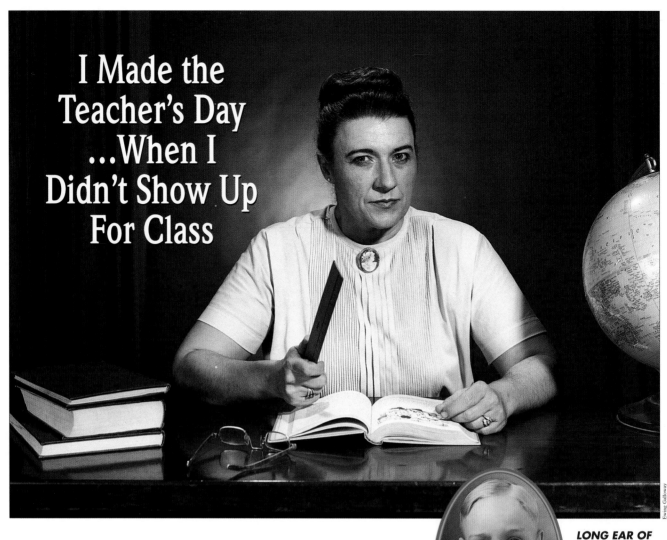

I Made the Teacher's Day ...When I Didn't Show Up For Class

LONG EAR OF THE LAW? Dayne Shaw (left) claims his left ear is longer than his right because a stern teacher, such as the one above, grabbed it too often.

By Dayne Shaw, Germantown, Ohio

WHEN I started school in 1944, it was not a one-room schoolhouse. No, we were much more advanced than that—I started in a two-room school in Plattsburg, Ohio.

My first-grade teacher was Miss Brown. She and I did not exactly hit it off. Actually, I would say that whenever I was absent, it made her day.

I can remember one time I "sassed" the teacher. I didn't even know what "sass" was, but I soon found out.

Miss Brown, in her authoritative tone, directed me to quit looking around and get busy or I wouldn't be able to get my work done. I replied, "I don't care."

She grabbed my ear, pulling me up out of my seat and said through clenched teeth, "Don't sass me, young man."

She escorted me to the old upright piano in the back of the room while maintaining a tight grip on my ear. I can still feel it today, and my left ear is bigger than my right. I attribute that fact

to Miss Brown's tight grip and many more trips to the piano.

The year I finally made it to Mrs. Martendale's room, which housed the top three grades in our two-room schoolhouse, things began to improve.

Not everything went smoothly, however. One day, for punishment, Mrs. Martendale placed me in the cloakroom and closed the door. This room was not the warmest place to be in winter, and I decided I needed my coat.

Lunches Were Tempting

I went over to the wall where my coat was hanging. As I reached up to take it down from the hook, my eye wandered up to the shelf above the coats. The other kids' lunches were just sitting there, and here I was, cold with nothing to do.

I slipped on my coat and began to investigate the possibilities that life had presented me. No, I didn't eat the lunches, but I did open them and switch everyone's sandwiches around.

After a short time, Mrs. Martendale

opened the door and invited me to rejoin the class.

Since I lived across the road from school, I usually went home for lunch. I ate as fast as I could and hurried back to the schoolhouse. I didn't want to miss the fun.

One of my friends told me that no one could believe what their mothers had packed them for lunch, and there was a whole lot of complaining going on. A big smile broke out across my face, and I was about to brag about what I had done when Mrs. Martendale saw me. She motioned for me to come to her desk, and I knew she was on to me.

I had done the crime and was ready

to do the time, so I was happily surprised when all Mrs. Martendale did was ask some very pointed questions.

"Dayne, did you have a nice lunch?"

"Yes, I had tomato soup and grilled cheese sandwiches."

"Do you like tomato soup and grilled cheese sandwiches?"

"Yes, they're my favorites."

"Don't you think everyone should be able to eat the things their mothers have fixed them?"

I couldn't look her in the eye. I knew she had me. I lowered my head, staring at a glass filled with pencils that always sat on the front of her desk.

She said, "Dayne, I want you to go back to your seat and think about this."

I did go back to my seat and I did think about it. I still think about it today, and a big smile breaks out across my face.

One year Mrs. Martendale told us we could no longer climb the good-sized trees in the yard surrounding our school, although we did this all summer. When we asked why, she said it was because smaller children might follow us up a tree, fall and get hurt.

About the second week of school, my friend Bud and I thought it would be great fun to get a game of tree tag going. Some of the other boys in the upper grades were hesitant, but I explained that Mrs. Martendale probably didn't mean we couldn't climb the trees; she just didn't want the *little kids* to climb them.

Foiled Again!

When the bell rang, we raced back to the schoolhouse, only to see Mrs. Martendale and Miss Brown standing just inside the doors with their arms folded across their chests and frowning. Miss Brown was tapping her foot.

We—the tree tag players—were herded into the room and lined up. Mrs. Martendale approached each of us in turn, looked us straight in the eye and asked, "Didn't I tell you not to climb in the trees?"

As each boy answered, "Yes, ma'am," she directed him to lie facedown across a bench seat attached to a desk in the first-grade section.

Armed with a wide, thick yardstick, she gave each boy three good, solid cracks across the rump. There were about 15 of us, and she worked her way to the oldest, Bud and me.

Bud went just before me and got a couple of extra cracks for good measure. He took it like a man.

As I was starting to assume the position, I slipped. Bud snickered, and I

⸓―――――――⸓
"I had done the crime and was ready to do the time..."
⸓―――――――⸓

thought it was funny, too, and snickered just as the yardstick came down. The crack resounded, and I could picture the smile on Miss Brown's face; she had to be enjoying this.

Every time the yardstick crashed down, I let out a little laugh. I wasn't going to give Miss Brown the satisfaction. As I think back, this was not a smart thing to do. Mrs. Martendale did not seem to think anything was at all funny. She wore me out.

Our little two-room schoolhouse is now closed and gone. The local school district consolidated with other small districts, and we were bused all over the county. Only memories remain of the days we spent together in the small local school, where everyone knew one another and we shared in each other's joys and sorrows.

Something is missing in today's society, and no one is able to explain what it is. Maybe it's the little one- and two-room schools, where the children did not get lost as they do now in the mad rush through the halls of large, impersonal modern schools.

Or maybe it's the fact that the teacher is no longer permitted to use the yardstick when mischievous boys get into trouble. ⸓

STRETCHED GUM. Brenda Boldman (see arrow) and her classmates in Troy, Ohio had a creative way of getting extra mileage from their rationed gum.

Prized Bubble Gum Was Worth Retrieving

IN THE 1940s, sugar was rationed because of the war, so there was little candy available. We bought ours from the "candy man", a blind gentleman who operated a little stand in the basement of the Miami County Courthouse in Troy, Ohio.

Whenever the candy man got a delivery, the news spread through Edwards School like wildfire. At lunch break, we'd run down Main Street, pennies clutched in our mittens, to buy the wonderful candies that were so scarce. The candy man sold large ruby-red paraffin lips, paraffin teeth, little paraffin bottles filled with sweetened juice, and many other treats. All the paraffin was edible.

I still recall the taste of those "lips" after I'd worn them for several hours. My favorite, though, was the pink bubble gum.

We weren't permitted to chew gum during class. If we got caught, we had to march to the wastebasket and deposit it. By recess, there'd be numerous bright pink "deposits" in the basket. But each of us positioned our gum very carefully, so we'd remember exactly where it was.

During recess, we'd slip up the fire escape steps, sneak back into the classroom, retrieve our gum and start chewing it all over again. I have to laugh about it now—and wonder how many times I ended up with someone else's gum!

—*Brenda Boldman, LaVerne, California*

Path to Graduation Led Through the Boys' Room

By John Smith, Manchester, Connecticut

MY HIGH SCHOOL, the Vincentian Institute in Albany, New York, was staffed by Holy Cross brothers. Brother John was the principal, and Brother Quentain was my Latin instructor.

Somehow I got into the bad habit of skipping homework during my senior year, 1943. When I came to school without my homework for the third day in a row, Brother Quentain told me, "Take your books and go see Brother John."

In our school, this sentence had only one meaning: You were going to be expelled.

As I walked down the hall toward Brother John's office, I couldn't imagine how I'd explain this to my parents. Halfway to the office, I darted into the boys' room, where I waited for the bell to ring for the next class. Then I followed my regular schedule for the rest of the day.

The next day, on my way to school, I thought up a million excuses to give Brother Quentain for not having gone to Brother John's office the day before. But it was useless. None of my excuses made any sense.

My first-period class was Latin. I sat at my desk and waited glumly for Brother Quentain to come in and send me back to Brother John.

But when the door opened, the man who walked in was someone I'd never seen before. He walked to Brother Quentain's desk and said, "Good morning, boys. I'm Brother Romanus. Brother Quentain was taken to the hospital last night with a burst appendix. Let us bow our heads and say a prayer for him."

I bowed my head so low I nearly scratched my nose on my shoelaces! Thanks to Brother Quentain's appendicitis, I graduated from Vincentian that year.

Several years later, I was walking down Madison Avenue in Albany when I heard someone calling me. I turned around and saw Brother Quentain. We walked together for a while, reminiscing. Then Brother Quentain came to a sudden halt.

"Wait a minute," he said. "Did you say you graduated from our school? Didn't I send you to see Brother John?"

When I confessed what I'd done, Brother Quentain laughed, put a hand on my shoulder and said, "John, if you ever decide to go to the racetrack, come and get me first!"

DIVINE INTERVENTION? If not for a chance appendicitis, the author would have been expelled from high school by Brother John (right), the principal.

"Perhaps You'd Like to Share That with the Rest of Us"

MISS HOPE was our math teacher at A.G. Junior High School in Charlotte, North Carolina in 1933. She was a strict disciplinarian and was known for being "wicked with the ruler".

One day someone started humming during class. "Who is that?" Miss Hope asked. A boy in the back of the room raised his hand. It was George McCachren. George, better known as "Toad", was well-liked by the other students.

"Since you like to sing so much," Miss Hope told him, "come up to the front of the class and sing for all of us."

Toad walked to the front of the room, turned around and started to sing *Frankie and Johnny*. You may recall that there are many, many verses to that song, and Toad clearly intended to sing them all.

Finally Miss Hope realized that no one was being punished, as everyone was enjoying Toad's performance. "That's enough," she told him, "you may go back to your seat."

Toad turned to her and asked, "Could I please finish it? There's only one more verse."

Everyone in the room laughed—except Miss Hope, who raised her voice and said, "Go back to your seat!"

After that, any time the teacher left the room, all the students asked Toad to sing. He was always ready to oblige with his favorite song.   *—Gerald Palmer Rochester, New York*

Comparison to Siblings a Bitter Pill to Swallow

UNKINDEST CUT. The principal (standing, right) offered a cruel comment to the author (seated, left) when she was in fourth grade.

MY FOURTH-GRADE teacher in Danville, Illinois was madly in love and soon to be married, so she was very lenient. My friends and I wrote notes and copied each other's test answers. If the teacher saw any of this, she never let on.

One day the principal came in and just walked around the room. To my horror, she picked up a note I'd written and read it. Then she put it back on my desk and whispered to me, "I never had this problem with your brother and sister."

I was very upset. That was the worst possible thing she could have said to me. I would've preferred a spanking! Having older siblings did have its disadvantages.

—Josephine Bolerjack Green Valley, Arizona

Youthful Hijinks Snowballed Out of Control

By Jim MacNair, Littleton, Colorado

EVERYONE at Newton Junior High School in Iowa was excited when the last bell rang that Friday afternoon in 1939. It had snowed most of the day, and the snow was just right for making snowmen, snow forts and especially snowballs.

On the playground behind the school, my seventh-grade colleagues were already taking advantage of this perfect snow. I'd barely stepped outside before the first compacted missile hit my shoulder. This was an act of war!

I quickly scooped up some snow, squeezed it tight and let it fly at Jake, the most likely perpetrator. Soon each of us had a two-man brigade engaged in all-out battle.

Jake laughed as he planted one on my forehead. Suddenly he straightened out and bent backward, clutching his shoulder. His face was grim as he looked to see where the snowball had come from.

Then I spotted Big Bob as he fired another shot, almost knocking Jake off his feet. The appearance of Bob, a high school junior, shifted the balance of power. He pummeled us with missiles that felt like croquet balls.

The four of us took refuge behind a drift across from the playground. We threw snowballs at Bob as fast as we could, peering over the snowbank only to aim and throw. My arm was getting tired, but I formed a perfect, deadly snowball and hurled it straight at Bob's nose.

The snowball started out on target. Then it began to break to the left. Out of the corner of my eye, I saw a small, thin figure wrapped in a black coat—a

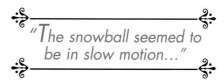

"The snowball seemed to be in slow motion..."

woman walking toward the playground. The snowball was still in flight and still breaking to the left. It was on a direct collision course with the woman. Even worse, the woman was our English teacher, Miss Channing.

The next moment was one of pure panic. The snowball seemed to continue its flight in slow motion, but my mind was racing. One more step, and Miss Channing and the snowball would reach the same destination at the same time. It was inevitable. I held my breath, closed my eyes and prayed.

Miraculously, the snowball whizzed within millimeters of Miss Channing's glasses. Tragedy had been averted.

The four of us slumped in relief be-hind the snowdrift. Our mittens were sopping wet, and we were sweating. It was time to go home.

In homeroom Monday, I was told to report to the principal. He looked very stern behind his dark oak desk.

"James, it's been reported that you and three other boys were throwing snowballs from across the street Friday after school," he said. "And that you threw one at Miss Channing."

"Yes, sir," I said. "No, sir. Not at her…"

"You know," the principal continued, "there is no snowballing allowed beyond the school playground when coming from or going to school."

"Yes, sir," I said. "We were in the school yard, but we were chased out."

The principal ignored this defense. "James," he said, "I'm sorry, but I have to expel you and your friends for 1 week. You know the rules about throwing snowballs, and you broke them."

The halls were empty as I walked to my locker. Everyone else was in class. I put on my heavy gloves and sheepskin coat, pulled on my aviator's helmet and stepped into the crisp morning air.

Considering the gravity of my punishment, I hate to think what the consequences would've been if the snowball had hit Miss Channing. ❧

LEFT ADRIFT. An afternoon snowball fight, such as the one shown here, had serious consequences for the author and three friends in junior high school.

If Losing Dolls Was Tough, Regaining Them Was Worse

DO YOU REMEMBER the "Boots" cartoon that ran in newspapers in the 1930s? Boots always wore the very latest clothes, and every week or so the papers printed a Boots paper doll with clothes to cut out.

My friends and I loved "designing" these clothes with our crayons and our vivid imaginations, and we competed to see who could make the best outfit. Unfortunately, these efforts sometimes spilled over into school hours. Even after I started junior high school, my best friend and I secretly fashioned outfits for Boots during class.

One day the teacher caught me and told me to bring my paper dolls to her. I was mortified but did as I was told. The teacher put the paper dolls in her desk. I thought that was the worst possible embarrassment—but I was wrong.

After several months passed, I felt too grown-up to play with paper dolls anymore. You can imagine how humiliated I was at the end of the school year, when the teacher called me up in front of the class to return the dolls to me!

—*Ruth Tuttle, Salt Lake City, Utah*

"Shave and Haircut" Weren't Appreciated

DURING the early '30s, the classrooms at McKinley Elementary School in Des Moines, Iowa were equipped with a buzzer system. It was used at the beginning and end of each class session and controlled from the school office.

One year when I was fortunate enough to own a wristwatch, I was chosen to operate the system.

Apparently upset over some trivial matter one day, I buzzed all the classrooms in the musical rhythm of "Shave and a haircut—two bits!"

Well, it wasn't long before I was called into the principal's office and promptly relieved of my prestigious "buzzer boy" position.

—*Charles Martin
Bartlesville, Oklahoma*

New Form of Punishment Was No Laughing Matter

I'LL NEVER FORGET the one time I was punished in school. Since I was a good little girl, it came as quite a shock.

The year was 1932, and I was in fourth grade. Our teacher, Miss Vining, announced that she had a new punishment for classroom offenses. She would draw a ring on the blackboard and have the offender stand with his or her nose in the ring. This sounded funny to me, and I began giggling. Miss Vining promptly drew a ring on the board for my nose!

This was no longer a laughing matter. The blackboard soon was dripping with my tears.

I believe this experience helped me feel a little more compassion for those who were punished. —*Florine Martin
Ruston, Louisiana*

Even Daily Report Card Couldn't Quiet Chatterbox

WHEN I WAS in second grade in Cedar Falls, Iowa in the 1930s, every day was report card day for me—much to my chagrin.

I usually finished my work quickly, and since I was a sociable only child, I would start talking to my classmates, who were still poring over their papers. No matter how many times Miss Raitt admonished me, I couldn't stop whispering while she was teaching. I always raised my hand first when she asked the class a question. In desperation, Miss Raitt drew a big chart with my name on top.

At the end of each school day, I had to stop by her desk and discuss whether I'd earned a black mark (for big transgressions), a purple mark (for trying, but failing, to follow the rules), or a gold star (for good behavior).

I can remember only one gold star, earned the day I was coming down with chicken pox and had a fever.

When my report card showed a low, low grade in deportment, my parents called on "Miss Rat", as I had begun to call her. She pulled out the chart, and they promised to try to repress my enthusiasm.

The solution came the next year, when I skipped a grade. I was so overwhelmed among the older and bigger kids that I scarcely said a word for months. But I did get an "A" in deportment.

—*Anita Hunter
Camarillo, California*

STAR-CROSSED. Sociable Anita Hunter tried hard to earn gold stars for deportment in second grade. She only remembers one, but her actions that day may have been impaired.

Nothing Like the Taste of Paste

WHEN my grandchildren ask me what years of school I liked best, I tell them kindergarten. That certainly doesn't say much for my intelligence—or my report cards from 12 years of schooling. Nevertheless, it's true.

And, after 68 years, what I remember most fondly is the large white jar of library paste that sat on the supply shelf. We were allowed to take a small wooden stick and get a glob of paste that we'd put on a piece of paper and then return to our desks.

I was (and still am) of the opinion that if a little is good, then a whole lot more is better. Therefore, my "creations" usually had big lumps of paste under the colored cutouts.

But my secret delight was to take a bite of the paste when no one was looking. It tasted as good as it smelled. Every now and then, that scent (was it peppermint?) takes me back to those long-ago days.

Strange, but I don't remember a single schoolmate. Guess I was so fired up with my own importance... being in love with the teacher...getting to work with all those colors...and sneaking bites of paste that I didn't need anyone else in my small world!

—Doris Hegeman
Santa Rosa, California

ONE RING PLUS TWO RINGS. Going to the circus could be a learning experience, as Martha Heist found out.

Some Things You Just Can't Learn in Class

OUR FAMILY always went to watch the circus set up when it came to our town, Harrisburg, Pennsylvania, in the '30s and '40s. So one day my mother took my friend and me to the circus.

When we didn't show up at school, the truant officer was called. The next day, we had to fill out excuse cards. My mother wrote that we'd gone to the circus, but the school wouldn't accept that as a valid excuse.

Mother, a teacher herself, told the school that I learned more going to the circus than I would've at school. Eventually, our excuses were accepted.

—Martha Heist, Harrisburg, Pennsylvania

Athlete Took the Snap Then He Took the Fall

I WAS NO ANGEL, which is probably why I was assigned a seat directly in front of the English teacher in high school at Tonawanda, New York. The year was 1938, and I was 18 years old. I was an end on the football team, and the fullback sat behind me.

Our desks had inkwells in the top corner, and one day my teammate removed his and set it inside the desk. While the teacher was facing the blackboard, my friend managed to slip my suspender off my right shoulder and insert it in the inkwell hole.

From beneath the desktop, he began pulling on the suspenders, forcing my torso backward at a 45-degree angle.

The teacher kept admonishing me to sit up straight. Whenever she did, the innocent-looking creature behind me would release the pressure on my suspenders. As soon as the teacher turned around, he'd start pulling me backward again.

It didn't take long for the teacher's patience to wear thin. After several warnings, she said, "The next time I have to speak to you about sitting up straight, you're out the door."

Just then, I glanced down and noticed the button attaching one of the suspenders was coming unraveled from all the pressure. I started giggling and couldn't stop. The button got looser and looser. When it finally broke free, it hit the ceiling as if it'd been shot from a rifle.

When the teacher kicked me out of class, I had to hold my pants up with my hands. The suspenders were no longer serviceable.

I was expelled from class and football practice for a week. The perpetrator got off scot-free, but at least the team didn't have to go without the services of its fullback. Ends like me were a dime a dozen.
—Frank Keller
Tonawanda, New York

Hooky Players Paid the Price

By Robert Stein, Osseo, Minnesota

I'LL NEVER FORGET the day during my childhood in Aberdeen, South Dakota when my twin sister, Janet, and I were the victims of a school day that went awry.

It all started innocently enough with us waking up and getting ready for school. With breakfast finished, we hurried out the door and went over to walk to school with two neighbor boys, Richard and Jack Oachs.

It was not unusual for us to have to wait for them to finish eating and getting ready, but on this particular day they seemed to be taking forever. As we sat there, we kept our eyes on the wall clock as the minutes ticked by.

We knew we'd have to run to make up for lost time, but we'd done it many times before so weren't worried all that much. The boys didn't seem to be making any effort to eat or get dressed, so finally I said, "Hey, you guys—it's getting late! Let's go!"

Just then their mother spoke up, "Oh, didn't I tell you? The boys won't be going to school today."

"What???" screamed Janet. "Why didn't you tell us that when we came to the door? We've got a mile to go and now we'll be late. Gosh! Our mom will be furious. C'mon, Bob, if we hurry, we just might make it."

Poised to Run

Like a shot, I was right behind her, when one of the boys said sarcastically, "You'll never make it before the tardy bell rings, then you'll be sent to the principal's office and what excuse will you give?"

Now the principal, Mr. Rathman, had a disposition to match his name. Woe to the student who said, "We didn't wake up in time!" Such an excuse was not only unacceptable—it was a bald-faced lie that would only bring out the worst in him.

Foolishly, we listened as the boys convinced us to skip school and stay there with them. "We'll play cards and games and have all sorts of fun," said Jack. "Then when noon comes, you can go home, and your mom will never know you skipped. C'mon, whaddya say?"

We knew better, but playing games and having fun sounded far better than studying and listening to boring teachers. So we decided to stay, promising ourselves we'd stay indoors and keep out of sight, lest our mom see us.

As it turned out, we did have fun, but there was always that nagging thought, "What if Mom finds out?" It bothered our consciences to the point where we didn't have as much fun as we'd anticipated.

Finally, the clock struck 12, and we left the neighbor boys' house and went home.

Big Mistake!

It would've worked out fine if we'd have waited another 10 minutes or so, but figuring we'd gotten away with it, I guess we felt a little overconfident.

For some reason, Dad hadn't gone to work that morning. Anyway, when we came into the house, Mom met us at the door and, looking at the clock, asked, "What are you kids doing home from school so early?"

Her question aroused Dad's curiosity, and when I stammered and stuttered trying to come up with an answer, he knew immediately what had happened. Before I could protest, he had me over his knee and was tanning my behind!

Meanwhile, Janet had secreted herself in the outhouse. When Dad finished with me, he went out to the privy and gave her the same punishment he'd given me.

You can be sure neither of us ever played hooky again—nor ever forgot the worst spanking of our lives. Although we missed school that day, we did learn a lesson! ♫

SKETCHY EXCUSE. Artist and reformed hooky player Robert Stein submitted this drawing to go with his story about skipping school and the reception he and his sister got back home.

Chapter 11

Oh, Those School Clothes

Oh, Those School Clothes

One of the major mysteries of the universe is not black holes or the theory of relativity, but how clothing fads among schoolkids are spread. Solve this and you could command a communications force that makes the Internet look as slow as smoke signals.

Some girl in Pasadena decides to wear bedroom slippers with bunny rabbit faces to school on Tuesday morning, and by Wednesday noon, every teenage girl in America is wearing them.

Or a boy in Seattle shows up at school today wearing his basketball shorts down around his ankles, and before sunset, guys in Lost Cow, Wyoming and Frozen Toe, Minnesota have dropped *their* shorts to half-mast.

I asked a grandson why he and his pals were so willing to dress funny. "Grandpa, we're showing our individuality," he answered.

"So if everyone dresses alike, they're showing their individuality?"

He sadly shook his head, disappointed but not surprised that Old Geezer Grandpa just didn't get it.

And he's right. I don't get it. I don't get it because being enslaved to fashion fads is a luxury, and I had the misfortune to be a schoolkid when parents couldn't even afford necessities, much less frills and fads.

Mine was the era of hand-me-down clothes, glue-on rubber half soles, feed sack dresses and cheap little cotton blouses that were made in home economics class.

It was the era when a boy's clothes were expected to last 3 years. Year One was the "Stop complaining—you'll grow into it" year. Year Two was the "Fits Just Right Year." Year Three was "So the sleeves are too short—just don't whine" year.

How I envied my sister. Mom was an accomplished seamstress who could whip up a coronation gown while waiting for the biscuits to come out of the oven. As a result, Mary's clothes always fit just fine every year, rather than 1 year out of every 3.

That was the era when socks and underwear and handkerchiefs under the Christmas tree were, well, not welcome, but not a shock either. We did, after all, understand the facts of the day.

Along about sixth grade, Grandfather Strock gave me the absolute, positively *ultimate* Christmas present, a pair of leather high-top boots! Yes, and with a little pocket that held a jackknife.

The whole family sat there in stunned disbelief. Grandpa Strock was a notorious grouch and tightwad. Was it possible that somewhere behind that perpetual scowl actually beat a heart?

Sometimes the best things—including shoes and clothing—come from the most unexpected places.

—*Clancy Strock*

Homemade Dress Was A School Sensation

By Ruth Gale Tuttle, St. George, Utah

WHEN I SAW the three-tiered dress on movie actress Anita Louise in a magazine, I knew that was what I wanted to make for my senior project in 1937. Miss Corliss, our very prim, very British sewing teacher at Ogden (Utah) High School was aghast. She refused to allow me to make the dress and said I had to make one from a commercial pattern.

But I loved the dress and was determined to have one like it. I bought three shades of blue taffeta and worked on the dress at school and at home. Miss Corliss didn't approve and said I would fail her class.

I began to think she was right when I found out I had cut the tiered pieces so that the skirt was more than twice my waist size!

My mother was ill at the time and wasn't able to make the dress for me. But she encouraged me and showed me how to gather all the extra material in the back with a dropped waist.

I will never forget the astonished look on Miss Corliss' face when I walked into the fashion show. Then, when I walked out onto the "runway", the audience went wild and clapped. To my surprise, they kept clapping until Miss Corliss had me walk around again. I got an A!

But the senior sewing class project and fashion show wasn't the end of the enjoyment in my dress.

It was the "thing" for all senior girls to wear white formals to the graduation program. We didn't have robes.

My folks couldn't afford another dress for me, so I wore my beautiful dress again. And when I walked across the stage to get my diploma, I got another round of applause from the audience!

I continued to wear the dress after graduation to local and church dances. In fact, I wore it until I joined the WAVES in 1944.

And even after the war, I still found many occasions to wear the dress, and I always felt wonderful in it. ❧

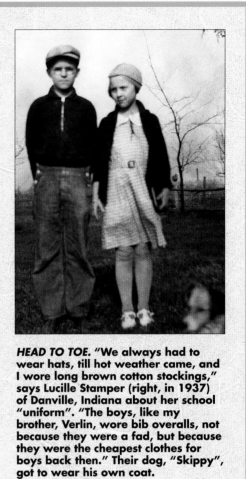

HEAD TO TOE. "We always had to wear hats, till hot weather came, and I wore long brown cotton stockings," says Lucille Stamper (right, in 1937) of Danville, Indiana about her school "uniform". "The boys, like my brother, Verlin, wore bib overalls, not because they were a fad, but because they were the cheapest clothes for boys back then." Their dog, "Skippy", got to wear his own coat.

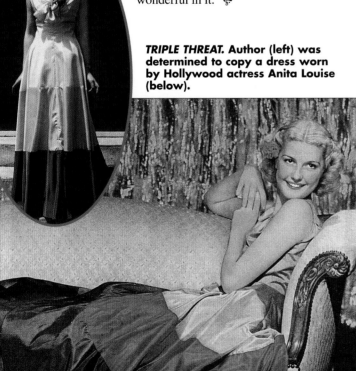

TRIPLE THREAT. Author (left) was determined to copy a dress worn by Hollywood actress Anita Louise (below).

Fresh Start, New Dress

MY FIRST DAY of school was in 1916. It was the day I got to wear a brand-new, blue and white checked gingham dress, with several rows of cross-stitching around the skirt, near the hem.

All though the eight grades of the one-room country school near Atkinsville, Missouri I attended, my mother made me a new dress for every first day.

I continued the tradition for my daughter, beginning in 1948. I made a new dress or blouse and skirt for her for every first day of school from kindergarten through high school.

When she was in second grade, I even made matching dresses for her and her favorite doll. During the year, I made matching dresses for my daughter and me.

But the dress-making tradition for the first day of school ended when my daughter had twin boys!
—*Marie Dilks, Holden, Missouri*

UNIFORMLY CUTE. "My daughters, Janette, 6 (left), and Ann, 9, are wearing their St. Vincent De Paul parochial school uniforms as they waited for the school bus on the first day of school in Mt. Vernon, Ohio in September 1961," writes Mary Jane McCann of Mt. Vernon. "They are also proudly showing their new school bags. My sons, George (top), 11, and John, 14, joined their sisters on the steps to wait."

Hot Wool, Warm Memories

EVEN WHEN THE temperature dropped to -10° in the Midwest, proper young girls were expected to wear inch-below-the-knees dresses to school in the '40s.

We prayed to avoid the inevitable. But after early-winter trial runs, and freezing our lower halves, we sadly yielded to wearing those itchy, double-ply woolen leggings.

Mine were made of the olive-drab material from Dad's World War II Army overcoat. But, pulled up under our cotton skirts, and tucked into our rubber boots, the leggings provided waist-to-ankle protection.

They also collected a crust of snow after a recess of making snow angels and snow forts. We had to pinch off these scales of snow before going back into school so as to not leave puddles that surely would have stained the hardwood floors.

The woolen leggings and wet mittens were placed on the radiator in the classroom. Even today, when we're deep into winter, I can still smell that homey, schoolhouse aroma of steaming wool. *—Judy Eshleman Onarga, Illinois*

Her First New Dress

BACK IN 1932, my family lived in a three-room house in Leavenworth, Washington. There were nine of us for Dad to feed and little work.

Then the WPA started, Dad got a job at the end of a pick and shovel and we got what was called relief, including commodities such as flour, canned meat and a few other things.

Along with the food items, all little girls got a new dress and boys got a new pair of pants and a denim shirt. My dress was black with little white flowers. That was my happiest day, as I had never had a new dress before, just hand-me-downs.

We got our clothes on Friday, but I just couldn't wait for Monday to show off my pretty dress. I carried it around, admiring it for the next 2 days and my mother kept saying, "If you don't hang that dress up, you will get it dirty and you won't be able to wear it to school."

Monday morning was such an exciting day. I must have been at the bus stop half an hour early to make sure I didn't miss my ride.

In the school cloakroom, I had a smile from ear to ear as I took off my shabby coat and hung it on a hook. I walked into my classroom so proud and so very happy, but soon my little heart was crushed.

As I looked around, almost every little girl had on the same dress, and all the boys had new pants and shirts just like my brothers'! *—Betty Formaz, Royal Oak, Michigan*

Stocking Had Its Place

WINTERTIME in my hometown of Kingston, Ontario meant cold, snow and ice for several months. I remember one of the things I hated most about winter were the long brown cotton stockings and garter belt worn by all schoolgirls in the 1940s.

My two sisters were 8 and 9 years younger than me, and they wore cute little white stockings.

The only time I didn't mind owning long brown stockings was on Christmas Eve, when we hung up our stockings for Santa Claus. Looking at the stockings of my sisters hanging next to my long brown stocking, I was glad I had long legs and didn't care what color sock I had to hang up! *—Elizabeth Dunbar, Lancaster, New York*

SAGGY WAS GOOD. Elizabeth Dunbar and her mother posed on Christmas 1943. The hated saggy cotton stockings were good only on Christmas Eve— when it took more gifts to fill them. "When this picture was taken, my two sisters hadn't been born yet, and my dad was overseas with the Canadian Infantry. He served for 3-1/2 years during the war."

'Cheap' Dress Gave Her Double Pleasure

By Dolly Smith Patterson
Laguna Hills, California

IT WAS THE RULE, back in 1925 when I was a high school senior in Covington, Ohio, that if you had a B or better average, you did not have to take the final exams. The exception was if you got a D or F in "Conduct".

I was always very mischievous, and my mother had warned me that if I got a bad grade in Conduct and had to take my final exams, I would have to wear a calico dress to the junior/senior prom.

Back then, calico was about the cheapest material you could buy. It was definitely not the fabric you'd choose for a prom dress. Sure enough, I got an F in Conduct. By the time that grade came out, Mother was wishing she hadn't promised me the punishment.

But when she asked me if I'd wear the calico dress if she made one, I said I sure would.

So Mother bought some yellow calico and made a dress with ruffles almost from top to bottom. She also made a bag to match, and my aunt, who was a milliner, made me a big picture hat rimmed in black velvet ribbon.

Arrival Was Anticipated

Everyone in high school and in the community had heard about my punishment, so they were looking forward to seeing me on prom night.

In those days, our mothers cooked the banquet dinner right at the school. So when I arrived, the mothers, as well as my classmates, were waiting to see what I was wearing.

"I knew you wouldn't wear calico," was the usual comment from those who got their first look at the dress.

"But this is calico," I was proud to reply. They couldn't believe calico could look so nice. In fact, all agreed the dress was the prettiest one at the prom *and* the cheapest.

My sister said I wasn't punished at all because Mother made a silk dress for me to wear at the baccalaureate service and commencement, so I got two dresses instead of one. ⚜

COVERED ALL CLOTHING. "We all wore our best clothes for this school picture taken in 1934 at the Bartlett Consolidated School, Bartlett, Iowa," shares Keith Eyler (first row, third from left) of El Cajon, California. "Overalls were the school clothing of choice. While they fit all right, school shoes were always two sizes too big so our feet could grow into them. When the soles wore out, we stuffed paper in the hole to keep our feet dry."

J.C. Allen and Son

She Recycled Her Dad's Clothes

WHEN I WAS a high school freshman in 1931, money for new clothes was hard to find. My dad had a job, but supporting our extended family was difficult.

My main concern was my inadequate wardrobe. I owned one decent skirt and two fairly nice blouses. But I could sew, and even if there was no money for fabric, I was determined to build an enviable wardrobe.

My father's office job required that he wear suits. When his trousers became too frayed to be worn, I carefully took them apart, cut off the legs and let down the cuffs, then used the material for a skirt. Luckily, I was petite.

If it happened to be a two-pair-of-pants suit, I could make a pleated or flared skirt or jumper. His worn-out shirts became tailored blouses.

This gave me several neat skirts and a rainbow of pretty blouses that were the envy of my friends, and all it cost was needle and thread!

—Betty Stoll, Hartville, Ohio

MORE THAN SEW-SEW. Enterprising young seamstresses like this girl and Betty Stoll could make their own school clothes when their families couldn't afford store-bought ones.

Saddle Shoes Made a Big Impression on Her

THERE WERE 24 girls in my class in 1942 in high school—23 had saddle shoes; I did not.

My feet were too big. If you wore a size 10, the only style was a sensible oxford with a Cuban heel, black in winter and, if you were lucky, white in summer. My mother wore them by choice, but I wore them because it was better than going barefoot.

One March day, my life changed. A Best and Co. catalog came, and it had saddle shoes in my size! My mother had carefully turned the page outward so I would see it immediately. I can still remember my joy when she told me she had mailed the order earlier in the day.

It took 6 days for the shoes to arrive, and those probably were the longest 6 days of my life. It was the custom in our house to wear anything new to church before wearing it anywhere else, but my mother said she didn't think I needed to wait until Sunday to wear my new shoes.

I could hardly wait until the next morning for school but, guess what? We had a nor'easter, and you never wore anything new in the rain. What a dilemma!

Should I risk ruining them in the rain or wait another day? I wore them and, fortunately, they were good quality and survived the storm. I was so proud of them, especially when the white part got dirty and I was like everyone else.

—Clare Mulqueen
East Falmouth, Massachusetts

Poetic Longing for "Longies"

WHEN MY BROTHER, Melford, was 9, in 1930, he wrote this poem, and it appeared in our local newspaper. We were living in Roosevelt, Minnesota at the time. Melford is gone now, but his memory and his poem live on.
—Earl Lofgren, San Diego, California

My Knicker Pants

I'm not worrying about my clothes,
Or the patches that I wear.
But these little knicker pants
I wish someone would tear.

Daddy says they're pretty,
And that they make boys grow,
And Mother makes me wear them
Every place I go.

To get a pair of "longies"
I'm saving all my cents.
For boys in school tease me
About my knicker pants.

If I live to be an old man,
And have a little boy,
To buy him a pair of "longies"
Will fill my heart with joy.

One Good Thing About Winter

By Lucille Ostman, Mora, Minnesota

IN THE '30s, when we went to Mora (Minnesota) Public School, we were not allowed to wear slacks in the winter. We had to wear long woolen underwear with a drop seat.

How we hated that long underwear! It was hard enough trying to get our long stockings to go over them smoothly. But by Friday, the legs were pretty well stretched, and a smooth look was all but impossible.

In the spring when we begged our mother to let us leave off the long underwear, her response was, "You wear them or you'll get rheumatism."

Outhouse Offered Solution

As pleading with our mother did no good, my two sisters and I got an idea. Halfway to school we passed a Swedish Lutheran church with an outhouse. We would stop in the outhouse, roll down our stockings, roll up our underwear, then pull our stockings back up. On the way home, we reversed the procedure.

All went well for a few weeks, then tragedy struck. While we were in the outhouse on the way home, rolling our long underwear back down, my youngest sister's hat fell down the hole!

The good news was everything down there was frozen solid. The bad news was we couldn't reach the hat, so we had to go home and tell our mother what happened.

She sent my older brother back with us. He took a hoe along and fished out the hat.

I don't remember what our punishment was for that transgression. But whenever I hear about long underwear, I recall that day and the long walk home, worrying over how we were going to tell our mother what happened. ❧

UP AND DOWN. Author (center) and her sisters, Rosalie and Evangeline, discovered a way to solve the long woolen underwear/stockings dilemma...for a while.

In Minnesota, Garter Belt Had Tentacles

By Bernie Young, Bishop, California

I HAVE MENTIONED the "garter belt" to many of my California friends and have always gotten the same response—"Huh?"

I grew up in Minnesota, where the winters were very cold and unusual measures were taken to keep small bodies warm and snug.

There were long scarves—one wrapped around the head like a babushka and the other wrapped around your mouth and neck, which allowed your glasses to get steamed up and icicles to form around your mouth. There were mittens strung through the sleeves of your bulky coat with a long piece of yarn. There were snow pants, sweaters, long underwear, socks and boots.

But the most awesome and memorable bit of paraphernalia was the blasted garter belt with its dangling tentacles.

And no matter how carefully the garter belt was hung on the radiator at night, it would take a contortionist to get it on with the first try in the morning. If you got the back in the back and the front in the front, it helped, but you weren't home free yet.

There was a strap over each shoulder, a strap around the tummy and a strap around the chest. Of course, at the bottom of the shoulder straps dangled four garters, two in the front and two in the back. The garters weren't used to hold up sheer beautiful nylons, but ugly brown stockings—another necessity on those cold winter days. ❧

Saddle Shoes Were a 'Must Have' Item

Rough 'n tough
thumps
'n scuffs
can't
throw

Rough Riders

Youngsters go for this
smart saddle shoe that's built
for rough 'n tumble wear. Full range of
widths and sizes for boys and girls. All
leather, genuine Goodyear welt construction.

TESTED AND
COMMENDED
by
PARENTS'
MAGAZINE
CONSUMER
SERVICE
BUREAU

Guaranteed by
Good Housekeeping

Smart and Sturdy Shoes for Boys and Girls

ROUGH RIDERS

CANNON SHOE COMPANY, BALTIMORE 17, MD.
252   See Good Housekeeping's Advertising Guaranty—Page 6

By Helena Ramage, Santa Barbara, California

JUNIOR HIGH SCHOOL in Fort Worth, Texas in the 1930s had a mixture of "oil barons' kids" and kids from families like mine—striving just to get along in the days of the Great Depression.

The rich kids were the style setters for the rest of us. The sporty look was "in", and brown and white saddle shoes exemplified it. I looked down at my black leather oxfords and hated them.

I envied the rich girls, dressed in expensive sweaters with skirts to match and saddle shoes, when they arrived in their chauffeur-driven limousines.

I knew we could never afford those clothes, but if only I could have shoes like theirs.

When the Montgomery Ward "wish book" came in the mail, I ran to show the saddle shoes to my mother.

"Look at these beautiful shoes. They're only

> *"I looked down at
> my black leather oxfords
> and hated them..."*

$2.98," I said. "Can we send for them? All the girls are wearing them," I added.

Mama looked sad and I thought she was going to cry, but she told me our family finances were tight right then.

"Right now, it's all we can do to pay the rent and eat," she said, giving me a hug. "Things will get better. You'll see."

I almost cried, but I didn't ask again. Still, I had to have those shoes!

The next morning, I was downstairs early and told Mama I wanted to go to school early to help my teacher. Every day I was late returning home, too, but she thought I was spending time with my girlfriend.

Instead, each day I was pocketing the bus fare. After a month, I showed Mama the $3 in nickels I had saved and the holes in my oxfords. I had been putting cardboard in the soles so I would be able to wear them for all my walking to and from school.

She didn't scold me for my deception, and she agreed to order the new saddle shoes.

When they came, I was walking on a cloud. Properly shoed, I was a member of the junior high "in" crowd.

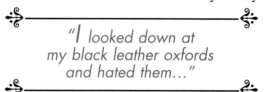

TWO-TONE TEMPTATIONS. Saddle shoes, such as the ones in this advertisement (left), were popular in the 1930s, '40s and '50s.

Senior Outfit Chronicled Her High School Career

SENIOR SKIRT. Erin White, a neighbor of Jan Morton's in Orlando, Florida, modeled Jan's senior skirt from Brookston High School. Erin borrowed the skirt and sweater for a "'50s day" at her school several years ago.

By Jan Morton, Orlando, Florida

ONE OF THE highlights of being a high school senior in the small Indiana town of Brookston in 1958 was getting to wear a "senior" skirt or pants.

Our school colors were black and gold, and in the summer before our senior year, every senior girl would buy a gold corduroy skirt and every senior boy would buy gold corduroy pants. We took them to someone who would personalize them by painting various identifying things on them.

My skirt had "Swing and Sway with Janice Kaye" across the back, and the imprint of my hand had my class ring painted to perfection. The skirt also contained all the organizations I belonged to and other personal information.

We would wear them nearly every day of our senior year, and even when they got dirty, we never washed them because the writing would fade.

Since all the schools in surrounding counties had senior skirts and pants, you immediately knew when you ran into a senior at a basketball game or other activity.

To this day, when you ask anyone in our small town about their senior skirt or pants, they're filled with great memories.

My senior skirt still holds a place in my heart and in my cedar chest. ♪

Comic Strip Adorned Skirt

DURING THE '50s, I went to Sweetser High School near Marion, Indiana and wore my senior "cords", a personalized skirt.

The characters on the front of my skirt were from the comic strip *Priscilla's Pop*.

Because of our namesake, I had a lot of fun wearing this skirt. —*Priscilla Beckett Marion, Indiana*

SENIOR "CORDS". Author models skirt showing her comic strip namesake.

CLASSMATE CLOTHES. "My father, Maurice Reisig, was always proud of our new (to us) cars and took this photo of one of them in 1942," explains Florence Reisig Chandler (above left) of Naples, Florida. "But my friend Evelyn Kill and I were just as proud of the look-alike outfits we made in our seventh-grade home economics class in Gasport, New York."

WELL SUITED. "Sewing was my favorite class in high school in northeast Washington, D.C.," says Elinor Rimar of Greenbelt, Maryland. "In 1941, I was 17 and made the Easter suit I'm wearing in front of my home there. I was very proud that the suit had turned out so well. The suit was navy blue, and my bag, hat and shoes were red. School was fun because I got to take the streetcar, and I also joined the girl cadets and practiced marching after school."

Good as a Taillight

I DON'T REMEMBER where I got the money for it, but as I watched my 6-year-old daughter, Doris, go off to school in Pleasant Valley, Iowa in her new green snowsuit, I felt so proud,

It was 1935, the height of the Depression, and Doris had been raised wearing hand-me-downs. It felt good to see her dressed in the warm snowsuit—the first brand-new one that she ever had—on this cold winter morning.

But when my little red-haired daughter came home, it was a different story. She was in tears, and the seat of that new snowsuit was completely in tatters.

There was a short, steep hill behind her country school. It was just right for sliding, and that's what the kids with sleds or pieces of cardboard did after school.

Having nothing else to slide on, Doris just sat down and slid on her bottom.

What could I do? There was no money for another snowsuit, and the only piece of material I had for repairs was a piece of blanket.

So that's what I used, and for the rest of the winter, Doris went to school in a bright green snowsuit, with a red plaid bottom.

We both remember it with a laugh, although it wasn't funny at the time.

—*Vern Berry, Bettendorf, Iowa*

SUITABLY ATTIRED. Doris Berry (center, front row) appears happier in this photograph than after her winter sliding escapade. See her mother's story above.

Sunday Best Made Weekday Appearance

FOR SOME REASON, I wanted to dress up for my afternoon classes one day in 1938 when I was in second grade at Berthelet School, in Montreal, Quebec.

When I went home for lunch, I sneaked my Sunday best dress, a light blue, see-through organdy, into the hall, and changed from the red print dress I had worn that morning.

When I got back to school, the teacher said, "My, what a pretty dress Rosalind is wearing. Come up and let us all see it."

As I proudly walked up the aisle, all the boys started snickering. It was then that it dawned on me. In my haste to change my dress, I had forgotten to wear my lace-trimmed matching slip, so my bright red print panties shone forth like a beacon!

—*Rosalind Haynes*
Barrie, Ontario

SAFE DRESS. Rosalind Haynes' red print dress (left) was a better choice for school than her organdy one.

Chapter 12

Our Most Memorable Teachers

Our Most Memorable Teachers

When you think back over your school days and, later, your childrens', you often discover something remarkable: The lucky ones came under the spell of one special teacher.

Not just a *good* teacher, because there are many more competent teachers than the school critics would lead us to believe. I'm talking about *great* teachers. Teachers who magically burrowed into our heads and hearts, showing us that learning was fun, not dreadful drudgery.

I didn't understand what was going on when I encountered my first truly great teacher. But years later I watched it happen to my own seven children.

In one case it was a man who taught fifth-grade mathematics. He was like no teacher they had encountered …offbeat, unconventional and—imagine it—*fun!*

What was going on here? Arithmetic was supposed to be sheer misery, not fun. But, gee, it actually was important in everyday life, whether you were making change at the store or discovering why playing the lottery was for chumps, thanks to something called *odds.*

Mr. Seiller upset a few parents, who thought you weren't being educated if you weren't being bored to tears. They just knew there was something wrong with a teacher who bet sticks of chewing gum on the outcome of football games…and kept the winnings.

But the kids had a ball in that class, learning lessons that they profited from during their whole lifetime.

Years later, three of my children fell under the spell of a lady English teacher at the Torrejon Air Base school outside Madrid, Spain. I knew something was out of whack when they came home actually bubbling with excitement over grammar, for pity's sake!

It wasn't right. One thing I had learned over the years was that most English teachers thought their mission in life was to turn children against their native language.

It was a mystery worth digging into. What I discovered was a lady who was convinced that language, whether spoken or written or sung, had only one purpose—to help people communicate. Not learn a bunch of stuffy rules.

And guess what? When the kids saw that she was right, *then* they wanted to learn the rules.

I didn't meet my own unforgettable teachers until high school and then college. One set me off on a delightful career that brings me pleasure to this day. Another got me excited about American history—lighting a fire that still burns 50 years later.

Yet another taught me about honesty and ethics, and why life was poor indeed without the presence of both virtues in your heart.

To be touched by an unforgettable teacher is a life-changing experience that affects you forever. Just read the following stories and see why. —*Clancy Strock*

'Tea Party' Taught Girl to Cherish Her Natural Beauty

By Frances Erb, Pittsburgh, Pennsylvania

DURING MY junior year of high school, back in the 1930s, I showed up for school one day with my hair dyed a flamboyant red. I wore oodles of makeup and painted my fingernails blood-red. My outfit was a tight emerald-green silk dress with a deep-cut back, green ankle socks and pumps.

I thought I looked glamorous. All the other girls in my class wore simple cotton dresses or skirts and blouses, and they all wore stockings.

My homeroom teacher did a double take when she saw me, but she didn't say anything. Born and raised in England, Miss Petty spoke with a clipped British accent and wore plain but elegant suits and dresses. She had expressive, beautiful hands, which she washed frequently in our cloakroom with a small hand brush.

One day shortly after I started wearing my flamboyant clothes, Miss Petty invited me to have tea with her after school in our homeroom. I was flattered.

She'd never done that for any other student, and I'd never been to a tea party. I thought it must be something like the coffee klatches my mother attended.

Stage Was Set

After school, I made a beeline for my homeroom and found Miss Petty setting up a large round card table. She covered it with a fine tablecloth of linen and lace, then put matching napkins at our places. The table was set with thin bone china and a silver tea service. In the center of the table were two lilies in a tall silver vase.

LOVELY LESSON. When Frances Erb, shown here at age 17, was invited to tea with a respected high school teacher in the 1930s, she got more than cookies and petit fours.

Miss Petty put tiny tea sandwiches on a plate and asked me to put the petit fours and cookies on another. She brewed the tea, sliced a lemon and stuck cloves in the slices, and filled the silver pitcher with cream. It all looked so lovely that I thanked her right then.

As we visited and enjoyed our tea, we had a lively conversation. Suddenly Miss Petty pointed to the vase and asked me which lily I liked best. I looked at the flowers closely. They were real, but one was pure white, and the other was painted gold. The gold lily looked stiff and unnatural, while the white one was fragrant and lovely.

"I like the white one best," I said.

"Why?" she asked.

"It looks right to me," I replied. "It smells divine, and it is so clean-looking."

A Pointed Question

"Then tell me," Miss Petty said, "why you are gilding a beautiful lily—you. Frances, take a good look at yourself. With all that makeup, your hair and your way-out clothes, you're spoiling something beautiful, and in the process making yourself look cheap."

I was so shocked I couldn't eat another bite. I was hurt and angry. How could she say such things to me? For days, I fretted and fumed every time I went to my homeroom.

Then one day it dawned on me how much trouble Miss Petty had taken to get her message across. After that, I became very thankful for her advice. I bought a copy of Emily Post's book on manners and studied it. I went back to wearing skirts and blouses, learned to apply makeup with a light touch and never colored my hair again.

Miss Petty and I became friends. I asked her about my problems, and she gave me sincere, straightforward answers. All her criticism was constructive. Miss Petty went the extra mile with me. I wish all students could be so lucky.

Reading Opened New World For Disadvantaged Farm Girl

WHEN I WAS YOUNG, my family moved around a lot, following the crops in season. As a result, my sister and I missed more school than we attended.

In 1955, we were put into foster care in Pulaski County, Arkansas. I was 8 years old and should have been in third grade, but I was placed in second grade because I could not yet read.

My teacher, Mrs. Welchman, was a miracle worker. She didn't just teach me to read—she opened up a whole new world for me.

BOOKS WERE KEY. Second-grade teacher introduced Sharron McDonald (above) to a lifetime of reading.

Mrs. Welchman introduced me to Dick, Jane, Sally and Spot. They became my friends, and I accompanied them on many exciting adventures.

As my skills improved, I devoured everything Mrs. Welchman gave me to read. She didn't scold me when I read ahead of our group—she knew I needed to explore beyond the day's assigned reading. To keep me challenged, she also let me help the students who were having trouble with reading.

Mrs. Welchman understood that poor, neglected farm girl's hunger for words. She introduced me to something that would inspire, encourage and sustain me for the rest of my life.

—*Sharron McDonald*
Springdale, Arkansas

"Banana Bash" Multiplied Child's Math Interest

WITH SIX hungry mouths to feed during the Depression, my parents couldn't afford any frills. Bananas were considered a luxury and were rarely seen at our house.

When I began third grade, my teacher, Mrs. Luke, had a plan to motivate us to master the multiplication tables. With colored chalk, she drew a lovely palm tree that reached the top of the blackboard. Next to the palm tree, she drew a ladder with 12 rungs and a great bunch of bananas at the top.

Each rung of the ladder represented one of the "times tables". The plan was to memorize each "rung", then step up to the next one. The first 10 students to reach the top would earn a reward—an after-school banana party.

Flash cards flipped furiously at my house as I studied the multiplication tables. I was determined to win.

In the 67 years since, nothing has ever tasted better than those bananas. I seldom peel one without thinking of Mrs. Luke's banana bash.

—*Irene Pollock, St. George, Utah*

Shared Books Whetted Girl's Appetite for Reading

OUR READING teacher in fifth grade read books to us every Friday. She would bring a novel from her well-stocked library at home and read it to us week after week until the book was finished.

I was so entranced that I never took my eyes off her. She must have noticed this, because she invited me to her home and let me pick out a book each week to take home and read on my own.

This whetted an appetite for reading that continues to this day. I'll never forget the influence that she had on my life.

—*Louise Perrin*
Idabel, Oklahoma

LATE LEARNER. Author (second boy from right) realized years later that his teacher was smarter than he thought.

"Forgetful" Teacher Was Smarter Than Pupils Knew

MY FIRST-GRADE teacher in Onslow, Iowa was marvelous and gave us a solid foundation for learning.

Miss McCune focused on new material in the early part of the school day, writing what we needed to remember on the blackboard. After recess, she often asked us to get out pencil and tablet, then gave us an oral quiz on the material she'd covered earlier that morning.

We thought Miss McCune was forgetful, because sometimes she neglected to unroll the large map that hung over the blackboard, so the test answers were in plain sight, right where she'd written them that morning. All we had to do was copy them.

Years later, I realized this "forgetfulness" had a purpose. While we thought we were getting away with something, Miss McCune was testing our ability to comprehend the lesson, read it on the blackboard and put it down on paper.

—*Floyd Streeper*
Gulfport, Mississippi

Meeting Tough Standards Paid Lifetime Of Dividends

By Katherine Patulski, Milwaukee, Wisconsin

MY HIGH-SCHOOL English teacher in Memphis, Tennessee was very demanding. But her toughness had a huge impact on my life.

Grace Mauzy made us write all our assignments in ink—either dip-pen or fountain pen. (There were no ballpoints in the early 1940s.) If you made a mistake, you couldn't scratch it out and continue. You had to use chlorine to remove the ink, then dry the paper and continue.

Miss Mauzy made no corrections when she marked our papers. Instead, she used abbreviations to indicate errors—"SP" for spelling, and "F" for a form error, like using an adjective instead of adverb form, for example. Errors requiring more explanation were numbed in the margin and described on the back of the paper, such as "No. 1—Your first statement is not a good introductory sentence."

When we got our papers back, we had to correct the errors. If we didn't understand them, we had a conference with Miss Mauzy.

Of course, this meant she had to grade every paper twice. But it also meant that we had to do more than just look at the test and throw it away.

After graduation, I began working in a defense plant, picking up invoices and recording them in a ledger in ink. I started on the night shift but was moved to day shift after 3 months.

I'd been on the day shift about 10 days when my supervisor told me Mr. Higley wanted to see me in his office. I gasped, "What did I do wrong? Why does the big boss want to see me?" My supervisor couldn't tell me.

What Did She Do Wrong?

By the time I got to Mr. Higley's office, my hands were shaking. He told me to sit down while he finished some paperwork. Beads of perspiration formed on my brow. When he finally put down his pen, I blurted, "Sir, what did I do wrong?"

He smiled and said, "What makes you think you did anything wrong? You've done things quite right! You're the first young person we've hired who could write with a pen without making a mistake. We're giving you a $5-a-week raise."

I was shocked. Five dollars was quite a lot of money then. I wrote to Miss Mauzy and thanked her for being tough.

The following January, I started night school and enrolled in a freshman English class. At the first class, the professor asked us to write an essay so he could determine our skill levels. Of course, I wrote mine in ink. I was the first to finish.

The next week, the professor returned my paper and said, "Miss Carpenter, you're a Memphis girl, aren't you?"

"Yes, sir, I am."

"And I suppose you attended Central High School," he said.

"Yes, sir, I did."

"And was Grace Mauzy ever your teacher?"

"Yes, sir, she was, for all three years I was there."

"Well, in that case, you do not need this class," he said. "Go to the office and sign up for the second-semester class."

Free Credit!

I couldn't believe it. I'd just received the equivalent of three college credits, at no cost in time, money or effort! Again, I wrote Miss Mauzy and thanked her for being tough. I kept in touch with her until she passed away.

In 1960, I was living in Milwaukee when my husband died, leaving me with two small children. I began working at a technical college, teaching English as a second language.

My students ranged in age from 16 to 76. Some had university degrees from their homelands; some were illiterate in their native languages. I had as many as 13 language groups in a class.

The job was fascinating, but not easy. I thought of Miss Mauzy and patterned my techniques after hers.

Sometimes a student would ask, "Teacher, do I have to do this? It is really important?"

I would reply, "Can you see down the road 5 years from now? Suppose you had a chance at a promotion or a better job if you had this skill. If you didn't have it, would you be unhappy that I hadn't taught it to you?

"Do me a favor. Learn it. Practice it. Then go out and work for 5 years. If, after that time, you think I've wasted your time, come back and tell me, and I promise I'll listen."

Over the next 20 years, many students came back after finishing their courses to thank me for being tough. Not one came back to say I'd wasted his or her time.

I wish I could write to Miss Mauzy to thank her again, but I will always thank her in my heart. She truly had a big impact on my life. ❧

NO MISTAKES. The author, shown above in a high school photo, learned life lessons that she later offered to her own students. Her teacher, Grace Mauzy (inset), taught much more

At This School, Students Wanted a Front-Row Seat!

THE FIRST 6 years of my education in the 1930s were at Koch's School, a one-room schoolhouse in Macungie, Pennsylvania. Our teacher was Charles Berger, a fine gentleman who loved kids. On the first day of every term, we all rushed to school in hopes of getting a seat in front.

There were 35 to 40 students in grades one through eight. Whenever Teacher called one of the classes up front for a lesson, the first pupil to get there was allowed to sit on his lap. You should've seen the rush!

Friday afternoons were devoted to "trapping". The pupils sat on class benches, and Teacher asked us about the material we'd covered that week, starting with the pupil at the left end of the bench.

When a student couldn't answer, Teacher moved on to the next one. If that pupil answered correctly, he or she moved to the left of the first student. Ultimately, the brightest pupils were at the left end of each bench, "at the head of the class". We all loved Teacher and paid close attention to him so we could sit at the head of our class.

Teacher paid two of the older boys 25¢ a week to carry drinking water from a nearby farmhouse. We also could earn money by carrying in buckets of coal, clapping erasers and emptying the wastepaper basket.

On the next-to-last day of the school year, Teacher took us for a walk through a pine forest. Whenever we spotted a wildflower, we showed it to Teacher, who identified it and recorded it on a tablet. The pupil who found the most flowers received a prize.

On the last day of school, Teacher treated us to a picnic and provided all the food. I especially remember his delicious fruit salad because it contained bananas, which were a rarity in those days.
—*Albert Schantz*
Reading, Pennsylvania

Truth Was Best Defense For Missing Homework

TO GRADUATE from my high school in Freeport, New York, we had to take American history, which was taught by the most feared teacher in school. We considered Miss Boardman humorless, intransigent and strict, plus, she assigned homework.

Appearing in class without having done one's assignment was not an option. And I never faltered—until an older cousin came up with an extra ticket to the Metropolitan Opera and asked me to go. I'd never been to the opera before.

Getting to the Met meant taking the Long Island Railroad to my cousin's place, then riding the subway to the city. I arrived home many hours past my normal bedtime, dreaming of Verdi rather than history.

The next day, as history class approached, I realized my predicament. Since I didn't want Miss Boardman to announce my delinquency to the whole class, I decided to face the dragon in her lair. On the way to my seat, I went up to her and confessed, "No homework."

Miss Boardman looked astonished. "Why not?" she said, eyebrows raised.

I didn't think she'd go for the "my dog ate it" routine, so I settled on a novel dodge—the truth.

I almost fell through the floor when Miss Boardman said, "I imagine you got more from the opera than from a history assignment."

I may have imagined it, but I thought for a moment that Miss Boardman almost smiled.
—*Jerome Nolan*
Wilmington, North Carolina

Teacher's Small Surprises Made Hard Times Easier

IN THE EARLY 1930s, most families in our Louisiana community had good farm food on their tables. But times were hard, and there were certain delicacies some of us had never tasted.

Our geography teacher must have guessed this. During our study of Italy, "Miss Della" brought in a jar of olives for us to sample. They were the first I'd ever eaten, and I immediately liked the taste.

Miss Della had other welcome surprises for her classroom. One was a penny pencil eraser awarded to those of us who could spell "Montezuma" correctly. And I was thrilled when she drew my name for a Christmas gift. I cherished the toy accordion she gave me.
—*Janie Griffith*
Shreveport, Louisiana

MISS DELLA. Author's teacher used creative methods to teach lessons.

Shy Student Fainted Away At Prospect of Reciting

I DIDN'T have much confidence in myself when I started sixth grade at Washington Elementary School in Manchester, Connecticut.

I'd never enjoyed school much to begin with, and I'd been confined to bed with rheumatic fever for most of fifth grade. There was no way I could ever catch up on all my subjects.

But my teacher, Miss Shea—who was also the school principal—had other ideas. She stayed with me after school every day, working for hours without overtime pay to make sure I passed on to seventh grade.

I made progress in the work I'd missed, but speaking before the class was my downfall. In those days, we had to memorize poetry and recite it. I loved the poems, but whenever I looked out at the faces in the classroom, I fainted.

This happened so often that it got to be a habit. I'd be standing in front of the class one minute, and the next thing I knew, I was waking up in the nurse's office.

Dynamic Teacher Brought Class Back Up to Speed

BETWEEN 1942 and '45, St. Petersburg, Florida had several wartime training bases that kept many people on the move, including teachers. My class had so many different teachers in a 2-year period that by the time we started fifth grade, we had lots of catching up to do.

Our teacher, Mrs. Della Reed, had her work cut out for her. Yet somehow she managed to teach us everything we should've learned in third and fourth grades, and covered our fifth-grade work besides.

One of her tricks was working on "times tables" all day. We could be in the middle of music class, when suddenly Mrs. Reed would call out, "Shirley! Four times five equals what?" We had to reply just as fast as she'd fired off the question, or we'd be writing the "four tables" several times.

This woman had eyes in the back of her head. She could be writing on the blackboard and, without turning around, catch Noble flying a paper airplane at Robert, or Ruth passing a note to Barbara. Punishments consisted of cleaning up the school yard with a stick that had a nail attached at the end, or standing with your nose pressed to the blackboard. The worst was being sent to the principal's office for a paddle across your behind.

We couldn't wait for the end of the school year so we could get away from this hard-driving woman. Maybe we'd have an easy teacher for sixth grade. But when September arrived and we stepped into our classroom, there was Mrs. Reed—again!

Looking back, Mrs. Reed was the best teacher we ever had. She was our doctor, with a needle for our sandspurs and bandages for our cuts. She was a psychiatrist, helping us with our problems. She prepared us for life's ups and downs, gave us the best 2 years of our lives, and sent us off to junior high with a dinner banquet and sixth-grade graduation I'll never forget.

I kept in touch with Mrs. Reed until she passed away in 1956. I lost a dear friend, but will always cherish my memories.
—*Ruth Davis*
Largo, Florida

PLAYED CATCH-UP. Despite wartime moves, one teacher worked hard to help Ruth Davis (front row, second from right) and other students bring their education up to date.

Miss Shea started having me recite my poems when everyone else was gone. She told me to look at the ceiling instead of the class. "I know you can do it," she'd say encouragingly.

This worked when it was just the two of us, but the first time I tried it in class, I was back on the nurse's cot.

At our next after-school session, Miss Shea had me turn my back to the empty classroom and recite. When I tried this in class the following day, I recited my poem without a hitch. The next face I saw wasn't the nurse's, but Miss Shea's. She was smiling. I got an A.

Learning to cope with this difficult situation enabled me in later years to give talks and address large groups of people. I owe it all to Miss Shea, the teacher who taught me self-confidence.
—*Dolores Eberhard, Bountiful, Utah*

Teacher Took Time To Take Chill Off

I REMEMBER my teacher from first and second grade very well. Her name was Marion Miller, and she taught at the one-room Powder Valley School in rural Pennsylvania.

One winter morning in the late 1920s, I arrived at school with my feet practically frozen. I was hurting so much that I couldn't help but cry.

So before starting classes, Miss Miller sat down with me, her hands in leather gloves, and vigorously massaged my feet for almost half an hour. It sure made them feel better.

Long after that, my teacher became my sister-in-law when I married her brother.
—*Beulah Miller*
Zionsville, Pennsylvania

TEACHER SHARED WARMTH. Author remembers a kind act of her teacher, Marion Miller (left), at Powder Valley School (below).

With Papa's Help, Value Of Math Began Adding Up

I HAD A LOT of trouble with mathematics my first 2 years at school in Beverly, Massachusetts. Fortunately, my father taught in another city and was able to tutor me in the evenings.

One night I got particularly frustrated with some subtraction problems and burst into tears. "I don't know why I have to learn math anyway," I sobbed. "I hate it!"

My father paused a moment, then said, "Well, I guess you could get along without arithmetic if you want to. I know a man who couldn't add or subtract, and he got by all right. Of course, if he went into a store and bought something that was, say, $1.53, and he only had a $5 bill, he never knew if the clerk was cheating him when he got his change."

Papa left me to think that over. It didn't take me long to realize I had to learn arithmetic. My allowance was only 5¢ or 10¢ a week, and I couldn't afford to be cheated out of even a penny at the candy store.

I went back to the problems with renewed vigor, and went on to get passing grades in math throughout my school years—even in trigonometry. Apparently, my father had a knack for using the power of suggestion. —*Patricia Munroe*
Madison, Maine

Students Worked Hard to Please Glamorous Teacher

EVERY STUDENT in our small public school in Gary, South Dakota remained in the same building all 12 years. After completing grades one through eight, we simply climbed the stairs to the high-school classrooms.

Catherine Clifford came to our school around 1930 to teach all 4 years of high school English. When she swept grandly into our classroom on the first day of English I, we greeted her with utter stillness. We were in awe.

Miss Clifford was a tall woman, beautifully dressed, with stylish shoes and sheer stockings. Her dazzling copper hair was smartly coiffed, and an ethereal fragrance enveloped her. I felt certain even the portrait of George Washington that hung in our classroom took notice.

Miss Clifford's wonderful fragrance wafted through the classroom every day. When she came down the aisle and bent near someone to answer a question, it was hard to remember the question you wanted to ask. We were overcome by her loveliness.

Her most remarkable attribute, however, was her knowledge of the English language and her skill and patience in imparting it. The more obtuse students worked valiantly to understand the material and please her. A little praise, a smile and the twinkle in her eyes were reward enough. All of us adored and respected her. —*Mildred Reinhardt*
Palisade, Minnesota

Teacher's Extra Effort Helped Child Catch Up

AS A YOUNG CHILD living on the edge of the Rocky Mountains in Montana, I had a hearing problem. People thought I was deaf, or nearly so.

When I was 9, we moved to the Puget Sound area and my hearing problem disappeared. Apparently the high altitude in Montana had been the culprit.

As soon as my wonderful third-grade teacher found out about my history, she began teaching me everything I should have learned in first and second grades. I am 84 now, but I will never forget Miss Monahan. She truly changed my life.

—*Margaret Hiscox, Tacoma, Washington*

No-Nonsense Teacher Ensured All Her Pupils Learned to Read

By Mary McCammon
Rolling Prairie, Indiana

MY FIRST-GRADE teacher's mission in life seemed to be making sure that all her pupils could read—and read well.

Lottie Pickerl taught a combined first- and second-grade classroom at Wagner School in South Bend, Indiana when I began school in 1955. To ensure our success at reading, Mrs. Pickerl used phonics cards, the "Dick and Jane" reader and a dark blue wooden pointer that she used at the blackboard. She also used the pointer to swat anyone who dared to talk during her presentations.

Under the blackboard were 10 small red chairs and one large oak chair. Each morning, Mrs. Pickerl would seat herself on the oak chair, and a row of students would fill the remaining chairs. One by one, we would read to her.

When Mrs. Pickerl was satisfied that a child knew the lesson, that child would return to his or her desk. Then the entire line of pupils would move down one chair until we'd all had a turn and the seats were empty.

Mothers volunteered to come in each day and cook our lunches in a cramped 6- x 12-foot kitchen. Bottled milk was delivered in wire racks.

A different student was chosen each day to puncture the lids with a special round tool and insert a straw in each bottle. We received chocolate milk about once every 2 weeks, much to our delight.

Boiler Room Off Limits

Our classroom was near the boiler room, which we were forbidden to enter. The only students who ever went into the boiler room were those accompanied by the principal and his paddle.

Directly outside the back door was a large boulder, which was used to beat the chalk dust out of the erasers. We were so disappointed when we moved to a new school in 1958 and found an electric eraser cleaner, complete with an attached dust bag.

Of all my experiences at Wagner, though, one stands out above all the others. My desk was directly in front of Mrs. Pickerl's, and from time to time I observed her discreetly reach into her desk, extract a gold pill case and place a tiny white pill in her mouth.

For a 6-year-old, this was frightening. I associated pills with sickness. Besides, Mrs. Pickerl was 64, which seemed very old to me. I feared she could die any day. And then who would teach me to read?

As it turned out, my fears were unfounded. Mrs. Pickerl not only lived to teach me to read, but outlived Wagner School, as well as the school that replaced it. She didn't pass away until 1999—at the age of 108! ✦

READING TIME. When students such as those at right sat in a row for reading lessons, they got special attention. Mary McCammon (above) remembers those lessons and other events from her school days in the 1950s.

Trolley Didn't Show Up, But Her Principal Did

IN THE 1930s, Bayonne, New Jersey had a citywide program in which children who tested above a certain level were allowed to complete seventh and eighth grades in a single year. I was one of those children.

Instead of attending a neighborhood school, I rode a trolley car to a special school 35 blocks away. One day the trolley didn't come. Missing school wasn't acceptable, so I started to walk. I met several classmates along the way.

Suddenly a big touring car pulled up alongside us and the driver called out, "Are you kids from Henry Harris School? Hop in!" It was our principal, C.S. Havens. He followed the trolley line and picked up all his students.

Mr. Havens loved children. Why else would he stand on the stage at our assemblies and teach the whole student body to sing *I'm a Yankee Doodle Dandy*—in Latin? I can still sing it!
—*Marjorie Varga*
Ormond Beach, Florida

Gifted Storyteller's Tales Kept Pupils Entranced

MRS. LYNCH, my fourth-grade teacher, was my favorite by far. She was a jolly, happy woman who gave each of us her love, time and attention. She made learning fun and was so good to us that we were all eager to please her.

As a mother herself, she was very aware of children's feelings. If there was a discipline problem, she would not embarrass a child in front of everyone. Instead, she'd call the child aside and take care of the matter quietly.

At the end of the school day, Mrs. Lynch would tell us stories. She was a wonderful storyteller and kept us on the edge of our seats with some of her tales. Even the more rowdy kids were spellbound, listening to every word she said.

Sometimes it took several days for her to finish a story, but we always remembered exactly where the story had stopped the day before.

In those days we had no TV, but Mrs. Lynch's stories were better than anything shown on television.
—*Nancy Hight, Jackson, Tennessee*

Bighearted Teacher Made Learning Fun

I STARTED first grade at a three-room country school in Flea Hop, Alabama. At the beginning of the year, we used the room on the north side of the building to stay as cool as possible, since the building had no electricity. In cold weather, we moved to the room on the south side of the building, where the potbellied stove burned you on one side while you froze on the other.

Fannie Lee Adams was our teacher. She drove an old 1928 Chevrolet with the back of the passenger seat removed so she could carry more children on rainy days. I had to walk 1-1/2 miles to school, and Mrs. Adams often gave me a ride home.

Mrs. Adams was a small lady with a big heart and a good sense of humor. Under her firm but gentle hand, school was fun as well as a place to learn.

HAPPY MEMORIES. Bertha Whetstone (above) enjoyed Flea Hop School. She sent a picture of a class from the 1890s, long before she was born.

I'll never forget the treasure hunt at Easter. Mrs. Adams went to a lot of trouble to make it fun, placing clues around the neighborhood. We were so excited as we ran from clue to clue. The hunt ended at school, with a basket of eggs for our treasure. The eggs were then hidden for our Easter egg hunt. After we found them, we sat on the grass, eating eggs and candy.

Before school was out in spring, we went on a picnic at Woodall Creek, between Flea Hop and Eclectic. Our mothers brought lemonade and baskets of food for lunch, and we played games and waded in the creek.

Our little schoolhouse had no sophisticated equipment, but we learned our lessons and didn't get promoted to the next grade unless we earned it. We were taught respect for our fellowman and for ourselves.

I miss that little school, the closeness of family and friends, and I miss Mrs. Adams most of all.
—*Bertha Whetstone*
Wetumpka, Alabama

Brown Brothers

TYRANT REMEMBERED FONDLY. Sewing classes, like the one pictured at left, remind Grace Baxter of the helpful lessons she learned from the feared "Iron Maiden". Her story is below.

In truth, she did have an iron character—no one would have been surprised to see her leading the Prussian Army!

But with all her bulk and muscle, this woman taught us the niceties and necessities of managing a home. She showed us how to make a bed (no wrinkles permitted!) and how to set a table. Silverware had to be exact inches from the dinner plate, and the water and wine glasses were each placed on marked outlines on a paper tablecloth.

She also taught us how to cook and clean, but most of all, she taught us how to sew. On old Singer treadle machines, we'd treadle in time to classical music played on an ancient phonograph.

I can still hear her saying, "Young ladies, you have no rhythm. How will you ever dance with a young gentleman?"

In eighth grade, under her exacting guidance, we made our own graduation dresses—machine-sewn seams exactly 5/8 of an inch from the edge. We hand-stitched the entire dress from the fancy collar to the hand-rolled hem.

And each tiny stitch had to be the same size—if it wasn't, you ripped it out and began again. How many times can you do that to white organdy before it becomes black organdy?

Now, each time I begin a project, hand- or machine-sewn, I recall Miss Euhlein and say a prayer for the "tyrant" who taught me to sew and would accept nothing less than perfection. ❖

My Years with the Iron Maiden

By Grace Baxter, Uniondale, New York

SHE WAS the most feared member of the faculty at Public School 71 in the Bronx, New York—even more feared than Dr. Kinney, the principal.

The boys called her "Iron Maiden"; the girls called her Miss Euhlein. She was the Home Economics teacher, and although we girls were afraid of her, we respected her, too.

Looking back on those days, I realize that her nickname described her very accurately. A large big-boned woman, she always dressed in gray and white or black and white.

Costumed appropriately, she could have been the diva in a Wagnerian opera. Her gray hair was drawn severely back from her face and tightly braided to form a crown on her head.

Steel-blue eyes peered from her fleshy face as she looked through you. And, if you were unfortunate enough to be caught breaking a rule, the roar of a lion would come from her narrow, prim mouth.

Her body was encased in an all-in-one corset, straining for release as could be seen by the pull on the seams of her dress.

Students Didn't Need This Kind of "Special Attention"

z z z z z z z

WHEN the weather started getting warm at the Red Hill School in southern Ontario during the '30s, time seemed to pass too slowly and lessons were getting boring. Our teacher, Miss Wilson, knew how to ease the situation.

She'd begin by asking questions at random to various students, boys being a favorite target. Sooner or later, one of them would respond with a stupid answer that would cause a ripple of laughter to go through the room.

Obviously, the poor kid had been half asleep. Some might say the humane thing would be to let him continue his slumber. But Miss Wilson was determined to bring him back to reality.

More questions followed in quick succession, keeping the boy off-balance and making for even more hilarious answers. Although the classroom was rocking with laughter, our teacher pressed on, undisturbed by the commotion.

Five minutes of this kind of grilling and the kid would be wide-awake—although he might barely remember his own name! But of one thing he was sure: He wouldn't go to sleep again in Miss Wilson's class.

—*Robert Dorman*
Burlington, Ontario

Struggling Student Excelled With Aunt's Loving Tutelage

By Marlon Rosenberger, Longwood, Florida

AFTER COMPLETING second grade at a school in town, I was passed "on trial" to third grade. I just wasn't making it, and I couldn't get any help from my teacher. If I couldn't read my lesson, she'd just tell me to sit down and then call on the next pupil.

My Aunt Myrtle lived on a farm with my uncle and grandmother and taught at a country school. When she heard about my problems, she said, "Now, this is just nonsense. You're a bright boy, Marlon, and there's no reason why you can't learn."

After talking with my mother, they agreed on a solution. I would go live on the farm and attend Aunt Myrtle's school. She would be my teacher.

Went to "Night School"

That fall, I began attending third-grade classes with Aunt Myrtle during the day and repeating the first two grades with her at night. I could be tough to handle during those "night shifts", but Aunt Myrtle was firm and reminded me that we were doing this for my benefit. She even taught me during our 1-mile walk to and from school.

Aunt Myrtle was relentless—the kids I see misbehaving today would never have had a ghost of a chance with her. But I loved her very much, and she began getting through to me. I never could have found or afforded an education like the one she gave me, because it was given with so much love.

I stayed on the farm and attended Aunt Myrtle's school through fifth grade. Then I was sent back to my widowed mother in town—and back to the town school.

With all the reading, writing, arithmetic and spelling Aunt Myrtle had drummed into me, I breezed through sixth grade and was promoted to eighth grade at the end of the year.

From then on, school was never a problem.

During my high school years, I finished all my work during the school day and never took a book home.

Loved the Library

In addition to the reading I did for classes, I probably read most of the books in the school library. I went on to have a good life and earn a good living, and I credit Aunt Myrtle for much of it.

When Aunt Myrtle died at age 91, after teaching 55 years in that same country school, I wrote a poem about my years with her. It's a long poem, but I think this one verse says it all:

Aunt Myrtle has gone
the way of all flesh
But her good works will live on
In the countless students
her life has touched
And in values they pass along.

Lunchtime Dance Lessons Gave Teen Self-Confidence

I NEVER had a male teacher until my freshman year of high school in Oneonta, New York. Mr. Reynolds decided that, as part of our general science course, we needed to know how the pistons in an engine worked.

I was a 14-year-old girl, and I did not care how the pistons in an engine worked.

But Mr. Reynolds made it so interesting that I found the topic fascinating and really enjoyed it. I got an A in the class—and I still remember how pistons work.

Teaching about pistons was just one of Mr. Reynolds' gifts. A few of us lived too far from school to go home for lunch, so Mr. Reynolds would turn on the jukebox in the gym so we could dance.

Since I'd never learned to dance, I just sat on the sidelines and watched. When Mr. Reynolds noticed this, he took me onto the gym floor and proceeded to teach me to waltz, two-step, polka and even jitterbug.

I was an awkward teenager, so the lessons took most of the school year. Mr. Reynolds must have had a lot of patience.

I loved those lunch hours in the gym. Mr. Reynolds not only gave a shy child some sorely needed confidence and self-esteem, but a skill to enjoy the rest of her life.

I was never able to tell him how much I appreciated what he'd done, but in my heart I've thanked him many times. He was a great teacher in more ways than one. —*Joye Satterfield*
Kildeer, Illinois

DANCING OPENED DOORS. When Joye Satterfield attended high school in Oneonta, New York (above), her teacher taught her about automotive pistons. But his dance lessons gave her confidence and self-esteem.

Kindergarten Teacher Was Ahead of Her Time in 1929

By William Loechel
Birminghan, Michigan

THE OLD PHOTOGRAPHS fixed in my albums with four tiny black gummed corners include several from my days in kindergarten in Baltimore, Maryland. Though it was 70 years ago, it's not difficult to recall the names of my classmates—and it's quite easy to recall the name of our teacher, who was young, pretty and inspiring. Her name was Berenice Cronin.

For Miss Cronin's pupils, kindergarten wasn't just time away from home. It wasn't just playing games, or taking naps on our mats, or drawing pictures. Miss Cronin believed in broadening the experiences of her children.

Miss Cronin had us listen to the music of great composers—Grieg, Mendelssohn, Beethoven. They were only short offerings, but they were meaningful nonetheless. I remember being able to play Mendelssohn's *Spring Song* on her piano.

Miss Cronin understood what would motivate children. Knowing that I was from a railroad family and often drew trains, she saw to it that I was able to make a train I'd told her about.

The boiler was a Morton's salt box; the smokestack was a large spool. The cab, undercarriage and tender were made of cheese boxes. She recruited Mr. Timmons, the janitor, to make the wheels. I assembled the train and painted it black.

Once Miss Cronin took the class to a small airport on a bus owned and operated by the father of one of my classmates. My mother came along with her box camera. Today these outings are called field trips.

Another time, we went to a local park via the same bus. We had a picnic and visited the zoo. What an adventure!

More than 40 years ago, I realized that it wasn't enough to just appreciate what Miss Cronin had done for me. I needed to do something more.

I wrote a letter to the Department of Education in Baltimore, explaining what an influence Miss Cronin had on me. I received an enthusiastic reply, along with her address. We exchanged letters for years, and I visited her whenever I could.

On one trip to Baltimore, I decided to stop at the old elementary school and relive my school days. The principal sensed I was there to reminisce. After a half-hour chat, she said she still had the inkwell from Miss Cronin's classroom and offered it to me. It is a real treasure. ♫

TRAINED AT SCHOOL. William Loechel (circled) was interested in trains while in kindergarten, so his teacher helped him make one (inset).

One Man's Interest Opened Door of Opportunity for Entire Family

OUR FAMILY had 14 children, and during the hard Depression years, our education ended when we completed eighth grade. After that, we were expected to go to work.

When I finished eighth grade, I started farming with teams of horses. After my 18th birthday, when I was "of age", I told my parents I intended to get a job in town and go to high school.

Dad suggested I remain at home instead and walk the 3-1/2 miles to school, so that's what I did. I never missed a day. I was never even tardy.

After 3 years, the high school superintendent, Mr. E.P. Ennis, came to our house. He told Dad our country school needed a teacher and that I was just the one for the job. I could take the teacher's exam, attend a 5-week session at Arkansas State University and start teaching the summer term. Imagine my surprise!

I began teaching July 23, 1935, at a salary of $55 a month for 8 months. Some of my little brothers and sisters were my fastest learners, and Dad was so pleased. After that, he insisted that the other 13 children attend high school, too.

Because of Mr. Ennis' interest, our extended family now includes 10 schoolteachers, three civil engineers, a pediatrician, a dentist and many others who have gone on to live prosperous lives. Mr. Ennis was a godsend to us.
—*Lena Mulhollen*
Corning, Arkansas

Butter, Paraffin Projects Made Second Grade Memorable

I LIKED my second-grade teacher in Shelton, Nebraska because she always had us doing unusual things.

Once she brought in a pint jar of cream from the farm where she lived and had each of us shake the jar vigorously until the cream turned to butter. Then she buttered soda crackers so each of us could have a taste.

Another time, she gave each of us a piece of the wax used to seal jam and jelly jars. We were told to chew the

HIS ATTENTION WAXED. Author (far left and circled) appreciated his second-grade teacher's creative lessons.

wax until it was nice and smooth, and then shape it into a heart to place on valentines for our mothers, who were visiting that day. —Bob Maase, Alhambra, California

---

Troublesome Kindergartner Found Principal a Soft Touch

THE START of my school career in Casper, Wyoming was very discouraging. I got off on the wrong foot right from the start with my kindergarten teacher. I couldn't even take a nap to suit her. I was sent to the principal's office often.

The principal had a reputation as a very strict old lady. If your case required punishment, it was harsh. But she never punished me. She'd read the note the teacher had sent with me, ask me a few questions, then sit me on her lap and let me punch the keys on her typewriter. Sometimes she would read to me.

I didn't care much for my teacher, but I loved that principal.
—Eugene Morehouse
Lilliwaup, Washington

Having an "in" with Teacher Brought No Special Favors

WHEN I began attending Mount Vernon School in Blount County, Tennessee in 1927, my teacher was a friend of the family. I was very pleased. This would be great.

Each student brought a small bar of soap and a towel from home so we could wash our hands before lunch. We lined up at the well in the school yard, and the boys pumped while each child washed and dried their hands.

When classes started after lunch, I held my towel up in front of my face. The other kids laughed. "Don't do that," the teacher said. When I thought she wasn't looking, I did it again.

I didn't see her coming, but I felt a sharp slap on my cheek through the towel. Everyone had a good laugh, including the teacher, and I quickly realized I would have no special privileges.
—John Russell, Clearwater, Florida

First Teacher Was a Pearl

MY FIRST TEACHER, Miss Pearl Gardner, was exceptional. Not only was she nice to all the pupils, she went beyond teaching us the three R's.

I started school in 1922, when we lived in the small town of Lyndon, Kansas. Miss Pearl had both the first and second grade in her class.

There was a Victrola in the room. We learned about the composers and conductors and marched around the room when she played band music.

We also played store. Miss Pearl brought empty boxes and cans for us to buy. She gave us real money to use so we'd know how to count change.

When it snowed, Miss Pearl would put on her black coat and take us out to the front steps of the school. There she'd catch snowflakes so we could see the different designs.

I shall never forget Miss Pearl.
—Dorothy Celender, Vinton, Iowa

KINDER-CARE. Kindergartners needed special attention, which Eugene Morehouse got from the principal.

MY ELEMENTARY education began in 1931, when my parents enrolled me in parochial school. At the time, I was unaware of the harsh stereotypes about nuns. The ones who taught me were stern but kind, demanding yet lenient, proud of their calling yet humble.

Looking back, I believe the sisters were assigned grade levels according to their temperament and the ages of their charges. Those who were gentle by nature taught the lower grades, while the tougher ones received classes where the students could be unruly.

In third grade, my teacher was a young, capable nun who demonstrated motherly care and compassion. She also had a unique method of teaching arithmetic, using hand signals to drill us in the multiplication tables and division.

By the end of the year, we were so skilled that we could multiply by 13, 14 and 15. I was grateful later, because I had little trouble with higher mathematics.

Her Pointer Ruled!

In sixth grade, I fell into the clutches of one of those stereotypical nuns. From the first day, she let us know who was in charge, and there was no deviating from her rules. She carried a heavy-duty pointer, which she waved before us during lessons. During question periods, she'd bring it down on the desk of any pupil who responded with a wrong answer. The sound sent shivers of fear into our hearts.

Outside the classroom, Sister used her stick to herd students into orderly lines for dismissal or recess. Although she was stern, she was an effective teacher—we learned all our lessons, completed our homework and behaved at all times.

The nuns were paid little or nothing during the Depression years, so they depended on the parish for their basic necessities. Many parishioners were facing lean times themselves, so church contributions were slim. As a result, the convent's cupboard was often empty.

Mother Superior solved this by posting a notice on the bulletin board every week, saying one of the sisters was about to celebrate her "Feast Day". This was to commemorate

Nuns Were More Caring Than Harsh Stereotype Suggests

By Robert Miller, Philadelphia, Pennsylvania

WATCHFUL SISTERS. Two nuns guide first communicants to church in this photo furnished by Robert Miller, who offers insights on the nuns who taught him in his story on this page.

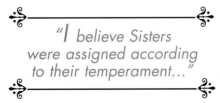

"I believe Sisters were assigned according to their temperament..."

something or someone that influenced the sister's life—a saint, the day she took her first or final vows or some blessing she'd received.

All the students were urged to bring a food item on the designated day. At the end of the day, the food-laden basket was taken to the convent kitchen, where all the nuns could share the contents.

My mother often found it difficult to put a nourishing meal on our own table, but she usually managed to contribute something—a can of soup, a jar of apple butter, a couple of apples, a few potatoes.

Pupils Did Cleaning

To keep the school clean without expending scarce funds, classes were suspended one afternoon a month so the students could clean the rooms.

Each pupil brought cleaning supplies from home. Some brought buckets and scrub brushes, some furnished yellow soap and rags, while others brought window cleaner.

The bigger kids washed windows, while the smaller ones cleaned blackboards, emptied wastebaskets and swept floors. Then all of us scrubbed the desks, chairs and floors. If Sister was satisfied, she usually rewarded us by announcing there'd be no homework that day.

Winter sometimes brought hardship to our school. Many homes in our poverty-stricken neighborhood ran short of coal in winter, so we'd trudge to school in hopes of having a warm place to spend the day.

But on many cold days, there was no fuel for the school furnaces, either. We sat in the classrooms wearing our hats, coats and gloves. Sister had no coat or sweater, only a hand-knit shawl that barely covered her shoulders. I guess the parish treasury didn't have funds to buy warm clothing for her.

Despite the hardships, we all managed to make it on to high school. Today's lawyers might argue that we were abused and exploited, but I would disagree. The nuns enabled us to cope with the harshness of the adult world. We're grateful for their concern, their compassion, and their insistence on perfection. Thank you, Sisters! ❧

Teachers' Devotion Was Blessing To Children

By Mary Heberly
Grand Junction, Colorado

IN THE LAST years of the Depression, there was a rule that female teachers had to be unmarried. The ones I recall from our rural school in Minneapolis, Kansas seemed to have a calling to teach and treated us as though we were their own children.

In kindergarten, Miss Lana Cameran had each of us bring a piece of printed fabric in a cigar box. From this, each girl made her own bib apron with straps that crossed in the back. It took us most of the year to hand-stitch the hems and straps. I still have mine, after 58 years.

We visited a family-run dairy on the edge of town, where the teacher bought a pint of cream. Each child took turns shaking the cream until chunks of butter appeared, then we ate the butter on crackers.

Miss Lana had a poster in the classroom with each child's name on it. If we had washed our faces and hands, cleaned our fingernails and combed our hair, we were given a star to place next to our names. We were taught to raise our hands for permission to speak or leave our chairs.

Bertha Brown, a 5-foot-tall redhead, took on about 36 of us in first grade. She taught us to read from the *Bob Merrill Reader*: "I am a gingerbread boy, I am

I am. I can run from a woman, I can run from a man."

Miss Brown showed her love for us with a hug and kiss every morning. She had "pretend kisses" of chocolate, caramel and peppermint, and always asked which flavor we were giving her. These flavored kisses were also her cure for minor injuries. Miss Brown and I lived a block and a half apart and often walked home together.

Teacher Felt Responsible

I was in second grade when one morning the sky grew dark, and then darker—it was a great dust storm. Some parents came to pick up their children in cars, but my widowed mother had a 2-year-old to care for, and no car. The teacher felt keen responsibility for us, so Miss Brown walked the 6 blocks home with me, then got her car to take the rest of her pupils home.

In later years, I was married and living in Pueblo, Colorado when I visited with Miss Brown, who was teaching in the mountain town of Beulah, 35 miles west. Years afterward, we both lived in Canon City, Colorado, where I was able to help her occasionally.

I visited her in the nursing home where she spent her remaining years,

TRIPLE TREAT. All children benefit from having exceptional teachers. Mary Heberly remembers three of her favorites in this story.

some 500 miles from where she'd taught me to read.

Our second-grade teacher, Constance Goodwin, had a sandbox with interesting plants and rocks. Whenever something new turned up in it, she told us that elves or fairies put it there. She also told us stories about what the elves and fairies did in the rock garden in her backyard.

On the last day of school, Miss Goodwin had "awards day". For having the second-highest grades in the class, I was awarded a piece of lovely lavender cotton in a flowered print. Mother used it to make me a pretty dress. I know some of the others who received "awards" were equally needy.

I could go on naming teachers from every grade, all the way through high school, who were devoted to us. Because they cared for us in such a tender way, it helps me reach out to less fortunate children today. I know it makes a difference to have someone who cares. ❧

She Waited 58 Years to 'Fess Up To Spoiling Classroom Paint Job

By Marcia Massey, Collinsville, Illinois

SISTER IRMINE probably doesn't remember me after all these years—58, to be exact. But she'd probably remember the day someone scratched the fresh green paint off our first-grade classroom wall.

We were lined up along the blackboard, hands clasped obediently behind our backs, eager for our weekly spelling bee. When my nails accidentally scraped into the soft, pliable paint, I couldn't help myself. The paint peeled off easily in long strips. As my nimble fingers began working at it, I honestly didn't think of the consequences.

Sister Irmine didn't notice my destruction right away, but as more students were eliminated from the spelling bee and returned to their seats, the gouges became obvious.

Suddenly Sister's eyes opened wide. "Who did that?" she demanded in a loud, angry voice. I was too terrified to speak. She might kill me!

Passed Inspection

When no one confessed, Sister shouted, "I'll get to the bottom of this. I'll find out who did this, and when I do…" She shook her finger at us as she paced back and forth, trying to come up with a plan that would expose the culprit.

She spun around quickly and said, "Hands on your desks!" Down the rows she marched, inspecting each child's fingernails for signs

of green paint. Numb with fear, I quickly dug at each nail to remove the evidence.

Sister finished her inspection without identifying the culprit. The class was so still you could've heard a pin drop.

After some thought, Sister declared, "Everyone is going to get a swat with my paddle until the guilty one confesses."

That really put me on the spot. I couldn't let everyone take swats for what I'd done. As soon as the first child was called up front for a swat, I'd confess.

Sister Irmine glared at us as she smacked the paddle against the palm of her hand. "Who gets the first paddling?" she asked. No one answered. I was sure I was going to faint.

Then Sister put the paddle down and said, "I can't paddle you all for the actions of one. That wouldn't be fair, would it?"

"No, Sister," we replied in unison.

But Sister had another idea. The whole class would stay after school until the guilty party confessed—even if it took all night.

Held Their Breath

As our day returned to normal, I decided to withhold my confession until the final bell rang. Even though I feared for my life, I wouldn't be a coward. I couldn't live with having others take my punishment.

When the last bell rang, Sister Irmine bowed her head as if in prayer. We all held our breath. After a long moment, Sister lifted her head and said, "I can't keep you all here because of what one child did. You may all leave."

The next day, the wall was repainted. There was no sign of my destruction, and Sister Irmine never asked again who was responsible. I was the only one who ever knew.

For all these years, I've wanted to see Sister Irmine and confess. Unless she's gone on to her heavenly reward, I'm sure she still wonders who did it. ✎

FINALLY! Marcia Massey, as a grade schooler and more recently, confesses to an unfortunate classroom incident in first grade.

Teacher's Lively Approach Kept Students Interested

THE MOST unforgettable person I've ever met was Mrs. Menzel, my fifth-grade teacher in Ingleside, Texas. She had a daughter in my class as well as three teenagers, so she knew a lot about children, and she enjoyed them.

During recess, she was always out on the playground with us, playing baseball or anything else we wanted. No game was too much for her physically.

Mrs. Menzel was an enthusiastic teacher. No subject was boring to her, so it wasn't boring for us. She had creative methods to help us remember facts in every subject. I especially enjoyed making a map of the United States out of salt dough and tinting it with food coloring.

She wasn't afraid to let us see her emotions, either. On the day President Kennedy was killed, Mrs. Menzel buried her face in her hands and cried when the principal made the announcement over the loudspeaker.

She was more than just a terrific teacher. She was a real human being, with feelings just like ours.

—*Candy Feathers, Bell Buckle, Tennessee*

'Ugly' Teacher Opened Teen's Eyes to New Sources of Beauty

By Grace Flitt
East Brunswick, New Jersey

AT THE START of school around 1929, when I was a budding teenager, we were assigned to a new music teacher. We were noisy and rambunctious as we filed into the music room of our school in Queens, New York, but the sight of our new teacher quickly struck us dumb. To us she looked so ugly, we didn't know what to say.

The first week, we just stared at her in silent fascination. She talked, but we did not hear. She played the piano, but we didn't sing. She assigned lessons, but we didn't do the homework. We were mesmerized by her looks.

In the weeks that followed, silence turned to snickers and whispers of "Schnozzola". Discipline gave way to pandemonium.

But our teacher staunchly stood her ground. She had a big voice that belied her small stature and defiantly told us that we were going to produce an abridged version of Smetana's operetta *The Bartered Bride*. We were stunned. We'd never heard of *The Bartered Bride*, and "Smetana" sounded like it might be a dirty word.

But our teacher persevered. She assigned the reluctant, rambunctious boys to create the scenery and props. She whipped the whiny girls into a working chorus. She chose a shy blond to be the "bartered bride" and the class bully to be her suitor.

As the days stretched into weeks, we became so absorbed in our project that we forgot to heckle the teacher. Inspired by her dogged determination, we actually began to appreciate this classic operetta. Her deep love of music began to seep into us, and we learned to love it, too.

I was unable to carry a tune, so I was stationed backstage to manage the

ORCHESTRA IN THE ROUND. Grace Flitt couldn't carry a tune, but she could operate the phonograph, so she became the "orchestra" for her school's operetta.

"canned" music. I was in charge of the phonograph and was the keeper of the 78-rpm records.

This noble project kept us busy for 6 full months. An assembly was held in the auditorium for our performance.

The hall was filled with noisy kids, but when the curtains went up and the "orchestra" began (that was me backstage, playing records), a hush fell. When the show was over, whoops of appreciation sounded loud and clear.

The cast proudly took its bows—except for me. I was huddled backstage.

I'll never forget that teacher rushing toward me, grabbing my hand and pulling me onto the stage for a bow. I was so embarrassed and overwhelmed by the sight of all those clapping kids that I just stood there, unable to move.

But deep down, I was proud—not only of my class, but of the woman who'd taught us so much. She was no longer "Schnozzola", but a beloved teacher.

Today, whenever I hear the music from *The Bartered Bride*, I think of her fondly and thank her for giving me the gift of music. ♫

First Graders "Buried" Ungrammatical Word

I ATTENDED first grade in Addicks, Texas in 1933. One day our teacher, Mrs. Gussie Patton, told us we were going to bury the word "ain't". She wasn't kidding!

Mrs. Patton wrote the word on a large white piece of cardboard, and we took it outside with a shovel. We dug a hole in the school yard, then put the cardboard in the hole and covered it with dirt. I have not used that word since.

Mrs. Patton was the sweetest teacher ever. Whenever a student had a birthday, she drew a birthday cake, complete with candles and flames, on the blackboard with colored chalk.

She still sends me cards and is a beautiful person to this day. Every first grader should have a teacher like her.

—*Willien Plackemeier*
Houston, Texas